Governance and
Changing American States

TRANSFORMING AMERICAN POLITICS

Lawrence C. Dodd, Series Editor

Dramatic changes in political institutions and behavior over the past three decades have underscored the dynamic nature of American politics, confronting political scientists with a new and pressing intellectual agenda. The pioneering work of early postwar scholars, while laying a firm empirical foundation for contemporary scholarship, failed to consider how American politics might change or recognize the forces that would make fundamental change inevitable. In reassessing the static interpretations fostered by these classic studies, political scientists are now examining the underlying dynamics that generate transformational change.

Transforming American Politics brings together texts and monographs that address four closely related aspects of change. A first concern is documenting and explaining recent changes in American politics—in institutions, processes, behavior, and policymaking. A second is reinterpreting classic studies and theories to provide a more accurate perspective on postwar politics. The series looks at historical change to identify recurring patterns of political transformation within and across the distinctive eras of American politics. Last and perhaps most important, the series presents new theories and interpretations that explain the dynamic processes at work and thus clarify the direction of contemporary politics. All of the books focus on the central theme of transformation—transformation in both the conduct of American politics and in the way we study and understand its many aspects.

BOOKS IN THIS SERIES

Governance and the Changing American States, David M. Hedge

Masters of the House: Congressional Leadership over Two Centuries,
Roger H. Davidson, Susan Webb Hammond, and Raymond W. Smock

Governing Partners: State-Local Relations in the United States,
Russell L. Hanson

The Parties Respond: Changes in American Parties and Campaigns,
Third Edition, L. Sandy Maisel

Revolving Gridlock: Politics and Policy from Carter to Clinton,
David W. Brady and Craig Volden

*Still Seeing Red: How the Cold War Shapes the
New American Politics,* John Kenneth White

*The Collapse of the Democratic Presidential Majority:
Realignment, Dealignment, and Electoral Change from
Franklin Roosevelt to Bill Clinton,* David G. Lawrence

*The Divided Democrats: Ideological Unity, Party Reform,
and Presidential Elections,* William G. Mayer

*Extraordinary Politics: How Protest and Dissent are
Changing American Democracy,* Charles C. Euchner

The Irony of Reform: Roots of American Disenchantment,
G. Calvin Mackenzie

Midterm: The Elections of 1994 in Context,
Philip A. Klinkner

*Broken Contract: Changing Relationships Between Americans
and Their Government,* Stephen C. Craig

Young Versus Old: Generational Combat in the 21st Century,
Susan A. MacManus

*The New American Politics: Reflections on Political Change
and the Clinton Administration,* Bryan D. Jones

Campaigns and Elections American Style,
James A. Thurber and Candice J. Nelson

Governance and the Changing American States

David M. Hedge

University of Florida

Westview Press
A Member of the Perseus Books Group

To my mother, Maida, and brother Richard
and in memory of my father, Carroll,
and brother Michael for a lifetime
of love and support

Transforming American Politics

Copyright © 1998 by Westview Press, A Member of the Perseus Books Group

Published in 1998 in the United States of America by Westview Press, 5500 Central Avenue,
Boulder, Colorado 80301-2877, and in the United Kingdom by Westview Press, 12 Hid's
Copse Road, Cumnor Hill, Oxford OX2 9JJ

Library of Congress Cataloging-in-Publication Data
Hedge, David.
  Governance and the changing American states / David M. Hedge.
    p.   cm. — (Transforming American politics)
  Includes bibliographical references and index.
  ISBN 0-8133-3193-5 (hardcover). — ISBN 0-8133-3194-3 (pbk)
  1. State governments—United States.   I. Title.   II. Series.
JK2408.H44   1998
320.973—dc21   98-11057
                                                                          CIP

The paper used in this publication meets the requirements of the American National
Standard for Permanence of Paper for Printed Library Materials Z39.48-1984.

10   9   8   7   6   5   4   3   2

Contents

Tables and Figures

Tables

Figures

Preface

America is in the midst of a "devolution revolution" as increasing amounts of the responsibility for governing the nation are shifted to the American states. For many this is how it should be. The new conventional wisdom of American politics is that the states are much better suited to governing than their federal counterparts. Part of the rationale for that assertion is the apparent resurgence of state governments. On the demand side, more citizens now have more opportunities to influence the decisions of state policymakers. On the supply side, the states' political institutions and those who serve in those institutions are more capable, enjoy more resources, and are more willing to use those resources to govern. Not everyone, however, accepts the new conventional wisdom. Over the past several years a more critical view of the American states has emerged, one in which state governments, for all their reforms, are viewed as suffering the same kinds of political pathologies that we encounter elsewhere in American politics, including gridlock, inordinate interest group influence, excessive partisanship, and political selfishness.

This book is an attempt to navigate between these competing views of the states and to address one of the more fundamental questions of governance in the years ahead—can the states govern and govern wisely in the new century? In the chapters that follow, I essentially do two things: (1) chronicle the kinds of changes that have occurred on the "demand" and "supply" sides of state government and (2) assess the consequences of those developments for the quality of statehouse democracy and the ability of state governments to govern responsibly and effectively.

This book was written for the serious student of state government. Undergraduates should leave this text with a sense of how state governments have changed in recent decades and with an analytic framework for viewing those changes. Scholars, including graduate students attempting to come to grips with the ever growing body of literature on state governments, may also appreciate my efforts at pulling together seemingly disparate literatures in sorting out some of the consequences of developments in state government and politics. Those who labor in or around state government may benefit as well from the insights that are offered by an outsider who, unfettered by the demands of actually doing government, has the luxury (and temerity) of stepping back and looking broadly at issues of politics and governing.

Like most works of this type, this book builds upon a solid foundation of prior scholarship and analysis. First, I owe a tremendous intellectual debt to those scholars who initially "rediscovered" the American states and their constituent parts. Two books—Ann Bowman and Richard Kearney's *The Resurgence of the States* and the first edition of Carl Van Horn's edited volume *The State of the States*—were particularly influential. The Bowman and Kearney text first alerted me to the fact that state governments had undergone a fundamental transition. For its part, the Van Horn reader underscored that point while suggesting some of the limits to the states' resurgence. Second, this book benefits from the literally dozens of studies that have looked systematically at the consequences of various reforms and developments. As the reader will note, I offer very little in the way of original research in this volume, in part because there is so little need to do so. In the last decade or so there has been not only a resurgence of the states but a resurgence in the research that looks systematically (and well) at the states. And although gaps remain in those respective literatures, there is now a sizable body of well-crafted research on state politics and policy. Taken together, that research demonstrates that the states can serve not only as "laboratories of democracy," but as laboratories within which scholars can examine fundamental questions of governance.

I am particularly indebted to those who reviewed all or parts of the manuscript. Several scholars gave me the benefit of their critiques of individual chapters, including Richard Brisbin, M. Margaret Conway, Robert Dilger, Keith Hamm, David Hill, Paul Kramer, John Kilwein, Richard Scher, Katrina Schochet-Cooper, Mike Scicchitano, Joseph Stewart, Betty Waldron, and various anonymous reviewers. Special thanks go to Christopher Mooney, James Sheffield, and an anonymous reviewer, who generously offered their advice and constructive criticism on the entire manuscript. I am especially grateful to my colleague and series editor, Larry Dodd, and to Leo Wiegman, senior editor at Westview Press, for their continuous support and encouragement. Additional thanks go to the project editor, Kristin Milavec, for keeping the book (and its author) on schedule. Finally, my family continued to dole out generous portions of love and support throughout the writing process. My son, Ken, and daughter, Meghan, always help me to keep things in perspective (not an easy task), and my wife, Jody, remains, after nearly three decades, my closest confidante and friend.

David M. Hedge

1

Introduction

American federalism is being turned on its head. After decades of federal dominance, a realignment is occurring in the respective roles of the states and the federal government. Increasingly, the states are becoming the principal focus for policy initiatives in areas as diverse as education, health care, welfare reform, economic development, and insurance reform. Indeed, the major long-term legacy of the tumultuous politics of the 1990s may be the transfer of substantial responsibility for governing to the American states.

The states' increasing prominence is both planned and unplanned. Throughout the 1980s, the Reagan administration's efforts to achieve a less active federal government and a New Federalism shifted considerable responsibility for governing to the states. As the decade wore on, a growing and seemingly uncontrollable federal debt, divided control of Congress and the White House, a lack of presidential leadership, and a Congress that was growing more and more dysfunctional further guaranteed that fewer policy initiatives, particularly spending initiatives, came from the nation's capital. Moreover, what federal policy prescriptions were put forward frequently had a distinctive state "flavor" to them. The centerpiece of Congress's 1988 overhaul of welfare policy, for example, was the workfare program that had been operating in many of the states for well over a decade.

The trend toward a more state-centered federalism continued into the Clinton administration as well. During its first term, many of the administration's proposals, including family leave legislation, managed competition in health care, urban enterprise zones, and national service, were all initiatives that had already been put forward in a number of states. Even when the Clinton White House proposed major new federal initiatives (the president's ill-fated health care proposal, for example), the states were often slated to play a major role in their implementation. Perhaps the clearest signal of the administration's willingness to transfer authority to the states was the president's decision to sign off on the 1996 welfare reform bill, despite misgivings about the harshness of the legislation.

Any doubts that the responsibilities of the states would continue to grow in the next few decades were erased in the wake of the 1994 election and the apparent rejection of a Democratic Congress and an active federal government. Elements of the Republican "Contract with America," as well as the overarching ideological thrust of the new congressional majority, sought to give the states more freedom from federal intrusion and to shift major responsibility back to the states. Once again, the case of welfare reform is instructive. Initially, the welfare reforms contained in the Republican's Contract with America included a series of controversial proposals that amounted to federally prescribed mandates on the states, including provisions that would have removed unwed mothers from the welfare rolls. However, after meeting with more than a dozen GOP governors, Republican leaders in the House agreed to drop many of those requirements and to recast welfare reform in block grant terms that allow the states greater flexibility in implementation.

The political fallout from the 1994 elections has been every bit as dramatic and potentially far reaching at the state level. Following the 1994 elections, Republicans held the governorships in thirty-one states (up from twenty) and controlled half the states' legislatures. In many of those states, governors and legislators have pursued the new conservative agenda with the same vigor as their counterparts in Congress. According to one source (*Washington Post,* January 29, 1995, p. A18):

> The same conservative themes of less government, lower taxes, and the devolution of power that now animate the legislative agenda in Washington are resonating with even greater volume in state capitals across the country. Newly fortified by the November election, Republican governors have outlined aggressive agendas for cutting taxes, shrinking government, reforming welfare and education, and rearranging the balance of power among Washington, the states, and local governments.

Several states considered their own "contracts," and a new round of budget and tax cuts were debated and, in many states, adopted. Newly elected governors George Pataki of New York and John Rowland of Connecticut, for instance, pledged to reduce taxes, and incumbent governors, including Howard Dean of Vermont and Christine Todd Whitman of New Jersey, sought additional cuts in their states' taxes. For the first time in more than a decade, state tax cuts in 1995 actually exceeded state tax increases (Van Horn 1996b).

Although the 1996 elections signaled the public's desire for a more moderate approach to solving the nation's problems, the partisan alignment of the 1994 election remained largely intact (Democrats experienced a net gain of five state legislatures, but Congress remained in Republican hands and Republicans controlled the governorship in thirty-two states), and no one expects power to flow back to Washington, D.C. Indeed, the political dynamics of the 1980s and 1990s point to a sea change in the nation's political thinking. Increasingly, the prevailing wisdom is that the states and not the federal government should take the lead in solving the nation's problems. Part of that reflects dissatisfaction with the federal government. But it also reflects a growing respect for the states. Many would agree with Carl Van Horn's (1989: 1) assertion that state governments "are arguably the most responsive, innovative, and effective level of government in the American federal system."

The reader will note an irony in all of this. The dramatic growth in the reach of the federal government following World War II came about in large part because state and local governments were either unwilling or unable (or both) to deal with a wide range of social and economic problems—civil rights, poverty, education, workplace safety, consumer protection, health care, and environmental protection. Yet, as the twentieth century comes to a close, it is to state governments that we now look for solutions to many of these same problems. But are the states up to the task? Can the "sometimes governments" provide the political and policy leadership so sorely needed in the United States? Many would say yes.

The Resurgence of the States

There is considerable consensus among scholars and practitioners alike that the states have undergone a dramatic resurgence in recent decades. As a result of forces operating at both the national and subnational levels, state governments have become more representative and better able and more willing to govern. A variety of initiatives and reforms have increased citizen participation and input into state government; blacks, Hispanics, and women enjoy considerably greater representation at the state and local level; and higher levels of interparty competition and a growing diversity of interest groups promise a better linkage between public opinion and public policy. Parallel changes have occurred in the states' political institutions. Governors now have more power than ever before and are more willing to use that power to effect innovative policy solutions. That influence is evidenced by their prominence and visibility; no fewer than a dozen governors and former governors have been serious contenders for the presidency in the past four elections. During the 104th Congress, Republican governors such as Tommy Thompson of Wisconsin and John Engler of Michigan seemed to spend as much time in Washington, D.C., as they did in their state capitals, as they sought to shape and reshape elements of the Republican legislative agenda. For their part, state legislatures are more professional, better staffed, and more assertive. There is a new kind of career legislator who comes to the legislature at an earlier age, stays longer, and is much less willing to defer to governors or party leaders. State courts have also undergone significant structural reform and have demonstrated a willingness to intervene in the decisions and actions of the executive and legislative branches.

Most importantly, the states have taken the lead in addressing a wide range of policy problems, becoming what one author (Osborne 1988) refers to as "laboratories of democracy." When a national education commission declared in the early 1980s that America was a "Nation at Risk," for example, it was the states that adopted innovative educational reforms including curriculum changes, teacher competency requirements, aid equalization, and increased spending. In a parallel fashion, by the time Congress put the final touches on its first major attempt at developing a national AIDS policy in 1988, several of the states had already passed legislation dealing with the more controversial aspects of the AIDS crisis, including confidentiality, discrimination, and AIDS education in the public schools (Bingham and Hedge 1991). More recently, in the wake of the administration's abortive attempt to pass national health care reform, several states, including Florida, Minnesota, Oregon, Washington, and Hawaii, have already considered, and in many cases adopted, dramatic new reforms. Similarly, even before Congress and the president agreed on the 1996 welfare bill, a majority of the states had already sought federal exemptions that allowed them to, among other things, set limits on welfare receipt, extend transitional services and support for families leaving welfare for work, and encourage teen welfare recipients to finish high school (see, e.g., Strawn, Dacey, and McCart 1994).

What prompted the resurgence of the states? Much of the credit lies, ironically, with the federal government. A half century of federal grants-in-aid has increased both the technical capacity and aspirations of state and local officials. Federal grants, together with federal mandates, have also expanded the policy scope of the states. Two other federal actions have been particularly important. Federal civil rights policy and the reapportionment "revolution" triggered by the 1962 *Baker v. Carr* decision have ensured that minorities and urban areas are better represented in state legislatures and have contributed to increased legislative activism, particularly on behalf of the cities. More recently, the Reagan administration's New Federalism, with its emphasis on devolution, deregulation, and "defunding," forced the states to do more with less, a trend that continues today. And if the cohort of new Republican governors and legislators elected in 1994 have their way, the states will enjoy even more flexibility in programming with fewer mandates in the years ahead.

The states have contributed to their own resurgence as well. First, since the 1960s over three-fourths of the states have either enacted new or revised existing constitutions that strengthen their governors, increase legislative sessions and compensation, establish greater fiscal discipline, and provide a basis for protecting individual rights and liberties (Van Horn 1996a). Second, the greater use of the initiative and referendum, efforts to make voting and registration less burdensome, and reforms that increase citizen participation in government between elections, together with state policies that comply with federal reapportionment and civil rights policies, have increased the opportunities for ordinary citizens to access and influence state government. Third, over the last few decades the states have restructured their revenue systems to make them more diverse, less prone to economic cycles, and, in many cases, more equitable. Prodded by the three Rs—tax revolts, recessions, and reductions in federal aid— many states in the 1980s increased existing taxes, most notably income and sales taxes, and found new sources of revenues, including state lotteries and additional user charges.

Perhaps nothing better illustrates the realignment of federal and state policy responsibilities than current models of federalism. Although the particulars may differ, recent visions of federalism afford the states the dominant role in governing America, something unheard of two decades ago. Two models are particularly illustrative of the states' resurgence. Linda Tarr-Whelan has argued that a *progressive federalism* may be emerging in America.[1] According to Tarr-Whelan, states serve as laboratories for policy innovations that are eventually diffused to others through federal incentives and negotiation. Progressive federalism unfolds in several stages. At the outset, a handful of states take the lead in fashioning new and innovative approaches to issues as diverse as welfare, health care reform, and consumer protection. At the federal level, progressives push to extend new state initiatives to the remainder of the states. The result is federal legislation that sets minimum program standards, provides limited federal resources as an incentive to participate, and allows the states maximum flexibility in implementation. The states are then allowed to further innovate beyond the prescribed minimum.

Thomas Dye's (1988) model of *competitive federalism* also views the states as the locus of governing in the United States and provides an even smaller role for the federal government. Extending Charles Tiebout's model of local government to the states, Dye argues that federalism is usefully viewed as a marketplace where states compete with one another for residents and firms by offering the most attractive package of taxes and services. Acting as consumers, voters and firms, armed with the necessary information, can "vote with their feet" and through the ballot box for the state policy package that best satisfies their policy preferences. Competition and the prospect of losing firms and citizens to other states forces the states to be more efficient, responsive, and innovative. Federalism as a marketplace of governments also blunts the federal government's tendency to overproduce goods and services and to respond to narrow interests at the expense of the larger public.

New theories of federalism are increasingly finding their way into more concrete proposals for rearranging functional responsibilities within the United States. Just prior to joining the Clinton administration, Alice Rivlin (1992) proposed a fundamental realignment in the respective policy roles of the federal and state governments. Under Rivlin's proposal, state governments would assume primary responsibility for economic development, including education, job training, infrastructure development, and child care, while the federal government would assume sole responsibility for national health insurance. As part of that, Rivlin proposed eliminating most federal programs in the areas of housing, social services, education, and economic development. On the fiscal side, she proposed that the federal government run a budget surplus and that the states cooperate in developing a common tax pool that would be shared among the states on a formula basis. What is particularly striking about Rivlin's proposal is that it rests less on conventional notions of politics and economics and more on a pragmatic view of American politics. States governments should shoulder greater responsibility for governing because they are better able to do so and federal authorities have demonstrated that they are not.

Passage of the 1996 welfare reform bill reflected that kind of pragmatism as well. The conventional wisdom, supplied by public finance theorists, has long held that programs that redistribute wealth, most notably welfare, are best left at the national level for both equity and efficiency reasons. Yet by replacing the open-end entitlement program that had guaranteed the poor assistance since the 1930s with a closed-end block grant, the president and Congress discarded the conventional wisdom in lieu of a number of more practical considerations—the size of the federal deficit and a corresponding desire to reduce spending, the political clout of Republican governors and the new conservative Republican congressional majority, and Bill Clinton's need to deliver on his 1992 campaign promise to "end welfare as we know it." In addition, as Richard Nathan (1996) points out, the discussion of welfare reform in the 1990s has less to do with the redistribution of wealth than with fashioning effective intervention strategies that will move individuals off welfare rolls and into jobs, a task that many feel the states are better suited to do.

The Irony of Reform: An Alternative View

Despite the apparent resurgence of the states, recent events and developments suggest a less benign view of the states' capacity to govern. Many have argued that political developments and policy activism in the states have produced new problems. As state governments address a wider range of issues, as those issues become more controversial, as each branch of government becomes more assertive, and as the states' political systems become further decentralized and fragmented, a number of political pathologies—political gridlock, parochialism, and political action committee (PAC)–dominated politics—threaten the states' resurgence. As the 1990s unfolded, a number of developments signaled that all was not well with the American states.

- The nation's recession that lingered into the early 1990s caused an overwhelming majority of the American states to face their most severe budget crises in recent history. Politically unable to raise taxes and fees significantly (having done so in the 1980s), faced with rising welfare, education, prison, and Medicaid costs, and limited by constitutional requirements to maintain balanced operating budgets, state lawmakers were forced to make painful cuts in many areas of their budgets. Many states faced crisis levels in several policy areas. In California, for example, the recession, tax limitations, and a population explosion produced serious school overcrowding, teacher layoffs, a real decline in per pupil expenditures, and as one author (Meyer 1992: 70–71) notes, "a lost generation of children." Similarly, in Florida, newly completed (and sorely needed) state prisons remained empty during the early 1990s because there was no money in the budget to staff and operate them.

  For many the recession of the late 1980s and early 1990s laid to rest any notion that the states' fiscal houses were in order. Despite the fiscal reforms and tax increases of the 1980s and the recent economic recovery, states in the 1990s still find themselves scrambling to generate new resources to meet escalating costs in a political climate that is even less supportive of new taxes than it was during the Reagan years. And analysts worry that in balancing their operating budgets and providing tax relief to their citizens, too many states have incurred too much short- and long-term debt. New Jersey's popular governor Christine Todd Whitman, for example, was able to deliver on her 1993 promise to cut taxes by 15 percent and balance the budget only by delaying payments to the state employees' retirement fund (payments that will have to be made later) and refinancing 10-year state road bonds to a 20-year maturity. Already analysts and political leaders are warning of potentially bleak days ahead for the states should the nation enter a new recession.

- Some worry that political reforms and other developments have produced new pathologies. Although the increased use of initiatives and referenda, for instance, has ensured that issues such as term limits and tax relief are placed on the public agenda, there is a concern that citizens are being crowded out of issue elections by special interests. Within legislatures, greater careerism and the demands of reelection contribute to legislative fragmentation, open the door to inordinate PAC influence, make leadership more difficult, and undercut the ability of legislatures to reach consensus or fashion coherent public policy. More broadly, developments and reforms on both the supply and demand side of state government magnify the role and importance of money in state politics, producing new ethical challenges and threatening the quality of representation and the ability of state governments to make difficult policy choices. In addition, as each branch of state government grows stronger and more assertive, conflicts between governors, legislatures, and the courts have grown more frequent and intense and too often lead to policy gridlock and inaction. That tendency toward gridlock is further accentuated by increases in the rate of divided government. A more recent development, the adoption of term limits in half of the American states, may also blunt the states' resurgence by reversing the trend toward greater legislative professionalism and making lawmakers more dependent on staff, governors, and interest groups.

- The new Republican majorities in the 104th Congress moved toward a much less restrictive federal presence in state government. One of the earliest elements of the Contract with America to be enacted was legislation limiting the ability of the federal government to impose new mandates on the states. Nonetheless, if elements of the Contract with America are a guide to what will unfold in the next few years, inconsistencies in federal policies toward the states will continue. In the series of crime bills passed in February 1995, for example, House Republicans managed to eliminate one set of mandates (the provision that localities use federal grant monies to hire new police officers) in one piece of legislation while at the same time imposing others (e.g., a requirement that states adopt truth-in-sentencing requirements as a condition for receiving federal prison dollars) in another. In a related fashion, tort reforms adopted in the House in March of 1995 would preempt state liability laws by limiting the amount of punitive damages that can be awarded to successful litigants.

- Perhaps most distressing, there is growing evidence that many of the states' policy initiatives have simply not worked or not worked as well as advocates had hoped. Despite two decades of school reform, for example, many contend that America's schools are still in crisis. The uneven record of state policy initiatives is seen elsewhere as well—studies in the mid-1980s gave a majority of the states low marks in managing the environment (see, e.g., Ridley 1987); critics charge that the states are doing a poor job of enforcing workplace safety standards (Victor 1990); and analyses of economic development policy raise fundamental questions about the ability of state governments to nurture and sustain long-term economic growth (Brace 1993). Moreover, even where state and local policies seem to be working, a lack of resources frequently limits policy effectiveness as services can only be provided to a portion of eligible recipients.

Taken together, the evidence suggests an alternative view of the states' resurgence, one in which the capacity of the states is limited and where state politics and policy frequently mirror the larger political climate of political stalemate and malaise that we have come to associate with politics in Washington, D.C. That should come as a shock to no one. The federal government has long served as the model by which we often reform and judge the states. State legislatures, for example, are given high marks for achieving the kind of "institutionalization" typical of the U.S. Congress. No one should be surprised, therefore, when state legislatures begin to exhibit the same kinds of frailties as the U.S. House and the Senate. Similarly, while state courts are applauded for their activism, that activism contributes to the policy dilemmas and conflict many states now face. In summary, by the mid-1990s state legislative politics looked surprisingly similar to congressional dynamics, governors faced the same kinds of limits with which modern presidents must contend, state courts find themselves at odds with the executive and legislative branches, political gridlock occurs frequently, and a skeptical public still expects governments to solve their problems without raising their taxes.

None of this is meant to suggest that the states have not enjoyed a resurgence (they have) or that they are not more capable of governing than they were three decades ago (they are). Rather, the politics of the 1980s and 1990s illustrate that the resurgent states face a number of limits—a more fragmented and contentious political climate, revenue constraints, citizen dissatisfaction, and a fiscally strapped federal partner—that make governing the states more difficult and complex. Moreover, decades of social programming have demonstrated, if nothing else, that the problems governments must now deal with, including poverty, health care for the poor and the aged, crime, and environmental management, are more intractable than we had first imagined. These are not problems that beg simple solutions. Nor are solutions to these problems likely to come cheap. Cleaning up the environment, rebuilding America's infrastructure, fighting poverty and crime, taking care of the elderly, and meeting the needs of education in an increasingly competitive world economy are costly enterprises and demand a long-term commitment of state resources and attention. They may also require a new way of conducting politics and devising policy.

At a minimum, recent developments, both good and bad, suggest the need for a closer look at state political reforms and developments. The pages that follow look systematically at those changes in an effort to gauge the capacity of the states to govern in the twenty-first century. Over the next several chapters answers are sought to the following questions:

How has the character of state politics changed in recent decades? How much political reform has, in fact, taken place? What other changes have occurred in state politics and government? What are the consequences of those changes for the capacity of state governments to govern in the decades ahead? Are state governments capable of producing policies that effectively address the pressing problems of the day? Are state governments sufficiently representative of and responsive to their citizens?

In addressing these and other questions, I focus on two sets of changes in the states' politics. Chapters 2 and 3 look at changes on the "demand side" of state governments, at those processes, mechanisms, and actors that, ideally at least, connect citizens and their political and policy concerns to government. Chapter 2 looks at how elections and opportunities for citizens to influence government between elections have developed in recent years. Beginning with the reapportionment revolution and civil rights legislation and continuing through more recent efforts to make registration and voting simpler and accessing government less difficult, the states have provided more citizens with more opportunities to participate in governing than ever before. Chapter 3 reviews how two other traditional sources of linkages between citizens and their government, parties and interest groups, have evolved. Both parties and interests groups have proven remarkably resilient, both adapting to and shaping the states' changing political climates. Chapters 4, 5, and 6 shift our attention to the "supply side" of state governments—those institutions that singly and collectively are responsible for making public policies within the states. Chapter 4 traces the evolution of the states' governors and focuses on how the informal and formal aspects of the states' chief executives have developed in the last several decades. Chapter 5 reviews the many changes that have occurred in state legislatures, including the emergence of careerism, increases in the rate at which women and minorities serve as lawmakers, and the growing assertiveness of legislatures. Chapter 6 documents how the states' highest courts have both reformed themselves and taken a more active role in governing their states. Chapter 7 concludes our examination of the changing contours of state politics by summarizing how various supply- and demand-side changes affect the ability of the states to govern.

In discussing the changes that have occurred in state politics in recent decades, the intent is not only to document those changes but to assess their larger consequences for the quality of governing in the states. Toward that end, the remainder of this chapter outlines an analytic framework that will help us to systematically sort those impacts. That framework consists of two related elements: (1) a pair of benchmarks against which reforms and developments can be assessed and (2) a discussion of the conventional wisdom concerning the likely impacts on governing of the many changes that are documented throughout the remaining chapters.

Benchmarks for Governing

Identifying a set of criteria for gauging the governing capacity of the American states is a daunting task. Analytically, there is a need for a set of standards broad enough to encompass the wide range of developments that have occurred on the supply and demand sides of government. Making it easier to register and vote and restructuring the states' court systems are seemingly unrelated developments, yet each conditions the character and quality of state government. The task is made more difficult by a lack of consensus in the 1990s as to what constitutes wise governance. Over the last several years, political conflict has increasingly foundered on fundamental issues concerning the goals governments should pursue and the institutional arrangements appropriate to achieving those goals. Those analytic and normative difficulties aside, most would agree that democratic governments need to do two things—produce effective policies while responding to the needs and preferences of their citizens. Given those twin goals, two sets of criteria—responsibility and democratic quality—are useful benchmarks for assessing the implications for governing of recent political developments in state politics.[2]

Responsibility

Responsibility speaks to the ability of governments to govern wisely. As Leroy Rieselbach (1994: 18) notes: "Responsibility focuses on problem solving. A responsible institution makes policies that are reasonably successful in resolving the major issues confronting the nation." Ultimately, responsible government requires enacting and implementing policies that work, that achieve their goals in an effective and efficient manner. In this sense responsibility focuses on the *products* of government, on the outcomes and consequences of government activities. Against that benchmark, state governments are responsible only when their policies, among other things, improve the education of their children, ensure a clean environment, or maintain acceptable levels of public safety or health. But determining the ultimate impact of public policies can be problematic, particularly in the short run. Policy analysts and public officials have long understood how difficult it is to link policy outcomes to specific policies. Most of the things governments attend to are influenced by a number of variables, of which policies and programs are only a few. We know, for example, that educational outcomes not only reflect what it is that schools do but also what children bring to the classroom and their experiences outside of the school. Moreover, policy analysts have learned that the effects of public policies are often not realized for years. Head Start is a good example of that. Written off as a failure in its formative years, the program is now hailed by liberals and conservatives alike as a program that worked.

For these and other reasons, responsibility is also defined and judged in terms of the *processes* involved in making and carrying out public policies. For some, responsibility entails making policy in a timely fashion. Relatedly, critics of divided government and increasing partisanship often couch calls for greater responsibility in terms of avoiding inaction, gridlock, and stalemate. In recent decades citizens have become increasingly frustrated not so much by what the federal government does, but with the seeming inability of Congress and the president to act at all, to avoid the partisan gridlock that frequently immobilizes the federal government. The most dramatic example of that in recent years, of course, was the budget deadlock that shut down the federal government in the winter of 1995.

Others look for responsibility in innovative programming and policy solutions that represent major departures from the status quo. Inherent in that latter notion of responsibility is a dissatisfaction with incremental policies and an attendant policymaking process that places a premium on compromise. According to this view, although compromise often makes sense from a political perspective, the result is frequently policies that are more symbolic than real, pursue conflicting goals, and are unlikely to produce much change. A desire for what is often radical policy change is not inherently a liberal or conservative trademark. Whereas calls for major changes in policy in the 1960s and 1970s typically referenced liberal policy alternatives, efforts to substantially alter the policy status quo in the 1990s are, often as not, support for conservative policy prescriptions (e.g., calls for a flat tax or the welfare reforms that were enacted in 1996) that are every bit as radical as analogous policies two or three decades earlier.

Kent Weaver and Bert Rockman's (1993) analysis of the governing capacity of the industrial powers in Europe, North America, and Japan suggests additional procedural indicators of responsibility, including the ability of governments to (1) sustain policy innovations over time, (2) target resources, and (3) impose losses on powerful groups. The latter pair of standards usefully acknowledge the limited resources that governments at all levels must contend with in the 1990s. In an era of scarce resources, state governments cannot address every policy problem, and state policymakers must necessarily choose among competing public policy concerns. In the early 1990s, for example, the need to build new prisons to house their states' rapidly growing prison populations meant that states such as Florida and Texas had to place new initiatives in education and health care on hold. In addition, one of the painful realities of governing in the 1990s is the fact that finding responsible policy solutions often means imposing losses on particular, and often powerful, groups. Although policymakers are reluctant to admit as much, shrinking the federal budget deficit, for instance, has meant (or will mean) substantially reducing (in some cases eliminating) benefits to the poor, farmers, the elderly, and others.

Defining responsibility in terms of the processes of governing has considerable virtue; it avoids the difficult and often fruitless task of sorting out the ultimate effects of public policies and it makes it easier to design and judge institutional arrangements that promote program effectiveness. But, as the reader is well aware, there is less agreement on procedural benchmarks. Decisions that are made too quickly, for example, can also be viewed as impulsive, not well thought out, and pandering to the latest public opinion poll. Similarly, proposals that depart substantially from the status quo are often seen as extreme, reckless, and risky. There is also no guarantee that policies that move in big steps will necessarily succeed. Nonetheless, there is good reason to believe that governments that cannot respond in a timely fashion to pressing public problems do not serve their citizenry well. Moreover, there is an emerging consensus that governments at all levels need to find new approaches that depart substantially from the policies of the past. And in the face of scarce resources doing that probably entails saying no to some and yes to others.

Statehouse Democracy

Governing requires more than acting responsibly, however. State governments, as all governments, also need to be judged in terms of the quality of "statehouse democracy." For the most part, democracy in the states is representative democracy; citizen preferences, at least in the ideal, find their way into government policies and decisions through elected and, increasingly, nonelected intermediaries. For that to occur, Kim Quaile Hill (1994: 11–12) contends that four procedural conditions or requirements must be present: (1) equal political rights; (2) free and fair elections; (3) high levels of citizen participation in elections; and (4) the existence of "competing nongovernmental institutions" that will organize and articulate the policy preferences of like-minded citizens. Robert Erikson, Gerald Wright, and John McIver (1993: 1) maintain that democratic practices embody both democratic procedures and their results. As those authors note, "we often gauge the quality of democratic government by the responsiveness of public policy makers to the preferences of the mass public as well as by formal opportunities for, and the practice of, mass participation in political life." For Erikson, Wright, and McIver, a critical test of democratic governments is whether public policies are congruent with public opinion.

Taken together, the analyses of Hill and Erikson, Wright, and McIver, as well as a broader reading of democratic theory and practice, suggest that in gauging the democratic consequences of state political developments, we need to attend to the following:

- the extent to which citizens are able to and actually do participate both directly and indirectly in the decisions of government, through candidate and issue elections and through citizen participation devices that promote citizen input between elections;
- the quality of that participation in terms of the number and kinds of opportunities for participation, the extent to which individuals are presented with meaningful and real choices, and the quality of those choices (i.e., are citizens informed and do they choose in their own best interest?);
- the extent to which political minorities, most notably women and racial and language minorities, are represented in government;
- the extent to which the preferences of ordinary citizens are effectively and accurately transmitted to public officials; and
- the extent to which there is a fit between public opinion and public policy.

Achieving greater democracy and policy responsibility is difficult under the best of circumstances. The problem, however, is compounded by a tension that often emerges between the two benchmarks in the day-to-day workings of government. As we suggest throughout the chapters, providing more opportunities for more citizens and groups to have input into government promotes statehouse democracy but often detracts from the ability of governments to make responsible policy decisions by promoting delay, incrementalism, or stalemate. The tension between responsibility and "democraticness" is particularly troublesome for individual representatives who must somehow balance the needs and preferences of constituents with the broader needs of the state and the need for policy coherence. On the one hand, we expect our representatives to prosecute district and constituent interests. And, to their credit, state legislators in a number of states have become quite adept at doing just that. On the other hand, there is a concern that by focusing on the needs of constituents, lawmakers inevitably produce policies that ignore the broader needs of the state and substitute pork barrel and other particularized benefits for responsible, effective programs.

Political Change and the Art of Governing: The Conventional Wisdom

The critical question is how various reforms and developments on the demand and supply sides of government will affect the ability of the states to be both democratic and responsible. Obviously, there is much disagreement here as well, as recent debates over term limits and balanced budget amendments testify. Nonetheless, there is a growing body of evidence and speculation that the capacity to govern is shaped in large part by the degree to which power is centralized within political systems. The conventional wisdom that has emerged maintains that political and institutional changes that fragment or decentralize political authority contribute to statehouse democracy but also make government less responsible. According to this view, spreading the power and authority to govern across and among multiple political institutions and interests ensures that more citizens and groups, including political and social minorities, will have more opportunities to participate in more decisions. Political fragmentation also protects political minorities from majority rule by making it more difficult for majorities to act. And, therein lies the rub. Decentralizing political authority also makes it more difficult to fashion coherent policies in a timely fashion by (1) promoting compromise and incrementalism, (2) making it more difficult to target resources or impose losses on major interests, (3) encouraging the production of particularized benefits (e.g., pork barrel programs or tax breaks for special interests), and (4) contributing to policy delay and stalemate by making political agreements on major legislation and policy initiatives more difficult to obtain.

The genesis of the conventional wisdom is found, in large part, in the long-standing institutional critique of American government, a critique that is addressed to the national government but which has obvious implications for state governments as well.[3] As all of us learned in our civics and American government classes, the founding fathers purposely set out to create a complex set of checks and balances aimed at ensuring that governing would be difficult. A number of constitutional provisions, most notably a separation of powers, checks and balances, antimajority rules, bicameralism, and federalism, provided the means to check the worst impulses of those who would use government too capriciously and on behalf of narrow interests. Those constitutional features also ensured that diverse interests would have the opportunity to be heard in government. Yet, for decades scholars and practitioners alike have found the decentralization and shared authority inherent in America's constitutional framework cumbersome and unwieldy. In his classic study of Congress, Woodrow Wilson lamented a federal government that "lacks strength because its powers are divided, lacks promptness because its authorities are multiplied, lacks wieldiness because its processes are roundabout, lacks efficiency because its responsibility is indistinct and its actions without competent directions" (Wilson 1981: 206).

A century later, the bipartisan Committee on the Constitutional System (CCS) voiced similar concerns about America's constitutional system. As CCS cochair Lloyd Cutler (1985: 12) complained: "A particular shortcoming in need of a remedy is the structural inability of our government to propose, legislate, and administer a balanced program for governing. In parliamentary terms, one might say that under the U.S. Constitution it is not now feasible to 'form a government.' The separation of powers between the legislative and executive branches, whatever its merits in 1793, has become a structure that almost guarantees stalemate today." The problem of decentralization and fragmentation is made worse by recent political developments, including a more assertive Supreme Court, the increased decentralization of Congress, and most notably perhaps, the propensity toward divided government.

Although institutional critiques have been aimed at the national government, their relevance to state governments seems obvious. In the first place, state governments share a common constitutional framework. Like their national counterpart, the states have devised systems of separation of powers and checks and balances and, with the exception of Nebraska, have bicameral legislatures. In addition, many of the changes that have occurred in state government, including the growing diversity of interest groups, the resurgence of state parties, and institutional reforms and developments in each branch of state government, contribute to the centralization or decentralization of state government.

At the same time, the model of governance outlined here only begins to capture the kinds of changes that have occurred at the state level and their likely effects on governing. Many of the changes that have occurred, for example increased compensation for legislators or merit selection for judges, are as much about increasing institutional capacity as they are about centralization or decentralization. Nor does the brief discussion of the positive impacts of decentralization for democratic development address the complex issues and concerns surrounding representation. Moreover, not everyone agrees with the major premise of the framework, that is, that decentralization detracts from responsibility. There is some evidence, for example, that divided government can promote policy innovation by encouraging competition between branches of government and ensuring effective oversight of the executive branch (Weaver and Rockman 1993; Fiorina 1996). These and other caveats aside, the model of governance implicit in the conventional wisdom represents a useful reference point for making sense in a larger fashion of the changes that are occurring throughout the states. It is to those developments we now turn.

NOTES

1. Reported in Peirce 1991.

2. Readers who are familiar with Leroy Rieselbach's (1994) excellent text on congressional reform will instantly recognize my intellectual debt to that author. Rieselbach argues that three sets of criteria can be used to assess congressional behavior—responsibility, responsiveness, and accountability. Those same criteria, however, seem appropriate to the kinds of changes that have occurred in the states' political institutions and processes. However, in utilizing those concepts, I have chosen to subsume responsiveness and accountability under the rubric of democratic quality.

3. Similar conclusions regarding the governing implications of centralization and decentralization are found in the literature on comparative politics. Kent Weaver and Bert Rockman's (1993) edited volume on Western and Japanese democracies is an excellent example.

2

Demand-Side Changes: Elections and Citizen Participation

Much of the resurgence of the states has occurred on the supply side of state government, in the states' political institutions and in the kinds of policies those institutions create. Yet considerable change and reform has taken place on the demand side of the equation as well, in the linkage mechanisms that historically have served to connect the states' citizens to their governments and policies. In terms of elections and nonelectoral participation, major barriers to voting have been removed, and citizens have more opportunities to directly shape public policies both at the ballot box and as policies are being implemented. In addition, the candidate-centered, media-based campaigns of the 1990s bear little resemblance to contests waged three decades earlier. For their part, the states' political parties have proven amazingly resilient and have adapted their roles and functions to fit a new political environment. And as the reader is well aware, interest groups in the 1990s have become more numerous and varied and maintain a powerful (perhaps too powerful) influence on state governments.

This chapter and Chapter 3 examine how these three critical linkage mechanisms—elections and citizen participation devices, parties, and interest groups—have changed in recent decades. In doing that, I not only document many of the important demand-side developments that have occurred at the state level, but also consider the implications of those changes for politics and policies in the states. As we shall see, changes on the demand side of government have both contributed to and detracted from the quality of state government. In this chapter I begin by looking at changes in how individual citizens can connect to state government through elections and through a number of reforms that allow individuals to influence governments between elections, what is labeled here as nonelectoral participation. In Chapter 3 I consider how parties and interest groups are changing in the states and then draw out the larger implications of the states' demand-side changes for representation and responsibility.

Increasing Citizen Influence: An Overview

Elections and other opportunities for individual citizens to influence public policy making are at the very heart of representative democracy. It is not surprising then that a number of changes in elections and nonelectoral participation have been key elements of the states' resurgence. Over the last several decades, state and particularly federal officials have worked hard at making state governments more responsive to all of their citizens by removing barriers to and providing new opportunities for participation in politics and governing both during and after elections. Landmark U.S. Supreme Court rulings in the 1960s ensured that state legislative districts would be equally apportioned among the states' populations. Enforcement of the 1965 Voting Rights Act and its subsequent amendments by the courts and the federal government have extended the right to vote to many blacks and other minorities. State and federal authorities have passed legislation making it easier for voters to both register and vote. In addition, the increased used of initiatives and referenda and the development of various citizen participation devices have provided citizens with the means to more directly influence state governments. Those developments have contributed, often in dramatic ways, to the quality of representation. On balance, state governments today are considerably more representative of and open and accessible to their citizens than ever before. At the same time, those and other demand-side changes raise new issues and concerns. Recent Supreme Court decisions concerning the use of minority-majority districts, for instance, are just the latest chapter in an ongoing controversy over whether simply guaranteeing minorities the right to vote is sufficient to ensuring meaningful representation. The move to make elections and government more accessible to citizens raises additional concerns as well. Does placing complex policy issues on the ballot provide citizens with the information and options they need to make truly informed policy decisions? Do citizen participation devices really increase the influence of ordinary citizens? Will motor voter registration initiatives or voting by mail detract from the quality of representation by making it too easy to vote? All of this is made more problematic by the changing character of state elections. The emergence of candidate-centered campaigns, changes in the vote decision, and the dramatic increase in the role of money in state political campaigns are all developments whose implications for representation and responsibility are still not clear. In order to get at these and other questions we look more closely at a number of critical developments in the character of the states' elections and nonelectoral political participation.

A Reapportionment Revolution?

The right to have one's vote count the same as anyone else's vote is a fundamental given in a democratic society. Yet, for the first two-thirds of this century that right was effectively denied million of Americans in most of the states. As the nation moved into the twentieth century, its people moved to the cities. Increasingly we became an urban (and suburban) nation. Between 1860 and 1910, the population of America's cities grew sevenfold and by 1910 nearly half of the American people lived in urban areas (Bingham and Hedge 1991). State legislators, however, chose to ignore that development in drawing (and sometimes redrawing) legislative districts at the congressional and state level. Instead, state legislatures maintained districting schemes that protected rural interests by denying urban areas proportional representation. As the nation became less rural, malapportionment became particularly severe. By 1955, for example, it was possible for 18 percent of Florida's voters to elect a majority of the state senate and house (Bingham and Hedge 1991). That pattern, although not as extreme in most states, nonetheless repeated itself to some degree throughout the rest of the nation. During the 1940s one estimate was that the value of an urban vote was approximately half that of a vote cast in a rural area (David and Eisenberg 1961, reported in Hill 1994). The victims of malapportionment, of course, were those who lived in the nation's cities—particularly immigrants, blue-collar workers, and blacks.

Relief from malapportionment came in the 1960s following a series of U.S. Supreme Court rulings in which the Court held that districts of unequal population size violated the equal protection clause of the Fourteenth Amendment to the U.S. Constitution. In *Baker v. Carr* (1962) and *Reynolds v. Sims* (1964) the Court ruled that both houses of the states' legislatures must be apportioned on the basis of population (*Wesberry v. Sanders*, 1964, extended the Court's mandate to congressional districts). Although the Court has been reluctant to set an exact mathematical standard, the justices have made it clear that legislative districts must adhere closely to a standard of "one man, one vote." For state legislatures this has generally meant that districts must not vary by more than 10 percent and then only if there is a need to preserve political subdivisions, like county or city boundaries.

At the time, many predicted that the Court's rulings would spur a "reapportionment revolution." As state legislatures were forced to redraw their districts to more fairly reflect urban populations, the assumption was that state politics and policy would undergo dramatic change as legislators representing urban areas gained influence within the legislature and helped to enact more liberal policies aimed at the poor and the cities.

The immediate effect of the Court's rulings was to increase the rate of urban representation in state legislatures as districts became more equal in size. Reapportionment, at least initially, also increased member turnover (see, e.g., O'Rourke 1980) and increased the rate at which younger, better-educated individuals, and ethnic minorities served in the states' legislatures (Patterson 1976). The broader effects of reapportionment were less clear and dramatic, however. Earlier research linking malapportionment to state politics and policy consistently failed to uncover a relationship, leading many to be skeptical about reapportionment's likely impacts (see, e.g., Jacob 1964; Dye 1965; and Hofferbert 1966). Subsequent analyses of the effects of reapportionment, however, indicate that court-ordered reapportionment did alter the states' political landscapes and public policies. In general, reapportionment worked to the advantage of Democrats in the North and Republicans in the South (Erikson 1971; O'Rourke 1980; and Maggiotto et al. 1985). There is also reason to believe that reapportionment produced policy changes that benefited urban areas and the poor. Reapportionment often yielded greater state aid to urban areas and increased welfare spending (Feig 1978), and states with a longer history of reapportionment subsequently spent more on education, public health, hospitals, and highways (Frederickson and Cho 1974). For their part, many legislators perceived that policies in their states had taken a more liberal turn following reapportionment (O'Rourke 1980; Saffell 1982). Not surprisingly, the impacts of reapportionment were felt more strongly in some states than others and were often mitigated by the larger political context in which they took place. Timothy O'Rourke's analysis of reapportionment in six states revealed that the policy and political effects were most pronounced in those states, Tennessee and Kansas, that had been severely malapportioned. In addition, the impacts of reapportionment were often mitigated by the legislature's internal political dynamics. Despite substantial gains in the size of the metropolitan delegation, for instance, rural legislators in Kansas still constituted a majority of the dominant Republican party and, as a result, were able to hold onto key committee and chamber leadership positions in the years following reapportionment.

On balance, the Supreme Court's reapportionment rulings did not produce a revolution in state politics. They did, however, change the character of state politics and policies in many instances and their long-term legacy is the assurance that those who live in urban and suburban areas enjoy greater parity in representation.

Extending the Right to Vote

For blacks in the South and Hispanics and Native Americans in the Southwest, the more important revolution began with the federal civil rights policies of the 1960s that aimed at ensuring minorities the right to vote. In the decades following Reconstruction, states in the South systematically disenfranchised African Americans through violence, intimidation, and a variety of "legal" mechanisms—white primaries, poll taxes, literacy tests, and discriminatory registration practices. Although the percentage of blacks registered to vote in the South had increased to 39 percent by 1964 as many blacks moved to urban areas, in hundreds of rural counties black voting was almost nonexistent, and black registration was still just a little more than half that of whites (Dye 1994). In the Southwest, Hispanics and Native Americans frequently suffered the same kinds of discrimination as literacy tests, white primaries, and other practices effectively disenfranchised those groups in many of the region's states (Davidson 1992; Hill 1994).

Beginning in the 1960s, the federal government moved on several fronts to eliminate voting discrimination. The most crucial of those efforts was the Voting Rights Act of 1965 and its subsequent amendments and extensions in 1970, 1975, and 1982. Designed to enforce the Fifteenth Amendment's prohibition against racially based voting discrimination, the 1965 Voting Rights Act effectively brought elections in the South under federal control for the first time since Reconstruction. The original act initially targeted seven southern states—Alabama, Georgia, Louisiana, Mississippi, South Carolina, Virginia, and forty of the one hundred counties in North Carolina that still had literacy tests in place in 1964. Under Section 5, the act required each of those states to receive prior approval (the so-called preclearance requirement) from the Department of Justice or the federal courts before making any changes in their election laws or practices. The original act prohibited the use of literacy tests for five years and provided for federal poll watchers and examiners. In 1970, the act was extended for five years, additional states were brought under federal control, and literacy tests were prohibited in all states until 1975. The 1975 amendments extended the act seven more years,[1] made permanent the ban on literacy tests, and brought so-called language minorities (e.g., Hispanics, Asian Americans, Eskimos, and Native Americans) under federal protection (Davidson 1992).

The immediate results of the act on black registration were dramatic. In Mississippi, black voter registration increased from 6.7 percent just prior to the act to 60 percent in 1967. In the seven states originally targeted by the act, the percentage of blacks registered to vote increased from 29 percent in 1965 to nearly 60 percent in 1971 (Davidson 1992). But opposition to enfranchising blacks and others did not vanish and over the next several years public officials discovered and rediscovered other, more subtle, ways to discriminate against minorities. Part of that resistance entailed efforts to dilute minority votes by putting into place institutional arrangements that effectively limited the impact and value of African-American and other minority votes. Racial gerrymanders, the annexation of black and Hispanic populations, and the use of at-large elections and multimember districts were used throughout the South and Southwest both before and after the 1965 act to diminish black and Hispanic voting strength (Davidson 1992). In 1960 in *Gomillion v. Lightfoot*, the U.S. Supreme Court declared racial gerrymandering unconstitutional, but it would take the federal courts and Congress another twenty-five years to develop more fully the legal and legislative tools to effectively challenge more subtle forms of dilution. In 1969 in *Allen v. State Board of Elections*, the Supreme Court ruled that vote dilution was subject to the 1965 act and its preclearance requirements, a decision that made it considerably easier for civil rights advocates to challenge dilution efforts. In the 1982 amendments to the Voting Rights Act, Congress explicitly prohibited election arrangements designed to dilute minority voting and, reacting to an earlier Supreme Court ruling (*City of Mobile v. Bolden*, 1980), stipulated that plaintiffs need not demonstrate intent to discriminate in challenging vote dilution schemes but need only show that the results of such actions were discriminatory. Four years later in a case involving a challenge to the use of multimember districts in North Carolina, the Supreme Court in *Thornburg v. Gingles* outlined three criteria for determining whether vote dilution had occurred: (1) the minority group must be sufficiently large and geographically compact to constitute a majority in a legislative district; (2) the minority group must vote as a bloc; and (3) the majority too must vote as a bloc in opposition to the minority group (Davidson 1992). Multimember legislative districts have been a clear casualty of an evolving federal voting rights policy. In 1965, every state in the South used multimember districts to elect representatives to at least one chamber of the state's legislatures and, in doing that, effectively limited black representation, By the mid-1980s, however, multimember districts had virtually been eliminated in the region as a result of Justice Department actions and successful voting rights litigation under the Voting Rights Act (Grofman and Handley 1991).

The 1982 amendments and the Supreme Court's ruling in *Thornburg* provided not only a standard for detecting vote dilution but also, at least until recent Supreme Court rulings, an additional remedy as well—"affirmative" gerrymandering and the creation of minority-majority districts. In the 1980s and early 1990s state legislatures in the South and elsewhere found themselves increasingly under pressure from the federal courts and the Department of Justice to create minority-majority legislative districts to ensure that blacks and Hispanics would be elected to office in greater numbers. The results have been impressive, particularly for black state legislators. In 1969, only 172 African Americans served in their legislatures and only 32 served in the eleven states of the Confederacy. By 1993, the number of black state legislators stood at 511 and the number of blacks serving in the South had grown to 260, an eightfold increase.

Hispanic gains have been dramatic as well. In the state of Texas, for example, the total number of Hispanic legislators increased from 10 in 1971 to 24 by 1987. During that same period of time in Florida, Hispanic representation increased from 2 to 7 members (Bullock 1992). By 1994, 176 Hispanics served in state legislatures (NALEO 1994).

The practice of creating minority-majority districts has been challenged on a number of grounds, including the charge that, ironically, their creation violates the equal protection clause of the Fourteenth Amendment. The Supreme Court first addressed that issue in its landmark decision in *Shaw v. Reno* (1993), a case involving the newly created 12th congressional district in North Carolina. Reacting in part to the district's bizarre, elongated shape, Justice O'Connor, writing for the majority, maintained that "we believe that reapportionment is one area in which appearances do matter. A reapportionment plan that includes in one district individuals who belong to the same race, but who are otherwise widely separated by geographical and political boundaries, and who may have little in common with one another but the color of their skin, bears an uncomfortable resemblance to political apartheid." Two years later in a similar case involving a congressional district in Georgia (*Miller v. Johnson*, 1995) the Court was even clearer about where it stood on the issue: Districts based predominantly on race would no longer be considered constitutional. Subsequent decisions by the Court in 1996 in *Bush v. Vera* and *Shaw v. Hunt* maintained that position but still left unanswered the larger issue of whether racially conscious districting was unconstitutional in every instance (Idelson 1996). How the Court's rulings will affect racial gerrymandering at the state level is even less certain. According to one source, by mid-1996, minority-access-districts had been challenged in at least four states—Texas, Georgia, South Carolina, and Ohio—and lawmakers in Texas and Georgia had redrawn house and senate districts in response to those challenges.[2]

Although the Court's recent rulings represent a potential setback for minority office holding, by the 1990s minorities were serving in state governments in record numbers as Tables 2.1 and 2.2 attest. Table 2.1 reports data on the rate of Hispanic office holding at all levels of government during 1994 in those nine states that contain 86 percent of the Hispanic population and 98 percent of all Hispanic elected officials in the United States. As the data indicate, by the 1990s over 5,000 Hispanics had gained federal, state, or local office in the nine states referenced in the table. Most Hispanic elected officials serve at the local level, in city and county office and on local school boards. But a number serve at the state level as well, particularly in the state's legislatures and as members of Congress. Although the data attest to Hispanic gains in recent years, those figures indicate considerable variation across the states and point to limits on Hispanic political progress.

TABLE 2.1 Hispanic Elected Officials in Selected States, 1994

Office	AZ	CA	CO	FL	IL	NJ	NM	NY	TX
U.S. House	1	4	0	2	1	1	1	2	5
State Exec.	0	0	0	0	0	0	6	0	1
State Legisl.	10	12	9	14	6	1	43	10	35
County	16	14	24	7	3	3	106	1	222
Municipal	127	319	97	24	19	13	272	10	731
Judicial/Law	50	50	10	12	3	1	105	11	389
School Board	136	381	42	3	845[a]	17	151	47	763
Special Districts	1	16	19	2	4	1	32	2	69
TOTALS	341	796	201	64	881	37	716	83	2215
% State Pop. Latino	16%	23%	11%	12%	7%	9%	35%	11%	22%
% Elected Officials Hispanic	10%	4%	2%	1%	.1%	.4%	33%	.3%	8%

[a]includes local school councilmembers.

SOURCE: Compiled from Tables 7 and 9 in National Association of Latino Elected and Appointed Officials, 1994 *National Roster of Hispanic Elected Officials* (Washington, D.C.: NALEO, 1994).

Although Hispanic officials in New Mexico and Arizona serve in elected office at a rate that approaches their proportion in the population, elsewhere the gap between the two is still substantial. In Texas, for example, while Hispanics represented 22 percent of the population, only 8 percent of elected officials in 1994 were Hispanic. Moreover, the data illustrates how difficult it is for Hispanics to win statewide office. In 1994, no Hispanic served in the U.S. Senate and only one Hispanic outside of New Mexico held a statewide executive branch office.

Table 2.2 reports similar data and suggests similar conclusions. African Americans serve in record numbers throughout the South (the primary target of the changes documented in this chapter) and at all levels of government. But as was the case with Hispanics, there is still a sizable gap in most Southern states between the proportion of blacks in the voting-age population and the proportion who actually hold office. Although the two rates are relatively close in Georgia and Alabama, elsewhere blacks have a long way to go before they achieve representation in government proportionate to their numbers in the population. And, as the table indicates, it is still difficult for blacks to win statewide office.

Making the "Simple Act of Voting" Even Simpler

Federal and state efforts to make it easier to register and vote are an additional means of expanding political participation in the American states. Although not as dramatic as reapportionment or civil rights litigation, easing registration requirements and making voting more convenient addresses a puzzling and troubling attribute of American politics—low and declining voting turnout. Although most of us take great pride in America's role as a leader of the free world, a comparison with other democracies indicates that, with respect to voting, the United States falls well behind other nations. During the 1980s, the United States ranked a dismal nineteenth among twenty industrialized nations (Teixeira 1992). Throughout the 1980s only slightly over half of the voting-age population in the United States bothered to vote compared to over 80 percent of their counterparts throughout much of the world. That trend largely continued into the 1990s; in the 1996 presidential race, only 49 percent of registered voters bothered to vote. Equally distressing is the fact that the decline in the rate at which Americans vote has occurred despite the removal of the more odious barriers to voting, an easing of registration requirements, and higher levels of education and income. As you would expect, there is considerable variation among the states. In the period 1989–1994, for instance, average turnout in four states, Montana, North Dakota, Maine, and South Dakota, was above 60 percent, while during that same period fewer than 40 percent of the voting-age population bothered to vote in presidential,

TABLE 2.2 African American Elected Officials in the South, 1993

Office	AL	AR	FL	GA	LA	MS	NC	SC	TN	TX	VA
U.S. House	1	0	3	3	2	0	2	1	1	2	1
State Exec.	1	0	1	2	0	0	2	0	0	1	1
State Legisl.	22	13	19	40	31	42	25	25	15	16	12
County	94	0	28	105	139	158	49	81	49	17	47
Municipal	435	214	105	266	206	337	279	188	55	305	79
Judicial/Law Enforcement	58	51	28	32	104	88	31	15	24	40	15
Local School Boards	86	100	16	95	151	119	81	139	24	85	0
TOTALS[a]	699	380	200	545	636	751	468	450	168	472	155
Blacks as % of Voting Age Pop.	23%	14%	11%	25%	28%	32%	20%	27%	14%	11%	18%
% Elected Officials African American	16%	5%	4%	18%	13%	15%	9%	12%	3%	2%	5%

[a]may include elective offices not included in table.

SOURCE: Compiled from Tables 2, 5, 6, 7, 9, 10, 13, 15, and 17 in Joint Center for Political and Economic Studies, *Black Elected Officials: A National Roster 1993* (Washington, D.C.: Joint Center for Political and Economic Studies, 1993).

gubernatorial, and congressional races in Kentucky, Mississippi, Texas, South Carolina, Tennessee, and Georgia (Bibby and Holbrook 1996).

A number of factors have been cited to account for low turnout in the United States, including low and declining political efficacy, the lack of serious political competition in many instances, and the number and complexity of candidates and issues typically placed on U.S. ballots. Scholars have concluded that America's registration and voting laws are contributing factors as well. Unlike the United States, most countries assume the bulk of responsibility for voter registration by either automatically registering individuals or by conducting systematic canvassing efforts to enter citizens on the voting rolls. In the United States, however, "the entire burden of registration falls on the individual rather than the government" (Glass, Squire, and Wolfinger 1984: 52). The problem is made worse by the fact that registration typically occurs at a separate time and place than the more gratifying act of voting. There is no shortage of evidence linking registration requirements in the 1960s and 1970s to low turnout in the American states. Four registration provisions—shorter closing dates, regular registration office hours, weekend and evening registration office hours, and the availability of absentee registration—contributed to higher turnout during that period and, had those provisions been adopted in every state, turnout in the 1972 election would have increased by an estimated 9 percent (Rosenstone and Wolfinger 1978). Critics have also charged that American elections are needlessly inconvenient and have urged lawmakers to adopt reforms that would allow citizens to vote by mail or to vote at more convenient times and places.

To their credit, the states had adopted a number of reforms aimed at making registration and voting easier even before the U.S. Congress passed the National Voter Registration Act (NVRA) in 1993. By the early 1990s all but a handful of states allowed individuals to register to vote by mail (under the NVRA all states had to do so beginning in 1995). In some states mail registration is as simple as returning a postcard to the registrar, whereas other states require witnesses or a notary (Rhine 1995). In addition, thirty-nine states had adopted some form of motor voter registration (although only a dozen or so states actively implemented such a plan) prior to 1993 and the NVRA's passage. Interestingly enough, some of the states that already had motor voter registration plans, including Michigan, Pennsylvania, and Illinois, have challenged the 1993 act ostensibly because of the expense of implementing the federal plan (in their challenge to the NVRA, California officials estimated that it would cost the state an additional $20 million to implement the act) and because they felt it usurped the states' constitutional rights. In 1996 the U.S. Supreme Court ruled, however, that the federal act was in fact constitutional. The Court's decision aside, a number of states are still challenging the federal act by moving slowly and reluctantly to implement key provisions of the bill, most notably the provision for registering individuals who receive public assistance (Piven and Cloward 1996). Frances Fox Piven and Richard Cloward argue that this strategy is the "last line of defense" for many Republican governors who fear that registering the poor would swell the roll of Democratic voters.

Many states have also moved the closing date for registration so that individuals can register closer to the actual day of the election. Today, individuals typically must register 28–30 days before an election. A number of states have closing dates of two weeks or less and six states, Alaska, Maine, Minnesota, New Hampshire, Wisconsin, and Wyoming (primaries only), allow individuals to register on election day. Voting has been made easier in a handful of states as well. By the mid-1990s, a dozen states allowed "no-excuse" absentee balloting and seven states—Arizona, California, Colorado, Iowa, Nevada, Tennessee, and Texas—allowed individuals to vote early at satellite polling stations (Foster 1994; Busch 1996). Seventeen states allow individuals to vote by mail, although mail elections are typically limited to special or nonpartisan or noncandidate elections (Parker and Przybylski 1993; Busch 1996).

The states' efforts at making voting easier seem to be working. Allowing individuals to register on election day, for example, has increased voting by an estimated 5 percent in Minnesota, Wisconsin, and Maine (Fenster 1994). Similarly, those states that allowed individuals to register closer to election day, ensured that individuals could register at night and on weekends, and were less likely to purge voters from the rolls for not voting enjoyed higher rates of turnout over the 1960–1988 period (Teixeira 1992). Evidence from the 1970s, 1980s, and early 1990s indicates that state motor voter registration laws produced higher turnout as well (Rhine 1995; Knack 1995). There is also some evidence that mail elections and early voting have yielded higher turnout. When the state of Washington allowed selected counties to vote by mail in the state's 1994 primary, for instance, turnout was 53 percent in those counties, well over the statewide figure of 35 percent (Foster 1994). In a parallel fashion, Oregon officials reported increases of 15 to 40 percent in turnout in those counties that employed mail ballot elections (Parker and Przybylski 1993). As part of the same survey, Washington state officials reported similar increases; in the fifty-nine mail ballot elections held in that state, the average turnout was 55 percent (Parker and Przybylski, 1993). Finally, states with more permissive absentee voting provisions enjoy greater turnout but only when combined with efforts by the political parties to mobilize voters (Oliver 1996).

Although it is reasonably clear that electoral reforms have yielded higher turnout in the American states, the political and policy impacts of those increases are not as certain. Given the tendency for nonvoters to come from lower socioeconomic strata, the conventional wisdom is that increases in turnout should advantage Democrats and thus alter electoral outcomes. Yet scholars generally agree that under most scenarios mobilizing nonvoters is not likely to alter partisan electoral outcomes. The reason for that is fairly simple: Even under the most optimistic turnout scenarios, nonvoters are still not likely to vote so lopsidedly for any candidate that it would produce a different partisan outcome (Teixeira 1992). Mobilizing nonvoters is likely to alter electoral outcomes only under fairly unusual circumstances—high turnout, close elections, and very monolithic voting on the part of nonvoters (Cavanaugh 1991).

There is some evidence to suggest that increasing turnout has nonetheless altered the kinds of policies that the states produce. In the first instance, a number of studies suggest that nonvoters often have different policy preferences than do voters. Summarizing the literature Ruy Teixeira (1992: 100) concludes that "nonvoters are somewhat more liberal than voters on policy issues concerning the economic role of government and somewhat less liberal on defense, the environment, and social issues such as abortion." Some argue that those differences are fairly small in magnitude and not likely to alter the policy outcomes of governments (see, e.g., Teixeira 1992 and Bennett and Resnick 1990). But evidence reported elsewhere suggests that the taxing and spending decisions of state governments do respond to variations in turnout, particularly differences in the rate at which lower-class citizens enter the electorate. There is, for instance, a tendency for increases in turnout to be associated with greater welfare spending (see, e.g., Peterson and Rom 1989). Kim Quaile Hill and his colleagues' research (see Hill and Leighley 1992; Hill, Leighley, and Hinton-Anderson 1995; and Ringquist, Hill, Leighley, and Hinton-Anderson 1997) demonstrates that the link between turnout and welfare policy reflects the mobilization of the lower class and the tendency among governments to respond to increases in lower-class turnout with more redistributive policies. Hill, Leighley, and Hinton-Anderson discover, for example, that increases in lower-class turnout are associated with more generous and equitable AFDC grants over the period 1978 to 1990. Their analysis also illustrates that the ability of the poor to affect policy outcomes is conditioned by a number of considerations. In particular, the influence of lower-class turnout is diminished during difficult fiscal times, where lower-class turnout is particularly low, and in off-year elections. Similar dynamics may well be occurring on the revenue side of state government as well. One recent study demonstrates that increases in turnout are associated with greater tax progressivity among the American states even after controlling for ideology, party competition, and the states' historical tax structures (Martinez 1997).

Does all of this suggest that in the wake of recent efforts to increase turnout state policies will become more redistributive? Probably not. For one thing, it is not at all certain that increasing turnout in the late 1990s will necessarily produce a substantial net increase in Democratic voters. Republican party officials have worked hard to mobilize absentee and potential new voters in recent years (see, e.g., Oliver 1996) and are not likely to ignore the opportunities that the NVRA presents to the party. Moreover, in recent years state governments have taken a decided turn to the right and welfare reform is at the very center of those developments. Accordingly, legislators and governors on both sides of the aisle are currently more inclined to cut welfare spending than they are to expand programming. At best, increases in lower-class turnout (assuming that they occur) might ultimately act as a check on more drastic cuts in welfare as politicians seek to avoid a potential political backlash from lower-class voters.

Direct Democracy

The rules under which state elections are conducted have changed in important ways in recent decades. So too has the content of those elections. Increasingly, voters in several states are engaging in what scholars have labeled "direct" (versus representative) democracy by using initiatives and referenda to place public policy issues directly on the ballot. Unlike the other reforms we have discussed, initiatives and referenda are not of recent vintage. With few exceptions, most states adopted their initiative and referendum provisions in the early 1900s during the Progressive Era in American politics. Like the Populists who preceded them, Progressive reformers were convinced that the political parties and state and local governments had become captured by special interests (most notably the railroads and political bosses) and were unresponsive to the needs of ordinary citizens. Progressives sought to remedy this situation by increasing the citizens' role in government through a number of devices, including the direct primary, a series of municipal reforms aimed at wresting control from party bosses, the recall provision, and our focus here, the initiative and referendum.

A number of provisions provide for direct democracy in the American states. Every state but Delaware requires that constitutional amendments be approved by the state's voters. In twenty-four states, state lawmakers can put issues before the voters in a legislative referendum. For their part, citizens in a number of states can place policy issues on the ballot in a couple of ways. Under the initiative, now provided for in two dozen states, citizens can place issues on the ballot by gathering the requisite number of signatures on an initiative petition. (Three of those states use an indirect initiative and require that issues be first considered by the legislature. Should the legislature fail to approve the measure, it then goes before the voters.) Citizens in twenty-one states can also petition to force a vote on bills enacted by the state legislature through a popular referendum. In each case, the number of signatures required is a percentage of the vote cast in a preceding election. Signature requirements range from as low as 2 percent in North Dakota to a high of 15 percent in Wyoming. About half the states also require that signatures be geographically distributed across the state. Not surprisingly, states with the least restrictive signature requirements, including North Dakota, California, and Oregon, have historically had more issues on the ballot (Magleby 1984).

The use of the initiative and referendum has increased dramatically over the last decade or so. The growth in the use of citizen initiatives has been particularly striking. Between 1940 and 1980 only 248 initiatives appeared on statewide ballots. In the 1980s, however, the public rediscovered direct democracy and the number of policy issues placed on the ballot by citizens increased significantly. From 1981 to 1992, a total of 346 initiatives were placed on statewide ballots (Kehler and Stern 1994). That trend continues into the 1990s. In 1996, 94 initiatives were placed on the ballot in twenty states.

A number of factors account for the increase in the use of the initiative and referendum. First, that increase probably reflects the changing character of interest group politics in the states. Interest groups at the state level have not only become more numerous and diverse, but more specialized as well, focusing on single issues and causes. In that kind of interest group milieu, initiative and referendum become ideal mechanisms for pursuing the policy preferences of single-issue interest groups. Relatedly, greater use of direct democracy devices also stems from changing interest group tactics. Interest groups have discovered the virtues of "outsider" strategies and grassroots mobilization. Using the initiative process to bypass legislatures is very much in the same spirit as mobilization efforts aimed at legislators. Second, the increasing use of direct democracy no doubt reflects a growing dissatisfaction with governments at all levels. California's infamous Proposition 13 in 1978, for example, was essentially a protest on the part of Howard Jarvis and his supporters, as were many of the three dozen or so tax and spending limit initiatives that were placed on ballots elsewhere within the next two years (Moore 1988). Third, an increase in the rate of direct democracy no doubt stems from a growing willingness on the part of some state legislators to duck controversial issues. Of the 700 or so ballot issues placed before the voters between 1982 and 1986, 81 percent were placed there by state legislatures (Cronin 1989). Finally, initiatives and referenda are used more frequently today because the technologies for doing so are so readily available to those who can pay for them. Candidates and political parties have become experts at direct-mail fund-raising and running media campaigns. Those skills and capabilities are easily transferable to various ballot issues. A new industry has emerged that will provide, at a substantial cost, the skills and technologies necessary to gather the requisite signatures and wage highly sophisticated media campaigns on behalf of their clients. Indeed business is so good that some political consultants specialize solely in initiative campaigns. Many of those firms concentrate on just a single aspect of the process, signature gathering or media campaigns. Others provide a full range of service for initiative sponsors and opponents.

All of that is made possible by the substantial amount of money that finds its way into initiative campaigns. In 1988, for instance, insurance industry officials in California spent over $40 million dollars to defeat a trio of initiatives that would have reduced automobile insurance rates and attempted to enact two additional initiatives that were more favorable to the industry. Total spending by all groups on the issue, including consumers and trial-lawyer associations, was estimated to reach $75 million. Altogether, $129 million was spent on the dozen or so initiatives on the California ballot that year (Moore 1988). Funding for expensive initiative races comes from a number of sources, including industry groups, trade associations, unions, consumer and environmental groups, and religious groups. Not surprisingly, often the biggest contributors are those who have the most to gain or lose from the ballot proposition. In 1984, Scientific Games, an Atlanta firm that provides services to state lottery operations, spent over $2 million backing Proposition 37, an initiative creating a state lottery in California. That proposition was passed and Scientific Games subsequently received a $40 million contract to supply the state with lottery tickets (Kehler and Stern 1994). California is not the only state with expensive initiative contests. In 1986, $6.7 million dollars was spent by opponents and supporters of a tort reform initiative in Arizona. Altogether, PACs in that state spent well over four times as much on initiative campaigns as they did on candidate races, $12.7 million versus just $2.7 million. More recently, the gaming industry spent $16 million in 1994 in their unsuccessful bid to legalize casino gambling in the state of Florida (Bowman and Kearney 1996). And in 1996, opponents and supporters of a series of initiatives that would require the sugar industry to pick up the tab for cleaning up the Everglades spent an estimated $30 million on behalf of their positions.

As the preceding discussion makes clear, a wide range of issues have been the subject of state initiatives and referenda. In the early 1980s, initiatives that would limit taxes were of course very popular. Ten years later, initiatives requiring term limits for lawmakers appeared on several of the states' ballots. In the interim, voters have been asked to sort out difficult policy choices, including abortion, prayer in school, crime, the

TABLE 2.3   A Sampling of Statewide Ballot Propositions in the 1996 Elections

Campaign Finance Reform—Arkansas, California, Colorado, Maine, Montana, Nevada

Education—Arkansas, Montana, Nebraska, North Dakota, Oklahoma, Oregon, South Dakota, Utah, Washington

Environmental Protection/Hunting—Alabama, Alaska, Arkansas, California, Colorado, Florida, Idaho, Iowa, Maine, Massachusetts, Michigan, Missouri, Montana, New Jersey, New York, Oregon, Rhode Island, Washington, West Virginia

Gambling—Alabama, Arizona, Arkansas, Colorado, Michigan, Nebraska, Ohio, Washington

Health Care—Arizona, California, Nevada, Oregon

Taxes—Arizona, California, Colorado, Florida, Georgia, Idaho, Louisiana, Missouri, Nebraska, Nevada, Oklahoma, Oregon, South Dakota, Utah

Term Limits—Alaska, Colorado, Idaho, Maine, Missouri, Montana, Nebraska, Nevada, North Dakota, Oregon, South Dakota, Washington, Wyoming

Tort/Legal Reform—California, Michigan, North Dakota, Oregon, Virginia

Victims' Rights—Connecticut, Indiana, Nevada, North Carolina, Oklahoma, Oregon, South Carolina, Virginia

Note: Includes both citizen initiatives and legislative referenda
SOURCE: Compiled from AllPolitics, "Ballot Measures by Topic." On-line posting. Available: http://allpolitics.com/1996/news/9611/02/ ballots (November 11, 1996).

rights of gays, women, and minorities, and environmental protection. Table 2.3 lists the subject matter of many of the more than 200 ballot measures (including both citizen and legislative initiatives and referenda) that were placed before voters in forty-one states and the District of Columbia in the 1996 election (AllPolitics 1996). As the table reveals, a wide range of policy issues were addressed, including term limits, taxes, environmental protection, hunting, victims' rights, campaign finance reform, education, and health care.

Advocates of direct democracy contend that initiatives and referenda can contribute to the quality of governing in a number of ways (Cronin 1989: 10–11).

- Direct democracy will make governments more responsive.
- Direct democracy will reduce the role of special interests in government.
- Direct democracy will facilitate open, informed discussion of critical public issues.
- Direct democracy will increase voter interest and participation and, as a result, lessen voter alienation and apathy.

- Direct democracy provides a means for ordinary citizens to realize their policy preferences in the face of recalcitrant public officials.

The evidence to date, however, suggests that initiatives and referenda frequently fall short of those ideals and raises a number of concerns and issues about the efficacy of direct democracy. In most cases, initiatives and referenda have failed to engage voters in quite the way that propo nents of those devices had hoped. Turnout in states with initiatives and referenda is no higher than in states that lack those mechanisms (Everson 1981; Magleby 1984) and drop off on ballot issues (i.e., the tendency for voters to not vote on issues and candidates elsewhere on the ballot) can be as high as 25–30 percent (Magleby 1984; Cronin 1989). Nor is there much evidence that voters come to issue elections any better informed than they do on candidate races. As David Magleby (1984: 198) notes, "On the most salient initiatives, voters do tend to be about as informed, interested, and sure of their opinions as in statewide candidate elections. But on the more frequent propositions of low salience, a substantial pro- portion of voters drop off; and of those who vote, many rely on very lim- ited information or no information at all." Although the print media and public officials often provide reasonably good coverage of initiative is- sues (see, e.g., Zisk 1987 and Cronin 1989) too many voters get their in- formation from 30- and 60-second television spots that, at best, can only begin to provide the information necessary to understand complex pol- icy issues and, at worst, are simply deceptive.

Moreover, despite the hopes of progressive reformers and more recent proponents, direct democracy has not reduced the influence of interest groups on public policy. As Betty Zisk (1987: 250) points out, "Far from replacing group lobbying efforts vis-à-vis the legislature, the initiative and referenda campaigns provide an alternative channel for the very group activities the reformers denounced." What particularly troubles some observers of direct democracy is the ability of well-organized inter- ests to pour huge sums of money into initiative contests and the atten- dant fear that money will determine election outcomes. Unfortunately, a review of the evidence suggests those fears are often warranted. In forty of the fifty issue elections conducted between 1976 and 1980 in California, Massachusetts, Michigan, and Oregon, for instance, the side that spent the most money won (Zisk 1987). Other evidence suggests, however, that the ability of interest group money to "buy" issue elections is probably more limited than those figures would suggest. Magleby's (1984) analy- sis of statewide propositions in California between 1954 and 1982, for in- stance, indicates that although groups that outspent their opponents by a substantial margin were able to *defeat* proposed initiatives 87 percent of the time, *proponents* of initiatives who outspent their opposition by a two-to-one margin actually lost more than they won. And, as Zisk (1987) observes, the influence of high spending can be offset by well-organized, grassroots efforts.

Many analysts are also concerned that the initiative and referendum will be used to hurt minority groups, including women, gays, and racial and ethnic groups. Many fear that voting majorities will not be as protective or supportive as state legislatures of the rights of minorities. Although Thomas Cronin (1989: 212) is probably correct when he concludes that "direct democracy measures in recent years have not generally had the effect of diminishing minority rights," efforts to curtail those rights frequently appear on state (and local) ballots and have been successful in enough instances to warrant at least some concern. Over the past several years, for example, a number of local communities have passed initiatives that typically repeal recently enacted ordinances that would have extended civil rights protection to gays and lesbians. Similar initiatives have fared less well at the state level. California voters in 1978 and again in 1986 voted down initiatives that would have made it more difficult for gays to teach in the schools and would have authorized public health officials to quarantine those with AIDS, respectively. In 1992, voters in Oregon and Colorado voted on initiatives that would restrict statutory protection for gays. Oregon voters defeated their initiative whereas the Colorado initiative passed (only to be struck down as unconstitutional by the U.S. Supreme Court). In 1994, voters in Oregon again voted down a proposition that would have banned laws and ordinances protecting gays, while in Idaho voters rejected by a narrow margin a similar ban. In 1995 voters in Maine also rejected, by a 53–47 margin, an antigay initiative.

Immigrants and ethnic groups have also been the subject of statewide initiatives. In 1984, for example, California voters overwhelming supported a nonbinding proposition that recommended that the governor write federal officials urging the passage of legislation requiring voting materials, including ballots and information pamphlets, to be printed only in English (Cronin 1989). More recently, in 1994 Californians passed, by a 59–41 margin, Proposition 187 which denies public education and social services to illegal aliens (as this is being written, opponents are challenging the constitutionality of Proposition 187).

For many the problem of minority protection is made worse by the fact that the poor and the less well educated participate less frequently in issue elections (Magleby 1984; Cronin 1989). Indeed the gap between affluent and nonaffluent Americans may be even greater on ballot propositions than in candidate races (Magleby 1984). Not only do less-affluent Americans have more trouble understanding many ballot propositions, but that lack of understanding often leads to nonvoting and, equally distressing, may lead the poor to vote against their own self-interest. For example, in 1976 voters in Massachusetts were asked to vote on a proposition providing for flat-rate electricity pricing. Although 61 percent supported the idea (it was after all in their best interest to do so), only 22 percent of those earning less than $5,000 actually voted yes. Why? "Poor people were more likely to state that they would skip voting on the proposition because it was too long and complicated or because they did not know what a yes or no vote implied" (Magleby 1984: 116). Does the underrepresentation of the poor matter in terms of the final outcome of issue elections? In many cases, probably not. Frequently, the final outcome of initiative contests would be no different if the poor had been mobilized. Nonetheless, the available evidence suggests there are at least some instances in which had the poor and minorities voted in greater numbers and more in line with their own self-interest, issue election outcomes would have been different.

A final concern with the initiative and referendum has to do not so much with how well they connect citizens to state governments, but with the kinds of public policies that they produce. While acknowledging the democratic virtues of issue elections, some analysts maintain that direct democracy simply produces bad policy. In 1988, voters in California, for example, actually approved two contradictory propositions—Proposition 68, which provided for the public financing of campaigns and Proposition 73, which prohibited it. That same year, voters were offered not one but five propositions concerning insurance reform. Years earlier, one survey estimated that as many as three-fourths of those Californians voting on a rent-control initiative actually cast the wrong vote (reported in Magleby 1984). As one commentator (Moore 1988: 2296) noted: "Democracy never looked so ugly."

Part of the problem lies with the process by which decisions are necessarily made in issue elections. Unlike legislatures, issue elections typically must reduce often complex policy decisions down to a simple yes/no choice. Except in the most unusual circumstances, voters are not allowed to choose, for instance, between a 5 or a 10 or a 15 percent decrease in property taxes, but instead must decide on just one of those options. Nor is there any opportunity for opposing sides to reach the kinds of compromises that often make legislation more palatable to all sides. (Of course some would contend that it is those compromises that make for bad legislative policy.) Some worry further that there is no room in issue elections for the kind of thoughtful deliberation that, at least ideally, can take place within legislatures as policies are formulated over a period of time and through member interaction. One related concern is that initiatives have preempted legislatures in many states and in so doing further detract from good public policy. In commenting on the active initiative process in California, one analyst (Barnes 1990: 2047) contends that "the most important branch of government in California may be neither the legislature nor the executive but the initiative branch."

An additional concern is that voters simply lack the information they need to make sound policy decisions because of the complexity or wording of ballot propositions. Although there is some disagreement within the literature concerning how well prepared voters are in issue elections, a substantial number of voters typically admit difficulty in understanding complex, often technical propositions (see Magleby 1984 and Cronin 1989), and many of us have found ourselves in the position where we fear that we have cast the wrong vote in those elections in which a "yes" really means no and a "no" means yes. The problem is made worse by the character of many initiative and referendum campaigns. One strategy that initiative opponents frequently use is to produce so much uncertainty and confusion in the minds of voters that they will vote no mainly out of a sense of frustration (Moore 1988). That confusion is often heightened when opponents of initiatives offer their own counterinitiative, as was the case in 1988 when Californians ended up voting on no less than five insurance propositions. A particularly onerous instance of misleading or what has been called "stealth" campaigning occurred in 1994 when tobacco interests spent $18 million in support of what at first glance appeared to be an antismoking proposition, Proposition 188. Only when the press and antismoking groups blew the whistle did many California voters learn that the true intent of Proposition 188 was to weaken, not strengthen, the state's existing antismoking laws (PBS, September 3, 1996).

Not everyone agrees that direct democracy automatically produces bad public policy. As Cronin (1989: 229) contends: "Unwise legislation does get onto ballots, but the record indicates that voters reject most really unsound ideas." Moreover, the initiative and referendum have usefully expanded the policy agendas in a number of states, forcing elected officials to address policy problems that they probably would not have addressed (at least as quickly) if left to their own devices. Property tax limits in the late 1970s and early 1980s and term limits in the 1990s are just two examples of the agenda-setting role that the initiative and referendum have played. Relatedly, given the fact that most voters lack both the time and information to monitor the behavior of their elected officials on a day-to-day and session-to-session basis, the initiative and referendum are an effective means of structuring and constraining legislative decisions "before the fact." In addition, one could make the case that the decisions of voters are no more fragile than those made by their elected officials. Given the pervasive influence of interest groups in many state legislatures and given patterns of cue-taking and deference to committees and party leaders, it may be unfair to hold citizens to a higher standard of decisionmaking than we do those who represent them.

In the final analysis, Cronin and others are probably correct in asserting that the initiative and referendum are not as bad as critics maintain nor as good as advocates had hoped. Direct democracy has expanded the policy agenda of the states and provides citizens the opportunity to directly influence policy decisions. In those and other ways, direct democracy has contributed to both the responsiveness and responsibility of state government. At the same time, citizens could be much better informed and more engaged in initiative and referendum contests, and the predominant role of well-organized interest groups raises questions about the democratic viability of the process. Officials in a number of states have begun reexamining the initiative and referendum, but to date little progress has been made in making the process more rational or addressing the problems of big money and the influence of special interests. With respect to the role of money in issue elections, the courts have made it clear that limiting either the sources or the amounts of money spent on direct democracy will not be tolerated. Reformers have, however, pressed for tougher disclosure requirements. A trio of groups that reviewed the initiative in California have proposed that the names of major contributors to each side of an initiative campaign be provided on signature petitions and political advertisements (Kehler and Stern 1994). The California groups proposed additional changes aimed at ensuring that citizens are better informed and the process more rational, including: (1) the preparation of voter information pamphlets that would not only summarize the major provisions of the initiative but identify major supporters and opponents; (2) provisions that would allow legislatures to correct errors or to amend successful initiatives with a supermajority; and (3) establishing a "cooling-off period" during which initiative proponents would work with the state legislature to enact compromise legislation acceptable to proponents.

Nonelectoral Participation

The states and federal governments and their citizens have worked hard in the last few decades to remove barriers to voting and to provide citizens with the opportunity to directly shape policy at the ballot box. The states, often at the prodding of the federal government, have also sought to increase citizen input into government *between* elections. Open meeting and records laws, citizen participation requirements, and interest representation mechanisms are used throughout the states and their local governments to increase the public's involvement in government decisionmaking. Although found throughout both the executive and legislative branches of government, nonelectoral participation mechanisms have become especially prevalent and have frequently had their greatest impact within the executive branch of state governments, particularly among regulatory agencies. There are good reasons for that tendency. For a variety of reasons, public bureaucracies are typically afforded a great deal of discretion and autonomy and much policy is actually made at the implementation stage and after laws have been enacted. As a result, citizen participation require-ments and other means of increasing citizen input into administrative de-cisions fill a potential gap in the process of representation. Unfortunately, with a few notable exceptions, few studies exist concerning the incidence and impact of nonelectoral citizen participation at the state level. Nonetheless, what evidence there is suggests that participatory devices are used frequently throughout the states and often provide additional repre-sentation for citizens and citizen groups. Indeed, William Gormley (1986: 180) has argued that state regulatory agencies "have been caught up in what might be described as a 'representation revolution' aimed at making administrative agencies more accountable to broad, diffuse interests by facilitating public representation in administrative decision-making processes." We look briefly at three common participatory devices.

Open Meeting and Record Laws

Effective citizen participation in government requires, at a minimum, that citizens have access to public meetings and information about govern-ment actions. Open meeting and record laws adopted in each of the fifty states in the 1960s and 1970s began to meet those requisite needs. By the late 1970s every state had an open meeting law on the books and all but three had open record laws (ACIR 1980). Among the 50 state meeting laws, 42 required that the public receive advance warning of public meet-ings, 37 required that minutes be taken, and 35 provided for some kind of sanctions in those instances where the open meeting law has been vi-olated. State open meeting and record laws are frequently modeled after similar laws at the national level, most notably the Freedom of Information Act and the Government in the Sunshine Act. And like their national counterparts, state laws have probably gone a long way toward making state government more open and accessible to ordinary citizens. Nonetheless, what little evidence there is concerning the experience to date with both federal and state laws suggests that the impact of state open meeting and record laws may be limited by a number of consider-ations. A review of state open records laws in the mid-1970s by the University of Missouri's Freedom of Information Center (reported in ACIR 1980) found, for instance, that many state laws failed to provide for judicial and administrative review of the process, thus making it difficult, if not impossible, to enforce open record provisions. According to that same study, only a handful of states compensated citizens for the legal fees borne in the process of seeking public records. In addition, a number of state laws make it easy for agencies to delay or evade requests for information by either not setting deadlines for agency responses or by allowing agencies to charge substantial photocopying costs. A review of federal laws suggests additional problems as well, including the tendency for corporations to benefit more than citizens in seeking information under the Freedom of Information Act and the ability of some agencies to successfully drag their feet in meeting citizen requests for information (Gormley 1989). In general, studies indicate that open meeting and record laws are likely to work only for attentive publics.

Public Hearings

The idea of public hearings is hardly new to state governments. However their use has increased substantially in recent years as part of the larger movement toward increasing citizen participation in government at all levels (Gormley 1989). Much of the impetus for that comes from the federal government. Throughout the 1970s and 1980s dozens of federal grants across a wide range of programming mandated some form of citizen participation as a condition for aid receipt. By the late 1970s 155 federal grant programs required some form of citizen participation, typically advisory committees or public hearings (ACIR 1980). In addition, various federal and state environmental laws require public participation in implementing federal and state environmental programs (Gormley 1993).

How effective are public hearings? Again, despite their widespread use and potential importance, few studies look systematically at their impact. Early evidence on federal grant programs, including General Revenue Sharing and the Community Development Block Grant (CDBG) program are not very reassuring. As the ACIR (1980: 5) notes in its review of federal grant programs in the late 1970s, "the impact of different kinds of federal citizen participation requirements varies, but overall it is modest." However, studies of environmental programming indicate that, under the right circumstances, public hearings can increase citizen influence over public policy. Analysis of over 1800 public hearings by three California coastal commissions in the mid-1970s, for example, indicated that the commissions were more likely to deny development permits in the face of citizen opposition (Rosener 1982). Similarly, environmental groups in Pennsylvania effectively opposed nearly half of the ninety-four hazardous waste permits they found objectionable in 1981–1982 (Rosenbaum 1983). Other studies (see, e.g., Godschalk and Stiftel 1981 and Mazmanian and Sabatier 1980) reach similar conclusions concerning the influence of citizen participation on environmental programming. Why have public hearings been more effective in the area of environmental protection? Gormley (1989: 77) argues that environmental policy exhibits a number of conditions that promote effective citizen participation, including "high issue salience, strong public support, well-organized citizens' groups, and in many instances, sympathetic administrative officials."

Proxy Advocates

Although public hearings, sunshine laws, and advisory committees provide citizens with access to and information about government decisions, those strategies are limited by the fact that most citizens have neither the time nor the expertise to effectively participate in government on a regular basis. Even where citizens are actual participants in regulatory decisionmaking, a lack of expertise frequently undermines citizen influence on actual decisions. Many states, for example, require public membership on state occupational licensing boards and in several instances require that citizens constitute a majority. Yet analysis by Schutz (1983) of licensing board decisions following passage of legislation in California requiring public membership found little evidence that the character of board decisions had changed even in those instances where citizens represented a majority of the board's membership.

Proxy advocates, public officials whose job it is to represent consumer interests in public utility regulation, were established in a number of states during the 1970s as a response to sharp rate increases following the OPEC oil embargo. Designed as an alternative to direct citizen involvement in regulatory decisions, the use of proxy advocates assumes that citizens lack the incentives to organize and the resources and knowledge to participate effectively in regulatory decisionmaking, particularly where those decisions involve complex and technical matters. By the late 1970s, proxy advocates had been established in thirty-one states. In thirteen of those states, advocates were part of the attorney general's office. In the remaining states, proxy advocates operated out of newly created offices of consumer counsels (Gormley 1983). Gormley's analysis of public utility regulation during that period indicates that proxy advocates effectively represented consumer interests and were able to persuade utility commissioners in a number of states to, among other things, adopt late payment penalty bans and roll back rate increase requests by utilities. The influence of proxies varied by the context in which they operated—proxy advocates were more likely to be effective where utility decisions were complex, but less effective where there was a high degree of consumer conflict. The apparent success of proxy advocates in utility decisions has led analysts to urge the creation of advocates in other policy areas, including environmental protection and banking and insurance regulation (Gormley 1986).

Transformed Electoral Politics

Although the major thrust of our discussion of elections and political participation concerns how states have sought to increase citizen input into government, no discussion of the changing nature of elections would be complete without at least some attention to how state electoral politics have changed in recent years. In an insightful piece written in the early 1990s, Stephen Salmore and Barbara Salmore (1993) argue that state elections are looking surprisingly like similar contests at the national level. According to those authors, gubernatorial politics have become "presidentialized" and in an increasing number of cases state legislative contests have become "congressionalized." More particularly, those authors point to a number of trends in support of their thesis—the emergence of candidate-centered campaigns, the decline of political parties both in terms of their role in campaigns and in how individuals cast their votes, and the emergence of incumbency as a factor in gubernatorial and legislative elections. As I note in Chapters 4 and 5, those developments have substantial implications, both good and bad, for the character of state government. On the positive side, those trends help account for the resurgence of the states' governors and reinforce the increase in legislative professionalism. At the same time, the transformation of state electoral politics has also contributed to split control of state governments and the fragmentation of state legislatures, trends that some would argue undercut the ability of state governments to govern wisely.

Central to all of this has been a dramatic increase in the role of money in state elections, particularly in gubernatorial races. Between 1977 and 1993, the average race for governor cost $8.6 million dollars (in 1993 dollars) or $3.87 per registered voter. In sixteen states over $10 million was spent, and in seven states candidates spent in excess of $18 million (Beyle 1996). Although hyper-expensive campaigns are still the exception and not the rule, legislative races in a number of states have become expensive as well. In 1990, for instance, spending for legislative races in California totaled $23.9 million, down from $40 million in 1988, but still a hefty chunk of change. In New Jersey spending on legislative races in 1991 totaled $15 million and sixteen of those campaigns spent over $200,000. In 1990, a dozen state legislative races in the state of Washington topped the $200,000 plateau, and that same year fourteen candidates in Oregon spent more than $120,000 (Neal 1992). Where does that money come from? It depends. In states where gubernatorial and legislative contests are relatively inexpensive, the bulk of the money raised and spent in campaigns comes from individual contributors. Elsewhere, political action committees and the parties have become important sources of campaign dollars. According to one study (Cassie, Thompson, and Jewell

1993, reported in Herrmann and Michaelson 1994), PAC contributions represented from 12 to 43 percent of total receipts in the eleven states included in their analysis. Not surprisingly, the bulk of that money went to incumbents. Parties have also become a major source of campaign funding in a number of states, a trend examined in Chapter 3.

The increasing role of money in state campaigns raises a number of issues and fears. First, since the majority of that money typically goes to incumbents, elections are likely to become less competitive as stronger incumbents are able to preempt challengers who are unable to raise the money necessary to mount a viable campaign. Second, the increase in campaign funding, particularly money from political action committees, raises the fear of influence peddling or, at a minimum, inordinate interest group influence. Finally, as the costs of campaigning increase, there is a concern that an increasing amount of the time and effort of elected officials will be spent, not on their official duties, but raising campaign funds. These and similar concerns have led to renewed calls for more stringent and effective campaign finance laws. These efforts are discussed in the following chapter, but suffice it to say that state officials are under a great deal of pressure to reform existing regulations, and to their credit, lawmakers in several states are now attempting to do so.

Summary and Conclusions

As the preceding pages make clear, the character of the states' elections and nonelectoral participation has changed considerably. The reapportionment revolution that began in the 1960s has ensured that urban and suburban areas now have equal representation in their state legislatures. In addition, federal civil rights policies have yielded often dramatic increases in the rate at which blacks and other ethnic and racial minorities vote and serve in government. More recently, federal and state authorities have moved on a number of fronts to make the simple act of voting even simpler. Citizens also have more opportunities to *directly* influence government. As we have seen, there has been a substantial increase in the use of initiative and referendum to make state policy, and citizens now have more opportunities to speak on public issues between elections. Taken together those changes ensure that individual citizens now have more opportunities to influence public officials and public policies than ever before. And in that sense the linkage between governments and their citizens is much stronger.

At the same time, there have been a number of troubling developments and disappointments on the demand side of state government. Recent court rulings concerning minority-access districts and the realities of racial politics in America demonstrate that the issue of minority representation is far from being resolved. In addition, the states' experiences to date with initiatives and referenda raise questions about the quality of citizen participation and the role of interest groups in direct democracy. Relatedly, despite the best efforts of many state and federal authorities, too few citizens, armed with too little information, bother to vote in issue and candidate elections or participate in public hearings or other opportunities to influence government between elections. All of this is made more problematic by the changing electoral landscape of state politics, particularly the emergence of candidate-centered campaigns and the increasing role of money in state races.

Regardless of the impacts of recent changes on how citizens connect to government, many of us rely on other linkage mechanisms, most notably parties and interest groups, to make that connection. As one would expect, those pieces of the demand side of state government have changed as well. Chapter 3 reviews how the states' parties and interest groups have evolved in recent years, and then looks more broadly at the implications of changes in elections and political participation, parties, and interest groups for the quality of statehouse democracy and policy responsibility.

NOTES

1. The 1982 amendments extended the act for another 25 years.
2. Correspondence with Ronald Weber, August 24, 1996.

3

Demand-Side Changes: Political Parties and Interest Groups

Thanks to the kinds of changes documented in Chapter 2, more citizens in the states now have more opportunities to access and influence governments. Nonetheless in a fragmented political system in which citizens face a bewildering array of candidates and issues and in which substantial resources, most notably money, are necessary to effectively influence politics and policy, most of us need an additional intermediary to successfully connect to government. Parties and, increasingly, interest groups have filled that role throughout much of the history of the states by, among other means, mobilizing and structuring the vote, aggregating and articulating interests, recruiting political leadership, organizing governments, and formulating policy. In the 1990s, however, they perform those functions in often unique ways. Both parties and interest groups have changed in recent decades, demonstrating a surprising adaptability and resilience. After decades of decline, state party organizations are enjoying a resurgence of sorts. Traditional party organizations have seen their role shift from controlling nominations and campaigns to servicing state and local candidates. Within legislatures, leadership and party PACs have become central players in the process of raising and allocating campaign dollars. And, increasingly, the activities of national and state party organizations are merging. Interest groups in the states are experiencing considerable change as well. The states' interest groups represent a more diverse set of interests, and groups that once dominated their state's politics now share influence with others. Lobbyists have become more professional, PACs more numerous, and the strategies employed by groups to influence elections and government more sophisticated and much more expensive. All of these changes have reshaped the demand side of government and, together with the changes noted in Chapter 2, have implications, both good and bad, for how well the states govern. Those implications are examined later in this chapter. First we look more closely at how the states' parties and interest groups have changed in recent years.

Political Parties

The twentieth century has not been particularly kind to America's political parties. Earlier in the century, political reforms, most notably the introduction of the direct primary and civil service reforms, wrested control over nominations and elections from the state parties and denied party leaders an important means of rewarding party supporters. More recently, the dramatic growth in the role and influence of political action committees (PACs), a decline in the electorate's level of partisanship, the emergence of candidate-centered campaigns, the development of new campaign technologies, and a strengthening of the national party organizations have further weakened the states' political parties (Bibby 1994).

Despite these and other challenges, the states' parties, much like their national counterparts, have proven remarkably resilient and adaptable. State party organizations in the 1990s are stronger and more active than they have been in decades. Although political parties today no longer dominate electoral politics and governing as they once did, as John Bibby and Thomas Holbrook (1996: 118) conclude, "they nevertheless remain the principal agencies for making nominations, contesting elections, recruiting leaders, and providing a link between citizens and their governments." Three developments have transformed the states' parties—the development of stronger and more professional state party organizations, the emergence of legislative campaign committees and leadership PACs, and increases in national-state party integration. Each is discussed briefly.

Strengthened Party Organizations

In the late 1970s, a team of political scientists led by researchers at the University of Wisconsin at Milwaukee set out to gauge the health of state party organizations throughout the United States. What they discovered (reported in Gibson et al. 1983 and Cotter et al. 1984) was that state party organizations were in surprisingly good health. A few years later, analysts at the Advisory Commission on Intergovernmental Relations (ACIR) reached similar conclusions. In each case, researchers were able to point to two kinds of evidence to demonstrate the increased viability of state party organizations. First, by the 1970s and 1980s party organizations in a number of states had evolved into well-financed professional organizations. As the ACIR (1986: 112) noted: "As recently as the mid-1960s, most state party organizations operated on 'shoestring' budgets of $50,000 or less, and many were part-time, voluntary operations run out of the state party chair's home or office." That changed considerably within a decade and a half. By the late 1970s over 90 percent of the state parties included in Cotter et al.'s analysis had permanent headquarters, and state party budgets had increased appreciably. The average budget for the state party organizations was over a third of a million dollars and over two-thirds of those organizations reported budgets in excess of $100,000. State party organizations had become relatively well staffed as well. Nearly two-thirds of the party organizations had five or more staff and a majority had specialized staff, including comptrollers, public relations directors, and researchers. Not surprisingly perhaps, the Republicans have tended to enjoy greater organizational resources. The ACIR, for example, found that whereas over 90 percent of the thirty-nine Republican organizations they surveyed had three or more staff, only 56 percent of their Democratic counterparts could match those staffing levels. Similarly, the percentage of Democratic organizations reporting budgets in excess of $750,000 by the mid-1980s was just half of the Republican organizations. By the 1990s the Republican funding advantage had largely dissipated, however, and each of the parties enjoyed substantial financial resources. In 1990–1991, over half of each party's state organizations reported receipts in excess of one million dollars. Collectively, both partys' state organizations were able to raise slightly more than $90 million during that period (Bibby and Holbrook 1996).

Evidence of state party resurgence is also found in the range and kinds of activities that state party organizations now engage in and provide. Both Cotter et al. and the ACIR discovered that state party organizations were increasingly active in terms of both organizational building and candidate support activities. By the early 1980s, a majority of the states' party organizations included in Cotter and his associates' study were engaged in a full range of organizational efforts, including fund-raising, polling, get-out-the-vote efforts, and the publication of a party newsletter. In addition, a substantial majority of the states' party organizations provided campaign assistance to their party's candidates. Table 3.1 summarizes the ACIR's findings in this regard. As the data indicate, although Republicans were the more active party in the mid-1980s, in most instances a majority of each party's state organizations provided a full range of assistance, including campaign contributions, fund-raising assistance, and a number of in-kind campaign services (campaign seminars, polling, media consulting, and coordinating PAC contributions).

State party organizations have undergone a dramatic transformation in the last two to three decades. Writing in the mid-1980s, Timothy Conlan, Ann Martino, and Robert Dilger (1984: 6) observe the state parties are "undergoing a complex process of adaptation to new electoral conditions

TABLE 3.1   State Party Campaign Assistance to Candidates for State Office
(entries are percentage of state parties providing assistance)

Form of Assistance	Republicans	Democrats
Campaign Contributions	90%	70%
Fundraising Assistance	95	63
Polling	78	50
Media Consulting	75	46
Campaign Seminars	100	76
Coordinating PAC Contributions	52	31

SOURCE: Compiled from U.S. Advisory Commission on Intergovernmental Relations, *The Transformation of American Politics* (Washington, D.C.: U.S. Government Printing Office, 1986), p. 115.

and are emerging in many states as vigorous entities capable of performing a mix of both modern and traditional tasks." At the same time, campaigns remain candidate-centered and there is little chance that the parties will ever enjoy the kind of hegemony over campaigns and elections that they did in many states and communities at the turn of the century. Instead, they have evolved into "service agencies for candidates and local parties" (Bibby and Holbrook 1996: 84). Moreover, as I note later, state party organizations increasingly share the limelight with, and in some cases are being overshadowed by, party organizations operating out of their state's legislatures as well as the nation's capital.

Legislative Campaign Committees and Leadership PACs

For many, the emergence of legislative campaign committees (LCCs) and leadership PACs provides additional evidence of the viability and adaptability of the states' party organizations. Legislative campaign committees are subdivisions of each party's legislative caucuses and coordinate the party's campaign efforts. LCCs first emerged in the late 1970s in a number of states, including New York, Illinois, Wisconsin, Minnesota, and California, and currently exist in at least forty states (Gierzynski 1992). Leadership PACs, found in many of the same states, are created by individual legislators for the purpose of distributing surplus campaign funds to their party colleagues, ostensibly in an effort to garner member support for their leadership ambitions and efforts.

A number of factors have been linked to the emergence of LCCs and leadership PACs. There is general agreement that the ever-increasing costs of political campaigns, coupled with a corresponding increase in electoral uncertainty occasioned by greater party competition and declining party loyalties among the electorate, create a need for the campaign support provided by the LCCs and leadership PACs. In the first instance,

LCCs are more likely to be found among those states with greater party competition and higher campaign expenditures (Gierzynski 1992; Rosenthal 1994). There is also reason to believe that their emergence is linked to the growing professionalism of state legislatures (Shea 1995). Apparently, as legislatures grow more professional, more members have more at stake in their legislative careers and more resources that can be devoted to campaign committee activities (Rosenthal 1994). Relatedly, the development of party committees and leadership PACs may also reflect the efforts of entrepreneurial party leaders such as former speakers Tom Loftus of Wisconsin and Willie Brown of California. Finally, LCCs often emerge where the state central committees are relatively weak, a tendency that suggests that LCCs fill voids left by their state party organizations (Gierzynski 1992; Rosenthal 1994).

Legislative party committees engage in a number of campaign-related activities. From the very beginning, LCCs and leadership PACs have been a source of campaign funds for their party's legislative candidates. Table 3.2 summarizes some of the findings from Anthony Gierzynski's (1992) ten-state analysis of LCCs and suggests a number of conclusions concerning committee giving. First, the amount of money expended by LCCs varies dramatically across the states. In some states, most notably California, Illinois, and New York, party committees allocate substantial amounts of money. In 1986, LCCs in the California legislature allocated over $4.5 million to party candidates (leadership PACs handed out an additional $3.7 million). In the remaining states, party giving is more modest, often amounting, on average, to just a few hundred dollars per candidate. Second, with the exception of states such as California and New York, state party giving represents only a fraction of total receipts, typically less than 10 percent of total funds raised by the candidates and the parties. Third, nonincumbents do quite well in terms of party receipt. In slightly less than half of the chambers, at least 50 percent of nonincumbents received caucus monies, a tendency that reflects the fact that state parties often concentrate the bulk of their contributions in competitive races. That targeting is often substantial. In 1986, for instance, California Assembly Democrats spent roughly a fifth of their receipts in a single assembly race.

In addition to allocating money to their colleagues' campaigns, LCCs are increasingly performing additional campaign-related activities and, in doing so, becoming full-scale party organizations. A number of state LCCs are engaged in actively recruiting candidates for their legislatures. In many cases, the goal of party leaders is simply to ensure that the party will have a candidate in each legislative race. In key races, potential candidates are often offered party money and campaign assistance as an enticement to run. In addition to recruitment, many state parties now offer a full range of in-kind campaign services, including polling, campaign

TABLE 3.2   Allocating Party Monies: Legislative Party Campaign Committees (LCCs) in Selected States in 1986

State	Democrats		Republicans	
	House	Senate	House	Senate
California				
Total $ Allocated	$2,518,068	$91,074	$1,256,873	$819,489
As % of Total Receipts	22.3%	1.4%	13.5%	19.5%
Mean Contribution	33,574	4,828	15,910	43,131
% Nonincumbents Funded	22.9%	23.8%	37.3%	40.0%
Illinois				
Total $ Allocated	$444,474	$240,878	$551,509	$806,640
Mean Contribution	4,154	7,299	4,758	22,407
% Nonincumbents Funded	29.3%	75.0%	27.8%	35.3%
Indiana				
Total $ Allocated	$76,950	$22,650	$74,500	$70,750
Mean Contribution	905	985	847	3,724
% Nonincumbents Funded	34.0%	25.0%	40.6%	63.6%
Minnesota				
Total $ Allocated	$45,000	$79,108	$28,300	$83,417
As % of Total Receipts	2.2%	3.5%	1.3%	4.3%
Mean Contribution	363	1,217	232	1,390
% Nonincumbents Funded	65.1%	46.4%	48.4%	52.5%
Missouri				
Total $ Allocated	$78,078		$12,500	
As % of Total Receipts	6.3%		1.8%	
Mean Contribution	550		159	
% Nonincumbents Funded	40.0%		40.7%	
New York				
Total $ Allocated	$944,042	$665,108	$632,984	$1,617,789
As % of Total Receipts	28.9%	49.2%	35.5%	70.8%
Mean Contribution	6,891	12,549	4,620	30,524
% Nonincumbents Funded	46.0%	18.5%	23.5%	38.1%
Oregon				
Total $ Allocated	$40,111	$24,485	$102,152	$53,217
As % of Total Receipts	3.7%	5.1%	7.9%	9.0%
Mean Contribution	692	1,775	1,792	3,801
% Nonincumbents Funded	51.7%	66.7%	58.8%	70.0%
Tennessee				
Total $ Allocated	$129,250	$55,000	$83,919	$72,000
Mean Contribution	1,701	3,929	1,399	6,545
% Nonincumbents Funded	87.5%	100.0%	56.5%	88.9%

(continues)

TABLE 3.2　(*continued*)

State	Democrats		Republicans	
	House	*Senate*	*House*	*Senate*
Washington				
Total $ Allocated	$46,207	$75,076	$39,145	$123,427
As % of Total Receipts	1.7%	2.7%	2.0%	4.0%
Mean Contribution	481	3,128	425	5,610
% Nonincumbents Funded	33.3%	91.7%	40.7%	42.9%
Wisconsin				
Total $ Allocated	$56,680	$48,415	$41,415	$49,840
As % of Total Receipts	5.1%	7.8%	3.7%	8.9%
Mean Contribution	683	2,848	441	3,115
% Nonincumbents Funded	67.6%	100.0%	74.5%	88.9%

SOURCE: Compiled from Anthony Gierzynski, *Legislative Party Campaign Committees in the American States* (Lexington: University of Kentucky Press, 1992), pp. 34–38.

consultants, mailing lists, research, and campaign seminars, to party candidates. LCCs are also more involved in fund-raising for candidates, either by actively soliciting contributions on behalf of candidates or by referring potential contributors to particular candidates (Gierzynski 1992).

The emergence of LCCs and leadership PACs is likely to have implications for not only electoral politics in the states, but the role of parties and interests groups as well. From an electoral standpoint, the existence of legislative campaign committees is likely to increase competition as party committees redistribute campaign monies and services from incumbents to nonincumbents. Currently, legislative incumbents enjoy a substantial funding advantage, and as a result, the bulk of campaign monies is poured into noncompetitive races. By targeting monies to competitive races, the giving behavior of LCCs not only levels the playing field a bit but ensures that more money goes to more races and to races where the outcome is less certain.

The presence of viable party campaign committees also has the potential to offset the growing influence of interest groups and PACs on state electoral politics, as parties become a significant source of campaign support. Ideally, as the amount of party support (both in terms of cash and in-kind contributions) increases, individual candidates become less dependent on PAC contributions. Even where PACs are the initial source of party monies, the fact that those monies are distributed by the parties and not received directly from PACs means that there is a layer of party officials between interest groups and individual candidates. Others worry, however, that the parties' reliance on PAC dollars will simply work to centralize interest group influence and make it easier for groups to access and influence elected officials. Those and similar concerns have led to calls for campaign reform in a number of states. In California, for example, Proposition 73 temporarily halted LCC activity in the late 1980s but was subsequently ruled unconstitutional by the state's supreme court. In New York, the practice of redistributing campaign funds has led to hearings and investigations. And in Florida, leadership PACs were banned in 1990 (leaders simply shifted responsibilities for raising and distributing money for legislative races to the state party organization; see Shea 1995).

The emergence of LCCs and leadership PACs also speaks to the ability of the states' political parties to perform their traditional role as a source of coherence and cohesion in the politics of the states. A separation of powers, bicameral legislatures, federalism, interest group politics, and candidate-centered politics all contribute to political fragmentation and policy incoherence. Throughout the nation's history, the parties have represented a centripetal force in this otherwise fragmented political system. To the extent that the legislative campaign committees can make campaigns less candidate-centered and more party-centered, then there is a potential for parties to again serve as a source of political integration and cohesion.

For that to occur requires, among other things, that the emergence and operation of LCCs and leadership PACs promote party unity and cooperation both within and without legislatures. With respect to how LCCs relate to party units external to the legislature, a crucial issue concerns whether and to what extent legislative campaign committees are integrated within the traditional party organizations. One noteworthy study suggests little integration actually takes place. Based on a case study of New York and interviews with state and local party leaders nationally, Daniel Shea (1995) finds only moderate amounts of LCC interdependence, interaction, and cooperation with state and local party organizations. That tendency toward independence is especially pronounced in those states with professional legislatures. Given the apparent autonomy of LCCs and their tendency to focus solely on electing members within their legislative chamber, Shea concludes that "state LCCs should be considered distinct organizations, at best nominally linked to traditional geographic party organizations" (p. 166). Moreover, while acknowledging their potential value to the party organizations, Shea expresses the concern that LCCs may actually prove harmful for the parties by competing for scarce resources, undercutting local party organizations, and by contributing to disunity within the party. Although those conclusions and concerns are well taken, an alternative view is that the emergence of LCCs and leadership PACs reflect the adaptive nature of the states' parties and a division of labor in which state parties focus more on institutional support activities and statewide races and LCCs focus solely on legislative races. In that kind of arrangement, one would expect LCCs and traditional party organizations to have somewhat different goals, engage in different kinds of activities, and to exhibit the moderate levels of interaction and cooperation that Shea uncovers.

National-State Party Integration

Throughout much of this century, the two parties have operated as loose confederations of state and local party organizations.[1] And, as we have just seen, some contend that the development of LCCs adds to the parties' decentralization. At the same time, the state-level activities of the two national parties in recent decades have worked against that trend and have produced heightened levels of national-state party integration. Beginning in the 1960s the two national parties began transferring substantial resources, both money and in-kind assistance, to state party organizations for use in party-building activities and in support of party candidates at all levels of government. Not surprisingly, Republicans provided the earliest support. As early as the 1960s, the national Republican party provided modest assistance to selected state party organizations. By the 1980s, however, each of the parties was providing millions of dollars of support to state and local party organizations and to various candidates throughout the states. In the 1990 elections, Democrats created coordinated campaign organizations in thirty-six states that provided a broad range of campaign services (voter registration and get-out-the-vote efforts, polling, media purchasing, etc.) to the party's candidates. The Republicans have operated similar programs in recent elections and like their Democratic counterparts have placed national party operatives within many states to coordinate campaign activities in those instances where the state party was considered weak (Bibby and Holbrook 1996).

The transfer of millions of dollars in cash from the national parties to the state party organizations has been at the center of the two parties' programs of assistance as well as the recent controversy over "soft money." Federal election laws place limits on the amount of direct assistance each party can provide individual federal candidates. Federal campaign laws, however, allow federal, state, and local parties to both raise and spend virtually unlimited amounts of money on party-building activities, including voter registration and mobilization efforts that nonetheless benefit each party's candidates for national office. Moreover, a 1996 ruling by the U.S. Supreme Court effectively allows the two parties to run "independent" campaigns on behalf of their party's candidates. In 1996, the two national parties raised a record $260 million in soft money (aka nonfederal funds). Roughly half of that money was transferred to state party committees or, to a much lesser extent, given directly to state and local candidates (see Table 3.3).

TABLE 3.3   National Party "Soft Money" (Nonfederal) Disbursements, 1995–1996

	Transfers to State Party Organizations	*Contributions to State and Local Candidates*	*Share of Joint Activity*
Democratic			
National Committee	$54,193,497	$318,684	$27,592,503
Senate Committee	5,859,770	3,049,918	2,385,324
House Committee	4,545,199	1,070,500	3,313,879
Total	64,598,466	4,439,102	33,291,706
Republican			
National Committee	$48,218,708	$1,349,882	$40,325,732
Senate Committee	1,641,800	3,015,371	7,668,704
House Committee	385,000	834,500	9,180,754
Total	50,245,508	5,199,753	57,175,190

SOURCE: Compiled from on-line posting. Available: http://www.fec.gov/finance/demsoft.htm and http://www.fec.gov/finance/repsoft.htm. (June 12, 1997).

The infusion of national party support has no doubt strengthened the state parties by providing needed campaign assistance, helping the state parties to build their own organizations, and promoting intraparty cohesion. Nonetheless, all of that has come at a cost to the state parties' autonomy and independence. As Bibby and Holbrook (1996: 96–97) note:

> For state parties, especially those lacking in organizational strength, being the beneficiary of national party involvement holds other risks as well. Weak state party organizations can be quite literally taken over by national party operatives in presidential election years as staff are brought in to run the campaign effort. These personnel and their backup resources are usually pulled out just as soon as the election is over, leaving the state organization in about the same condition as before the campaign. State party organizations also run the risk of becoming overly dependent on the national party organizations, which periodically go through dry spells in fund-raising and have shifting priorities.

For good or bad, the state and national parties have become increasingly integrated and will probably continue to be so. The 1994 election demonstrated how closely the fortunes of state political figures are tied to national politics, and the role of the Republican governors in shaping federal initiatives in the 104th Congress simply reinforces those ties. However, there are limits to the amount of integration that is likely to occur. Although the two parties are more homogeneous ideologically in the 1990s, a trend that is particularly evident within the national congressional parties (see, e.g., Rohde 1991), there are still significant ideological divisions within each of the parties and those schisms often play out and reflect regional and state-by-state differences. Moreover, for all that pulls parties together, other elements of the states' politics often work to pull parties apart. Some would argue that in the 1990s interest groups, our third linkage mechanism, play that kind of centrifugal role.

Interest Groups

Interest groups have long been a fixture in state government. Indeed, the political history of many of the states has been one of dominance by a single powerful interest: coal in West Virginia and Kentucky, oil in Louisiana and Oklahoma, and the railroads in nearly all of the states (Thomas and Hrebenar 1996). The desire to weaken those powerful interests was the impetus for much of the populist and progressive reforms a hundred years ago. Those reforms aside, interest groups are still very much a part of state government and continue to exert enormous political clout. But like much of state government, the character and impact of interest groups in the states is much transformed. Like political parties, the states' interest groups have proven very adaptable and as a result have experienced a number of changes, including a growth in the number and kinds of interest groups involved in state government, changes in the tactics and strategies employed by those groups, serious efforts to regulate interest group activities, and changing patterns of interest group influence.

Interest Group Growth

One of the more striking changes in recent years is the marked increase in the number and kinds of interest groups that approach state government seeking to influence the character of state policy. According to an Associated Press survey (reported in Rosenthal 1993), more than 42,000 lobbyists plied their trade in the states' capitals in 1990, a number that represented a 20 percent increase in just four years. Not only has there been a surge in the number of interest groups at the state level, but the range of interests that are represented by those groups has increased substantially as well. Table 3.4 illustrates that diversity by listing the interest groups mentioned as influential by legislators in the late 1980s in Maine, a state that just three decades ago was dominated by the "Big Three"—power, timber, and textile and shoe manufacturers (Hodgkin 1993). As the table illustrates, a much more diverse set of interests shape policy in that rural state today, including teacher unions, labor, environmentalists, business groups, utilities, and local governments. That diversity is even more evident throughout the nation. By the 1990s, no fewer than forty different

TABLE 3.4   Influential Interest Groups in Maine, 1987 (number of mentions in parentheses)

Labor (54)
Maine Teachers Assn. (40)
Environmentalists (30)
Sportsmen (27)
Utilities (21)
Business (21)
Maine Municipal Assn. (18)
Insurance (17)
Paper Companies (16)
Maine State Employees Assn. (15)
Health Care (14)
Banks (10)

NOTE: Cited by at least 10 legislators as "very" influential.
SOURCE: Compiled from Douglas I. Hodgkin, "Maine: From the Big Three to Diversity," in Hrebenar and Thomas, eds., *Interest Groups in the Northeastern States* (University Park: Pennsylvania State University Press, 1993), pp. 119–120.

types of groups representing a broad array of ideological, professional, economic, and social interests were continually or intermittently active in forty-five or more states while another twenty-seven kinds of groups were active in at least twenty-five states (Thomas and Hrebenar 1996).

That growth in the number and diversity of interest groups, in turn, stems from a number of developments. Much of that growth reflects the fact that state governments are involved in more activities affecting more people than ever before. As a result, more groups and interests are motivated today to become involved in state government. Other changes in state government, including electoral reforms, increases in direct democracy and citizen participation, and legislative professionalism provide citizens, but particularly organized groups, multiple opportunities to access governments. Those developments have promoted a greater diversity of interest groups as well. That diversity also reflects the states' changing economies; as the states' economies became more complex, the states' interest group system became diverse as well (Thomas and Hrebenar 1990; Gray and Lowery 1993).

Changing Strategy and Tactics

Whatever influence interest groups might have, and most commentators would agree that influence is substantial, stems from the fact that they do two things well—contributing campaign money to individuals seeking public office, and lobbying government officials (primarily legislators but also the courts and executive branch agencies). Both of these activities have undergone considerable change in recent years. As campaigns have become more candidate-centered and as candidates wage more sophisticated, media-based campaigns, the costs of seeking state office have skyrocketed. Increasingly, interest groups, through the contributions of lobbyists and PACs, have become a major source of campaign funds. The growth in the number of PACs has been particularly striking. Alan Rosenthal (1993), for example, reports evidence that PACs in Washington, Wisconsin, and New York doubled in number between the 1970s and early 1980s and increased by approximately sevenfold in Illinois and Oregon. As that has occurred PAC dollars have come to compose a larger proportion of the total monies raised in political campaigns at the state level. Analysis of PAC activity in eleven states (Cassie, Thompson, and Jewell 1992, reported in Herrmann and Michaelson 1994) indicates that PAC dollars represented anywhere from 12 to 43 percent of total candidate receipts in those states during the 1987–1988 election cycle. Perhaps more importantly, PAC dollars represented over 50 percent of total revenues for *incumbent* candidates in three of those states, including Idaho (57 percent), Oregon (63 percent), and Pennsylvania (53 percent), and over a third of total incumbent receipts in California (39 percent), North Carolina (49 percent), and Washington (37 percent). The actual sums of money are often staggering. According to one estimate, medical groups in Florida poured $2 million into state legislative campaigns in 1994, surpassing the $1 million put up by the state's lawyers (reported in Judd, *The Gainesville Sun*, February 18, 1996). PAC giving of that magnitude is rare, but a review of the evidence from other states indicates that it is not unusual for individual PACs to distribute hundreds of thousands of dollars to candidates they support (see, e.g., Hrebenar and Thomas 1987, 1993b).

What does that money buy? For many the answer is simple: PAC giving is a down payment on an elected official's subsequent decisions. And indeed, there is no shortage of anecdotal evidence indicating that groups that spend heavily on campaigns often receive favorable consideration from those in government. The same article that reported the $2 million in medical group campaign spending, for instance, also cited various pieces of health-care legislation that had been subsequently killed in the face of medical group opposition and noted that many of the members who had received significant amounts of medical PAC money had sponsored legislation ostensibly favoring at least some segment of the medical industry. Others counter that kind of evidence is merely circumstantial and proves little in the absence of additional information indicating a quid pro quo. Moreover, studies of PAC giving at the congressional level are mixed regarding the link between money and roll call voting.

Putting aside the elusive question of whether PAC money buys votes, there is some agreement among both congressional scholars and those who study state legislatures that campaign contributions ensure interest group access to members and, in some cases, ensure that member time, itself a scarce commodity, will be spent on activities important to those groups (Wright 1996; Hall and Wayman 1990). PAC giving is important for other, more subtle, reasons. PAC giving is often regarded as "table stakes" aimed at ensuring that members are part of the larger debate over particular policy questions. Relatedly, "the absence of contributions, where they are expected, may be more harmful than their presence is helpful" (Rosenthal 1993: 139).

In a real sense, PAC giving is simply an extension of the lobbying efforts of organized interests. And here too there has been considerable change in statehouse lobbying. The days of the stereotypical cigar-chomping, back-slapping, old-style lobbyists are largely gone. As legislatures and state governments become more professional, as the laws that regulate lobbyists grow more stringent and as the public becomes more aware, a new kind of lobbyist has emerged. Lobbying, and the men and women who do it, is becoming more professional and sophisticated, a tendency that manifests itself in a number of ways.

In the first place, more and more lobbying is done by full-time professionals who bring specialized skills and technologies to the task of accessing and persuading state officials. Although a plurality of lobbyists are still "in-house" and work for individual firms or associations, the state government relations divisions within which they work are better staffed and more professional. They are also increasingly likely to avail themselves of the services of contract lobbyists, individuals who lobby full-time on behalf of one or more clients. According to one estimate (Thomas and Hrebenar 1990), as many as a quarter of all lobbyists at the state level are contract lobbyists and their proportion and numbers continue to grow. The growing sophistication of lobbying is also evidenced by the emergence of large specialized firms, including law firms and groups of contract lobbyists, that can provide a full range of specialized legal and campaign services to their clients, including "research, budget analysis, bill drafting, grassroots organizing, legislative and regulatory monitoring, workshops, receptions, media and newsletters, and association management" (Rosenthal 1993: 24). A number of those groups, including firms like MultiState Associates and Stateside Associates operate out of Washington, D.C., monitoring state legislation and coordinating lobbying efforts throughout the states on behalf of national corporations. All of that is occasioned by the fact that a significant number of corporations and associations have interests in more than one state and need to have some sort of presence in several of those states. Contract lobbyists and those firms that can connect contract lobbyists with individual corporations facilitate and provide that presence.

The changing character of the states' lobbyists is also evidenced by a greater reliance on alternative means of lobbying, including grassroots campaigns and the development of well-organized coalitions of interest groups. In the wake of ethics reforms and the public's disdain for some of the techniques of the "insider" game, groups are finding the former alternative especially attractive. Although developing a personal relationship with elected officials and their staff is still the stock-in-trade of effective lobbying, an "outsider" strategy can bring additional pressures to bear on legislators as interest groups mobilize their members and constituents back in the district and throughout the state. And as you would expect, there are no shortage of consulting firms that offer the necessary expertise and technical services needed to mount effective mobilization efforts. Coalitions of groups have also become more common as lobbyists work to identify and recruit various groups in support or in opposition to legislation. The advantage here is obvious. As Rosenthal (1993: 150) notes: "The greater and more broad-based the support, the more likely that legislators will see the wisdom of a particular policy direction. At the very least, they will have the rationale of widespread support to justify their position." But building and maintaining coalitions is not always easy. Even among organizations and groups that seemingly share common interests, the health care industry for instance, there are often major policy disagreements that make coordination and negotiation difficult.

Perhaps the best indication of the growing sophistication and professionalism of statehouse lobbying is found in the amount of money that is involved in that effort. It is not unusual, for instance, for the states' top lobbyists to earn six-figure salaries (Rosenthal 1993). In addition, as Table 3.5 suggests, various interests devote considerable sums of money to lobbying state government. The reader should approach the dollar figures in the table with some caution. States vary in terms of what expenditures groups must report, and even in states with stringent disclosure requirements, groups need not report all of their actual expenses. As a result, the dollar figures in the table in all likelihood represent a low-end estimate of how much is spent on lobbying in the states. Nonetheless, the experiences of the states included in the table point to a number of conclusions. Not surprisingly, it is economic and business interests, including various business and trade associations, utilities, and insurance companies, that dominate lobby spending. In that regard the reader will note that spending by health care groups is invariably near the top of each state's spending list, a tendency that reflects the continuing role and importance of the states in health care issues. Although economic and business interests tend to represent the biggest spenders on lobbying, the fact that labor, educational, and citizen groups are also included in the table speaks to the growing diversity of interests that has already been noted. What is par-

TABLE 3.5 Lobbying Expenditures in Selected States (entries are lobbying expenditures by type of interest group, top ten groups per state, years vary)

Maryland[a]		New York[b]		Washington[c]	
Interest	Expend.	Interest	Expend.	Interest	Expend.
Banking, Finance, Insurance	$1,286,536	Business, Commerce, Industry	$ 4,300,000	Medicine & Health Care	$623,000
Health Groups	683,473	Health	1,400,000	Utilities	599,000
Trade Assoc.	479,232	Labor	1,400,000	Banking and Finance	523,000
Building & Construction Companies	420,163	Education	1,100,000	Education	427,000
Business Assoc.	409,018	Insurance	1,100,000	Insurance	408,000
Professional Occupational Groups, Health	390,268	Energy	960,000	Timber & Forest Products	401,000
Utilities	364,445	Banking and Finance	940,000	Transportation	366,000
Citizens Groups	336,551	Public and Community Interest	810,000	Labor	353,000
Petroleum, Coal, Chemicals	304,187	Local Government	740,000	Business and Trade Assoc.	334,000
Communications Companies	244,855	Racing and Wagering	680,000	Manufacturing	327,000

[a]November 1, 1986 through October 31, 1987.
[b]FY 1986.
[c]1981.

SOURCE: Compiled from: Ronald C. Lippincott and Larry W. Thomas, "Maryland: The Struggle for Power in the Midst of Change, Complexity, and Institutional Constraints," in Hrebenar and Thomas, eds., Interest Group Politics in the Northeastern States (University Park: Pennsylvania State University Press, 1993), pp. 143–144.

David L. Cingranelli, "New York: Powerful Groups and Powerful Parties," in Hrebenar and Thomas, eds., Interest Group Politics in the Northeastern States (University Park: Pennsylvania State University Press, 1993), p. 261.

Walfred H. Peterson, "Washington: The Impact of Public Disclosure Laws," in Hrebenar and Thomas, eds., Interest Group Politics in the American West (Salt Lake City: University of Utah Press, 1987), p. 125.

ticularly important about the values in Table 3.5 is their relation to actual group influence in those states. In Maryland, for instance, fourteen of the top twenty individual groups in lobbying expenditures fell into those categories of groups perceived by legislators and lobbyists as the most effective groups in the late 1980s (Lippincott and Thomas 1993). That pattern holds in other states as well.

Regulating Political Interests

In recent years, the states have entered into a new round of reforms aimed in large part at regulating the lobbying and campaign activities of political interests. In 1994 and 1995, over half the states enacted legislation aimed at strengthening lobbying regulation (Boulard 1996). Similar efforts have been aimed at reforming the states' campaign finance laws. State reform efforts reflect a number of trends, including the often dramatic growth in the number, velocity, and reach of political interests, the sharp increases in campaign spending, and most importantly perhaps, recent scandals involving organized interests and public officials in a number of states, including South Carolina, Arizona, Kentucky, New Mexico, and California. In correcting those and other abuses, state officials have concentrated on three broad areas of reform: ethics regulations governing the behavior of elected officials, the regulation of lobbying, and campaign finance. On balance, those efforts go a long way in making state governments more ethical and limiting the influence of powerful interests and political money. But not every state has enacted meaningful reform; in some instances loopholes make controls less effective, and in many states enforcement is still problematic. Ethics legislation is discussed in Chapter 5. However, lobby and campaign finance reform are considered here in some detail.

Lobby Reform.   Some of the worst political scandals involving private interests and public officials have occurred at the state level. In the 1790s lobbyists in Georgia used cash, land, barrels of rice, and slaves to bribe state officials into selling developers 50 million acres of land in the western part of the state. In one of the earliest exercises in lobby regulation, the state's voters turned out every sitting member of the legislature and added a clause to the state constitution declaring lobbying a crime, a clause that remained in effect until 1945 (Boulard 1996). The wrath of Georgia's voters notwithstanding, unholy alliances between public officials and private interests continued into the next two centuries. Following the Watergate scandals, legislators in a number of states enacted ethics and conflict of interests bills, but even in the wake of these reforms questionable and suspect lobbying practices persisted. Providing legislators and their staff with gifts, free meals, entertainment, favors, and travel became standard practices for developing long-term relationships with public officials in many states. That generosity has often been excessive. Until recently, for instance, it was not uncommon in Florida for organized interests to treat state legislators to all-expense paid hunting trips to Georgia, Texas, Alaska, Mexico, and Wyoming and pleasure trips to destinations such as New Orleans, Lake Tahoe, San Francisco, Paris, and Zurich. That practice was called into question in 1990 when two dozen Florida state legislators were charged with failing to reports trips and gifts under the state's lobbying laws (a second-degree misdemeanor at the time) and is now prohibited under legislation adopted in the early 1990s (Rosenthal 1993). Florida lobbyists are and were not that atypical. Groups and their lobbyists elsewhere often provide travel to friendly legislators, pick up the tabs for the members' and their staff's meals, and do favors for members and their constituents, all of this in addition to their often sizable contributions to political campaigns and leadership PACs.

In recent years, many of the states have attempted to rein in this kind of behavior. First, a number of states have set limits on gift giving by lobbyists and their clients. By 1992, fifteen states had adopted legislation that limited lobbyists to gifts valued at $100 or less (Bullock 1994). Three states, Wisconsin, South Carolina, and Minnesota, have adopted "no cup of coffee" provisions prohibiting any gifts, and Iowa prohibits all gifts except for food and drink valued at $3 or less. Other states are only slightly less restrictive. In Connecticut, for example, limits are placed on how much lobbyists can give members—$50 in gifts and $150 for meals per year per member. In a parallel fashion, legislation in Kentucky prohibits gifts to members or their families with the exception of meals (limited to $100 annually per member). In addition, a number of states, including Ohio, Michigan, California, and Illinois, have recently banned members from receiving honoraria from organized interests and others (Neal 1995, 1996). A number of states also require lobbyists to disclose gifts valued at more than a token amount. Second, several states have considered or adopted rules that would also limit lobbyists from contributing to political campaigns. At least four states, Colorado, Kentucky, South Carolina, and Vermont, simply prohibit the practice. Nearly half of the states forbid lobbyists from making contributions while the legislature is in session (Bullock 1994).

Strengthening disclosure requirements is for many the most effective means of controlling lobbying behavior. Every state but Wyoming requires lobbyists to provide reports of their expenditures, but the states vary in what expenditures must be included and how often those reports must be provided. In recent years, a number of states have sought to tighten disclosure requirements. At least eleven states now require more frequent reporting during the legislative session. As part of its ambitious effort to curtail the role of special interests in the wake of recent political scandals, for instance, Kentucky now requires lobbyists to file expenditure reports six times a year when the legislature is in session (Boulard 1996). In addition to more frequent reports, a number of states, ten by 1993, are requiring detailed itemization of expenses. In Illinois, for example, lobbyists must report expenditures by category—travel, gifts, honoraria, entertainment, and so forth.

Most analysts would agree that new and proposed lobbying regulations have gone a long way toward ensuring a more ethical climate for lobbying. Thomas and Hrebenar (1996: 138) argue that public disclosure requirements in particular have altered the character of statehouse lobbying by promoting "restraint in dealings with public officials, greater concern for their group's public image, and increasing professionalism." Clearly the more blatant instances of influence peddling are largely gone as are the old "wheeler-dealer" lobbyists of the not-so-recent past. Nonetheless, there are limits to what the states have accomplished. In the first place, many states have not adopted the tougher standards seen elsewhere. Obviously if ten states require itemized expenditures, for example, forty do not. Similarly, if half the states forbid campaign contributions during the session, the other half do not. More broadly, research from a number of quarters indicates that considerable variation exists across the states and that the toughest laws are in those states that may need regulation the least, that is, states with weaker interest groups systems and more professional legislatures (see Morehouse 1981; Opheim 1991; Thomas and Hrebenar 1996). In addition, newly enacted state laws are only effective if they are enforced. Unfortunately, states typically spend little to monitor the actions of their lobbyists, and according to one source (Bullock 1994), half of the states in 1994 had only one or a part-time staffer monitoring lobbyist activity.

Campaign Finance Reform.   Lobbying regulation is ineffective if it is not coupled with serious campaign finance reform. As we have seen, campaign spending has reached all-time highs, and in many states PACs are a major source of campaign monies. Given the concerns we noted earlier, public officials have moved on a number of fronts to regulate the flow of money into campaigns, regulations that touch not only on PACs but other political actors as well. Three major strategies have been pursued in recent years: disclosure requirements, limits on campaign contributions, and public financing. First, every state now requires candidates and PACs to submit reports on campaign receipts and expenditures. All but two states require state parties to do so. And a majority of states require unions and corporations to comply with state disclosure provisions. Second, many states have put into place a series of limits on the amount, kinds, and sources of campaign contributions. Limits are an attempt to curtail the role of money in campaigns and to provide challengers a better chance of competing. By 1996, two-thirds of the states had placed limits on the maximum amount individuals could contribute to campaigns. In addition, thirty-four states had placed limits on PAC giving, ranging from $500 to $6,000 per candidate. Twenty-one states prohibited corporate contributions whereas nineteen limited the amount corporations can contribute. Twenty-six states placed limits on labor union spending, and a handful of states prohibited union contributions altogether (Council of State Governments 1996). Finally, a number of states are currently experimenting with some form of public financing of campaigns. By the early 1990s, roughly half of the states provided public financing for some statewide offices. However, several of those states reported difficulties in collecting sufficient funds for their public financing efforts and only a handful funded legislative races (Chi 1992).

Yet for all this activity, there is a sense that campaign reforms are simply not working. As one observer of state politics (Gurwitt 1992: 50) notes, "It's hard to escape the feeling that much of the campaign reform effort has been a waste of time." Analysts point to a series of problems. Disclosure requirements are rendered less effective in a number of states because either too little information is collected or access to that information is limited. As of the early 1990s only twenty states, for example, required candidates and others to report the occupation or employment of contributors, an omission that makes it hard to track the contributions of organized interests. Less than half the states required independent committees to file spending reports (Alexander 1991). Moreover, the public's access to disclosed information is unnecessarily limited in many states. In Ohio, for example, during the early 1990s candidates needed only to submit information to their county clerks, making it more difficult to track the flow of money from PACs and others. According to Herbert Alexander (1991) only fifteen states published reports on campaign finance and only a little more than half of the states surveyed by Common Cause maintained a computerized data base on funding. Similar kinds of problems plague state laws that attempt to regulate campaign finance through contribution limits. Like their counterparts at the national level, PACs and others employ a variety of techniques including bundling, transfers, soft money, and independent campaign expenditures to get around state spending limits. Bundling occurs when political or private organizations take it upon themselves to solicit and distribute individual contributions. Enterprising journalists in Ohio, for instance, discovered that three-quarters of the money given to two prominent state legislators, over $2 million, had come from thousands of utility company employees (Alexander 1991). Not only were those contributions legal under Ohio law, but they were difficult to track. Ohio, like many other states, did not require disclosure of the occupation or employer of contributors. PACs are also able to channel additional dollars to candidates by either transferring money through the legislative leadership committees (so-called conduit contributions) or making contributions to the state party organizations (soft money). In California, for example, candidates in 1986 relied on transfers made through leadership committees for over a third of their total receipts (Alexander 1991). And, of course, where all else fails, PACs and others are allowed (with few limits) to mount independent campaigns.

Much of the problem with existing campaign finance reform is simply a lack of enforcement. As of the early 1990s, only thirty-one states had a regulatory commission responsible for enforcement (Herrman and Michaelson 1994), and where such an agency or commission existed, it often lacked the resources or the will to effectively enforce state campaign regulations. As Rob Gurwitt notes (1992: 55):

> In those states that have watchdog disclosure agencies, they are treated like poor stepchildren. They rarely have the staff or resources to analyze what is happening to the campaign finance system as a whole, to perform specific audits of candidates' returns, or even to make the data available in a form that allows people to figure out, say, how much the dairy industry has contributed to a particular candidate.

According to one report (Bullock 1993, reported in Herrmann and Michaelson 1994) half of the thirty-four state and local regulatory agencies included in the analysis suffered budget cuts between 1987 and 1992. An additional study conducted by the Center for Responsive Politics discovered that nine of the thirty-three enforcement agencies included in their review could not conduct hearings and twelve did not have the power to impose fines (Mallory and Hedlund 1993, reported in Herrmann and Michaelson 1994).

Perhaps the most troubling aspect of campaign reform in the states is that so little of it exists in many states: At least seven states place no limits on corporate contributions; unions are allowed to make unlimited contributions in eight or so states; and PACs can spend unlimited amounts in at least fifteen states. Even more serious, less than half the states prohibit regulated industries and interests from contributing to political campaigns (Council of State Governments 1996).

Although the record to date is hardly reassuring, there are some positive signs. Election agencies in California, Connecticut, Florida, Minnesota, Washington, and Wisconsin are frequently given high marks for integrity and effectiveness (see, e.g., Alexander 1991 and Gurwitt 1992). In addition, a number of states are currently considering a new round of reforms that, ideally, will further limit the influence of money in campaigns. One strategy has been to establish voluntary spending limits, a reform that would lessen the need for PAC dollars. In 1989 the New Hampshire legislature, for instance, set voluntary limits on statewide and federal elections, including a cap of $15,000 on state senate races and 25 cents per registered voter in state house contests. Candidates are enticed to accept limits through a waiver of filing fees and, once they have agreed to limits, nominal fines. Although the New Hampshire law faced a number of legal and legislative challenges in the ensuing years, the early evidence suggests that it has reduced the level of campaign spending in that state as all but a handful of candidates have voluntarily accepted the state's spending limits (Neal 1992). Others states are following New Hampshire's lead. By January 1996, thirteen states had established limits for at least some offices (Council of State Governments 1996). In the 1996 election, voters in three states, California, Colorado, and Maine, passed statewide initiatives providing for voluntary spending limits.

The states are pursuing other reforms as well. A number of states, including Alabama, Arkansas, Colorado, Florida, Minnesota, New Mexico, Washington, and Wisconsin, have considered or have passed legislation limiting contributions to specified periods and/or when the legislature is not in session. Some states are also attempting to further restrict PAC, union, and corporate giving. A 1993 Kentucky law limits a candidate's total PAC contributions to 35 percent of receipts or $5,000, whichever is greater. In a similar vein, in 1994 Massachusetts placed aggregate dollar limits on PAC contributions per state and local candidates. In the state of Washington, voters in 1992 approved an initiative that would restrict out-of-state contributions from unions, PACs, and corporations. Voters in Oregon approved a similar initiative in 1994. A number of states have also toughened disclosure requirements in recent years. Kentucky and Maine, for instance, have lowered the threshold beyond which committees must publicly disclose individual contributions. Other states, including Arkansas and New Mexico, now require frequent reporting of expenditures and receipts. In still other instances, states are considering or have passed legislation that would require additional information about the occupations or economic interests of contributors (Herrmann and Michaelson 1994; Prochnow 1994; Neal 1995, 1996).

The Question of Influence

Efforts to regulate the actions of organized interests are testimony to the kinds of influence that interest groups exercise in many of the states' capitals. That influence is evident at two levels: interest groups as a whole and the power of individual groups. With respect to interest groups collectively, the primary concern is with the extent to which state politics is dominated by those groups. With respect to individual groups, scholars have focused on the extent to which business groups dominate interest group politics in the states. Taken together, the evidence suggests that interest groups, particularly business groups, play a major role in the politics of a majority of the American states, a role that is not likely to abate any time soon.

Research reported by Ronald Hrebenar and Clive Thomas provides the most recent and comprehensive estimate of the role that interest groups play within the states (Hrebenar and Thomas 1987, 1992, 1993a, 1993b; Thomas and Hrebenar 1990, 1996). During the early to mid-1980s, these authors enlisted the aid of over seventy political scientists throughout the country to gather a mix of quantitative and qualitative evidence on interest group activity and influence in each of the states. The result is a series of insightful chapters on individual states as well as a sizable fifty-state data base (updated in 1994) from which the authors draw a number of conclusions concerning the character of state interest group politics. Some of the authors' most important conclusions are drawn from the evidence contained in Table 3.6. Thomas and Hrebenar classify the states into five categories of overall interest group influence. Dominant states are those in which interest groups "are the overwhelming and consistent influence" (p. 152) on state policymaking. Complementary states are those in which groups either must work with or, alternately, are constrained by other elements of the state's political system (e.g., the political culture of the state or a strong executive branch). A state is classified as subordinate if groups are, as the label implies, subordinate to elements of the state's political climate. States that fall into the dominant/complementary and complementary/subordinate groupings are simply those that alternate between the two categories. The findings suggest what many critics of state politics frequently lament: On a fairly regular basis, interest groups dominate policymaking in a majority of the American states. In seven states, groups consistently dominate state politics, and in another twenty-one states groups alternate between sharing power and dominating other political actors and influences. Equally important, only five states fall into one of the two subordinate categories.

There is a clear regional pattern in their data as well. With few exceptions, states in which interest groups dominate tend to be located in the South and the West. Those regional patterns, in turn, are suggestive of the conditions that promote or inhibit interest group dominance. The tendency for interest groups to be stronger in the South and West, for example, probably reflects the fact that those states tend to have traditionalistic and individualistic political cultures, cultures that are considered more amenable to interest group dominance. And, unlike much of the Northeast and Midwest, many of those states lack the economic diversity

TABLE 3.6 Classification of the Fifty States According to the Overall Impact of Interest Groups

		Impact of Interest Groups		
Dominant (7)	Dominant/ Complementary (21)	Complementary (17)	Complementary/ Subordinate (5)	Subordinate (0)
Alabama	Alaska	Colorado	Delaware	
Florida	Arizona	Connecticut	Minnesota	
Louisiana	Arkansas	Indiana	Rhode Island	
New Mexico	California	Maine	South Dakota	
Nevada	Georgia	Maryland	Vermont	
South Carolina	Hawaii	Massachusetts		
West Virgina	Idaho	Michigan		
	Illinois	Missouri		
	Iowa	New Hampshire		
	Kansas	New Jersey		
	Kentucky	New York		
	Mississippi	North Carolina		
	Montana	North Dakota		
	Nebraska	Pennsylvania		
	Ohio	Utah		
	Oklahoma	Washington		
	Oregon	Wisconsin		
	Tennessee			
	Texas			
	Virginia			
	Wyoming			

source: Clive S. Thomas and Ronald J. Hrebenar, "Interest Groups in the States," in Gray and Jacob, eds., *Politics in the American States*, 6th ed. (Washington, D.C.: CQ Press, 1996), p. 152. Reprinted by permission.

and complexity that would pit competing interest groups against one another and make it less likely for any single economic interest to dominate the state's politics. The propensity of interest groups to dominate in the South may also reflect the relative weakness of political parties in that region. Where political parties are weak or inactive, interest groups are likely to fill the resulting vacuum by performing many of the functions—fund-raising, the recruitment of candidates for office, and interest aggregation—traditionally performed by political parties. However, Hrebenar and Thomas suggest that the relationship between party competition and interest group influence is more complex than that. They contend that although a lack of competition is associated with strong interest groups, there are instances when states with strong and competitive parties, for example Illinois and New York, have powerful groups as well.

Other features of a state's political system are likely to condition the influence of interest groups. First, states with more professional legislatures and stronger governors are less likely to be dominated by interest groups, largely because public officials in those states are less dependent upon the information and technical expertise that organized groups often can offer (Ziegler 1983). Second, research on the legislative success of interest groups and other political actors in California, Iowa, and Texas in the late 1970s and early 1980s (Wiggins, Hamm, and Bell 1992) suggests that the likelihood of legislation passing increases with the level of group involvement and consensus. Legislation that enjoyed the support of interest groups was considerably more likely to pass than bills in which groups were not involved. That tendency was even greater in terms of group opposition, a finding that is consistent with the notion that groups are better at playing defense (i.e., opposing legislation) than offense. In addition, as the amount of consensus among groups increased, so too did the likelihood that legislation would pass or, in those instances where groups opposed legislation, be defeated. Third, that same research also indicates that governors and party leaders are frequently able to offset the influence of special interests. In Iowa and Texas, the majority party leadership and the governor, respectively, enjoyed greater influence over legislation than did interest group agents in those states. At the same time, the findings from the three states suggest that the ability of party-oriented leaders to serve as a check on interest groups is limited by two considerations: (1) governors and party leaders are typically involved in far fewer pieces of legislation than are interest groups and (2) when they do become involved with legislation, only rarely (roughly 20 percent of the time) do they find themselves in conflict with interest group agents. Finally, there are good reasons for believing that political systems that are more fragmented nurture interest group influence by providing multiple points of access for organized interests. Divided government, weak po-

litical parties, a decentralized executive branch and legislature, and conflict between the state's political institutions all contribute to that access
and make it more likely that more groups will have more opportunities
to shape the decisions of state officials.

There is a second dimension to interest group influence as well and that
concerns how individual groups fare in the tugging and pulling of state
politics. Given the historical influence of vested economic interests in the
states, it is not surprising that scholars have focused on business groups,
including corporations and trade associations, in examining the influence
of groups at the individual level. And for good reason. In looking at interest influence in the 1970s Sarah McCally Morehouse (1981) discovered
that business groups represented more than 70 percent of those groups
cited as powerful in the forty or so states in which interest groups were
strong or moderately strong. Other, more recent studies, however, suggest that although business groups still play a dominant role, a much
wider range of interests is now present in most state's interest group systems, and many of those groups are able to effectively compete with business interests. Once again, the research of Hrebenar and Thomas is particularly illuminating (see Table 3.7). Even a cursory glance at their listing
of the most influential groups in the states reveals a number of groups
representing interests that just three decades ago were rarely present in
most states, including senior citizen groups, environmental action
groups, groups opposed to or in favor of abortion, and taxpayer groups.
Even among economic interest groups there has been increasing diversity: witness the emergence of specialized groups representing various
sectors of the health care industry. Nevertheless, as Table 3.7 indicates,
business groups outnumber other interests. Table 3.7 lists the fourteen
groups cited as most or moderately influential in at least twenty-five
states in the Hrebenar and Thomas study. As the table indicates, business
organizations and trade associations still dominate interest group politics
in the 1990s. Of the fourteen groups listed in the table, eight represent
business or economic interests, including general business organizations,
utilities, lawyers, and representatives of the health care industry.
Interestingly enough, of the remaining six, two represent groups that traditionally have had influence at the state level, unions and farmers, and
three represent public employees (most notably teachers' unions) or local
governments. Only one "cause" group, environmentalists, was cited as
influential in at least half of the states. With the exception of senior
groups, cited as moderately effective in nineteen states, the influence of
cause groups was isolated in a smaller number of states. Taxpayer groups
were mentioned as influential in just twelve states, women and minorities in only ten states, religious groups in eleven states, "good government" groups in thirteen states, and pro-life and pro-choice groups in

TABLE 3.7   The Most Influential Interests in the American States (number of states where interest cited as "most" or "moderately" effective in parentheses; ordering reflects the rate at which interest was cited as "most" effective)

Teachers Associations (48)
General Business Associations (53)
Utility Companies (47)
Lawyers (40)
Traditional Labor Associations (35)
Physicians and State Medical Associations (34)
Insurance (36)
Manufacturers (35)
Health Care Organizations (39)
Bankers (32)
Local Government Organizations (37)
State and Local Government Employees (32)
Farm Organizations (34)
Environmentalists (25)

NOTE: Cited as most or moderately effective in 1994 in at least 25 states. Because it was possible for some groups to be mentioned as both "most" and "moderately" effective, numbers in parentheses can exceed 50.

SOURCE: Compiled from Clive S. Thomas and Ronald J. Hrebenar, "Interest Groups in the States," in Gray and Jacob, eds., *Politics in the American States,* 6th ed. (Washington, D.C.: CQ Press, 1996), pp. 149–150.

fewer than a half dozen states. Those patterns are hardly surprising. Groups that represent economic interests, whether trade associates or general business groups, have not only the motivation to organize that comes from seeking nondiffuse benefits, but also the resources to do so effectively. As Thomas and Hrebenar (1996: 154–155) conclude:

> The inescapable fact is that resources, and especially money, are at least three-fourths of the battle in building and maintaining good relations between lobbyists and public officials and in securing the other essential elements that lead to influence. In this regard, business and other well-financed lobbies are unsurpassed.... Experience and resources have enabled business groups to adapt more easily than the new interests to the new circumstances and demands of state political systems.

Studies that look at the influence of interest groups in regulatory decisionmaking reach similar conclusions. Despite a rich theoretical tradition that suggests otherwise (Huntington 1952; Bernstein 1955; Stigler 1971), the available research offers little evidence that state (or for that matter, federal) regulatory agencies have been captured by the interests they regulate (see, for example, Berry 1984 and Meier 1987). Instead, studies of state regulation seem to indicate that, on balance, to the extent that the

regulatory decisions of state officials are influenced by interest groups
(and they often are) those pressures are likely to derive from diverse and
competing interests. An early study of hazardous waste regulation, for
example, found that both industry *and* environmental groups were able
to influence the level of environmental spending in the early 1980s
(Williams and Matheny 1983). Similarly, a study of public utility regulatory decisionmaking in twelve states indicates that a variety of interests
bear on those decisions (Gormley 1982, 1983). Although utility companies
were typically cited as the first or second most important influence in
commission proceedings, in those half dozen states in which proxy advocates existed, advocates were often perceived to be as influential as the
utility companies. Moreover, other business groups, groups often in opposition to the utilities, as well as grassroots organizations, also enjoyed
moderate levels of influence over utility commission decisions.

   Other studies of regulation suggest that the influence of the regulated
industry is often offset by the professionalism and resources of both regulatory and legislative officials. William Berry (1984) discovered, for instance, that rate decisions were more likely to reflect cost-of-service considerations in those states with more professional commissioners. In a
parallel fashion, William Gormley (1983) found that commission staff
were often perceived as the most important influence on commission decisions. There is also evidence that states with more professional legislatures tend to regulate more vigorously (see, e.g., Lester et al. 1983 and
Ringquist 1993), a finding that suggests that more professional legislators
are better able to resist industry pressure.

An Assessment of State Linkage Mechanisms

As this chapter and the previous chapter reveal, the principal linkage
mechanisms by which citizens "connect" to state government have
changed considerably in recent decades. Those changes, in turn, have implications for how and how well state governments govern, most obviously in terms of their performance as democracies, but also in terms of
their ability to fashion coherent public policies.

   With respect to the quality of statehouse democracy, I have already presented evidence that demand-side changes have promoted greater responsiveness and representation. The reapportionment revolution of the
1960s increased urban representation in state government and probably
contributed to state policies that were more responsive to urban interests.
And of course, the Voting Rights Act has had a profound effect on minority voting rights and the extent to which minorities serve in government. Other changes, most notably the increased use of the initiative and
referendum, reforms making it easier to vote and register, and efforts that

allow citizens and groups to access government between elections, have also increased the opportunities for ordinary citizens to influence state government. Similarly, as state interest groups have become more diverse, power within the states has been more evenly dispersed to a wider range of interests and concerns.

One additional piece of evidence concerns whether and to what extent public policies in the states reflect public opinion. Research by Robert Erikson, Gerald Wright, and John McIver (1993) demonstrates that state policies are remarkably responsive to the policy preferences of the states' citizens. To arrive at that conclusion, the authors combined data from 122 CBS/*New York Times* polls over the period 1976–1988 in order to estimate public opinion liberalism in each of the states (with the exceptions of Alaska, Hawaii, and Nevada). That data was then linked to measures of policy liberalism during the 1980s. From the perspective of democratic theory, their findings are quite heartening. After controlling for the states' socioeconomic climate, public opinion is strongly and consistently related with public policies in the American states. In more substantive terms, states with more liberal publics adopt more liberal policies (and vice versa).

Equally important, the analysis of Erikson, Wright, and McIver suggests that the parties and elections are the principal mechanisms for linking public opinion to public policy. As the authors note, "Parties and elections are the central conduits for mass influence" (p. 245). The rather complex process by which parties and elections connect public opinion to public policy is depicted in Figure 3.1. According to the model and the author's analysis, party elites in each of the states have distinct ideologies; as you would expect, Democratic leaders tend to be liberal, Republicans conservative. However, as Anthony Downs (1957) predicted four decades ago, an issue-oriented electorate rewards those parties whose issue stands are closest to the electorate (and conversely punishes those whose stands are not; see the path between party elite liberalism and Democratic legislative strength). As a result, the desire to win elections motivates Democratic and Republicans alike to moderate their stands: Democrats will enjoy their greatest success when they move to the right, whereas Republicans will gain votes by assuming positions closer to their opponents in the Democratic party. The result of this is the seemingly contradictory paths between Democratic legislative strength and legislative liberalism on the one hand and policy liberalism on the other. As the model illustrates, increases in Democratic legislative strength yield more legislative liberalism, which in turn is associated (predictably) with greater policy liberalism. At the same time, the pressures to moderate party stands produces the situation depicted in the figure in which greater Democratic strength, once other variables are controlled for, actually produces more conservative policy.

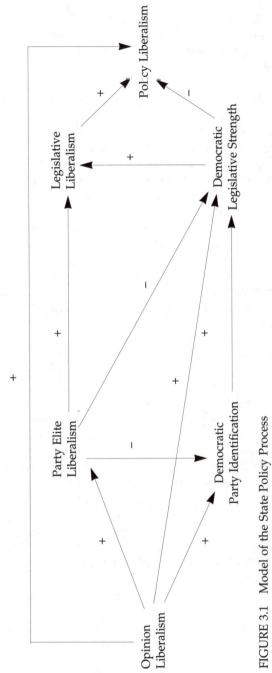

FIGURE 3.1 Model of the State Policy Process

SOURCE: Robert S. Erickson, Gerald C. Wright, and John P. McIver, *Statehouse Democracy: Public Opinion and Policy in the American States* (New York: Cambridge University Press, 1993), p. 126. Reprinted by permission.

What is particularly reassuring about the findings of Erikson, Wright, and McIver is the pivotal role that citizens play in the process of translating public opinion into public policy. As their evidence makes clear, voters play an active role in moving candidates and government policies toward the middle of the ideological spectrum. More generally, their findings point to an electorate that is more rational and informed in the aggregate than studies of individual voting have indicated.

Although recent developments have contributed to statehouse democracy, there is also reason to believe that the effects of demand-side changes have been limited in some respects. Students of voting behavior, for instance, remind us that most eligible voters still do not vote in most elections, and voters typically lack the information and interest necessary to make reasoned choices among political candidates, despite political reforms and the millions of dollars that are poured into state campaigns today. And as we have seen, voting in initiative and referendum contests in most cases is not much different in quality than in candidate elections. Research by Robert Jackson (1992) and Kim Quaile Hill (1994) further underscore the limits of recent demand-side reforms and developments. Using the data of Erikson, Wright, and McIver, Jackson looks at the mediating or conditional effects of several of the demand-side characteristics that we have touched on in this chapter and in Chapter 2 on the relationship between public opinion and public policy. Although many of those attributes exert a direct influence on policy liberalism (a finding consistent with what we have already seen) there is surprisingly little support in Jackson's data that various demand-side conditions promote a better fit between public opinion and public policy. Specifically, the extent to which public policy is driven by public opinion is not affected by levels of turnout or the character of the states' party and interest groups systems. That analysis does not, of course, preclude the possibility that other changes that we have documented here, including the Voting Rights Act, the reapportionment rulings, or the increased use of initiatives, improve the fit between opinion and policy, particularly for groups previously left out of the political system. It does, however, caution students of state government from assuming that demand-side reforms necessarily translate into greater responsiveness.

Research by Hill (1994) is also suggestive of the limits of recent demand-side reforms and developments. Using many of the variables we have already touched upon, Hill looks at three aspects of the states' democratic development—voting rights, interparty competition, and electoral participation—at two points in the time, the 1940s and the 1980s. On balance, the findings are disheartening: On two dimensions, interparty competition and electoral participation, the states either became less democratic or experienced, only a slight improvement. In terms of electoral participation, for example, although twenty-one states could be classified as undemocratic in the 1940s, by the 1980s that number had grown to thirty-four. In a parallel fashion, Hill's analysis indicates little progress in terms of party competition, a trend that owes much to the success of the Democratic party during this period. Only in terms of voting rights has there been significant movement in the right direction. As we have already seen, by the 1980s most vestiges of voter discrimination had been removed.

To get at the overall pattern of the states' democratic development, Hill develops a classification of statehouse democracy and combines data on the three components to assess how representative democracy has evolved in recent decades. The states are classified into four main regime types: (1) democracies—states exhibiting high levels of voting, voting rights, and two-party competition; (2) highly or moderately polyarchic—states approaching but falling short of democracy (e.g., moderate or high levels of competition and turnout but with somewhat restrictive voting rights); (3) closed party or relatively closed party oligarchies—states with restrictive voting rights and low-to-moderate competition and participation; and (4) those states that fall somewhere between polyarchic and oligarchic (what I have labeled as mediocracies in the table). Table 3.8 summarizes Hill's findings. As the table indicates, no state qualifies as a democracy in either time period. More importantly perhaps, fewer states are classified as polyarchic in the 1980s than in the late 1940s and early 1950s. Fifteen states approached democraticness in the earlier period, but only seven did so by the 1980s. On a more positive note, no states in the 1980s fell within the oligarchic categories, a development that reflects the elimination of racial restrictions on voting in the South. Further, most states in the 1980s fall within the middle category, neither polyarchic nor oligarchic.

Hill provides additional analysis that suggests that differences between the states do indeed matter. Employing a composite scale of the states' democraticness, Hill examines the relationship between that summary score and public policies in both the 1940s and the 1980s. For our purposes, the more important findings are those obtained for the 1980s. States that are more democratic tend to adopt more equitable policies, in this instance civil rights protections and more generous welfare benefits, a relationship that holds even after controlling for public opinion, the states' socioeconomic character, and federal influences. That and additional analysis leads Hill to conclude that "undemocratic regimes typically favor the interests of elites at the expense of the rest of society, especially the lower class. Democratization allows lower-class citizens to press legitimate new claims on government, and it encourages governmental responsiveness to those claims" (p. 128).

As insightful as Hill's analysis is, the reader should exercise some caution in drawing inferences from his findings. Hill's measurement strategy

TABLE 3.8   The States and Democratic Development (entries are number of states per regime type)

	1946–1952	1980–1986
Most democratic		
Democracies	0	0
Highly polyarchic	11	2
Moderately polyarchic	4	5
Mediocracies	21	43
Relatively closed party oligarchies	4	0
Closed party oligarchies	7	0
Least democratic		

SOURCE: Compiled from Kim Quaile Hill, *Democracy in the Fifty States* (Lincoln: University of Nebraska Press, 1994), pp. 96–98.

precludes other demand-side characteristics, including the fit between public opinion and policy, the diversity of interest groups, and the rate at which minorities are represented in state government, that might lead to different conclusions concerning the quality of statehouse democracy. In addition, interparty competition may well be increasing in the 1990s— witness the Republican victories in 1994. Assuming that this trend continues, it might be the case that a number of states will move into the moderately polyarchic category. Nonetheless, Hill's analysis underscores a broader conclusion. Over the last several decades public officials at both the state and federal levels have worked to increase the opportunities for citizens to participate in government by removing barriers to and offering more opportunities for participation. Unfortunately, all too frequently citizens have not taken advantage of those opportunities or have not always done so in a wise fashion. As a result, state governments are less democratic than they need be.

There is also the concern that at least some developments on the demand side have actually detracted from the quality of statehouse democracy. The increasing role of money in state politics comes immediately to mind. As we have seen, elections, both candidate and issue, have become increasingly expensive, lobbying has become a big money affair, and the resurgence of the parties is increasingly a resurgence in their ability to raise money. As a consequence, more and more of the political energy of the states is devoted not to representation and governing but to the business of raising and spending money. The result is that the influence of those who can provide that money, most notably interest groups, has increased at the expense of ordinary citizens and traditional party organizations. Although the influence of special interests is mitigated in part by the growing diversity of groups and the fact that a wider range of the citizenry is now represented in state politics, two considerations are worth noting: (1) many citizens are not represented by organized groups, and (2) narrow economic interests still enjoy disproportionate political influence. Indeed, evidence reported by Virginia Gray and David Lowery (1995) indicates that the proportion of noneconomic interest groups at the state level has not increased appreciably since the 1970s. According to their evidence, noneconomic groups represented less than 30 percent of all groups in 1990.

Resurgent state parties represent a potential antidote to an increasingly fragmented system of elections and influence. And indeed, there is at least some evidence that the parties are performing that role in the 1990s. As state party organizations grow stronger, for instance, interparty competition has often increased, offering voters real choices at election time. In a parallel fashion, the infusion of funding from the national party organizations holds out the promise of a cleaner fit between party and ideology and an easier vote decision for many citizens as they use party as a means of sorting among a long list of candidates for state and local office. Yet, there is also the possibility that developments within the states' parties, most notably the emergence of LCCs and national-state party integration, may actually detract from the ability of the parties to perform their traditional linkage functions. Daniel Shea (1995) argues that the emergence of legislative-based party organizations may undermine traditional party organizations by fragmenting the state party and preempting local party organizations. At the state level, the emergence of LCCs threatens to produce a situation where there is not one state party but several—the traditional party organization, the party in the lower chamber, and the party in the upper chamber. To the extent that the activities of LCCs remain isolated from one another and the state party organization, then the likelihood that the political parties will serve to aggregate diverse political interests is much reduced. The irony here, of course, is that instead of playing a centralizing role within an otherwise decentralized political system, resurgent political parties may end up promoting political fragmentation. At the local level, Shea charges that LCCs undercut local party organizations in a couple of ways. First, as LCCs become more active in recruiting candidates for state legislative races, local candidates have less of a need to work their way up through the ranks of the local party organization. Consequently, local parties are less likely to perform what Shea contends are valuable screening and socialization functions. Second, to the extent that LCCs and candidates rely on outside consultants and media-based campaigns, local party officials and the party rank and file become less relevant to campaigns, and the opportunities for the kinds of direct, grassroots mobilization involving cadres of party volunteers going door-to-door to solicit support for their party's candidates are foregone in lieu of less personal mass media efforts. The infusion of national party monies into the state party organizations may have parallel effects on state parties by nationalizing what heretofore were state contests.

Clearly most of the implications of demand-side changes for the quality of state governing fall on the democratic side of the equation. But there is also reason to believe that changes in elections, participation, parties, and interest groups also condition the ability of state governments to govern responsibly. We have already noted, for instance, the pros and cons of direct democracy for the quality of state policymaking. The available literature also suggests that a number of reforms and developments, including reapportionment, variations in turnout, and greater interparty competition directly impact state policy outputs. The question that remains is how, taken together and singly, demand-side changes have promoted or detracted from the ability of state governments to fashion coherent and effective policies.

The conventional wisdom outlined in Chapter 1 would suggest that by increasing the opportunities for more interests to participate more frequently in more public venues, the various demand-side changes documented in this chapter and in Chapter 2 ultimately add to the decentralization of state governments and, accordingly, undercut the ability of state governments to govern wisely. One scenario is that as reelection-driven public officials interact with an increasing number of specialized interests groups adept at prosecuting the interests of their members, more and more of the energies of state government will be devoted to providing particularized benefits to specialized interests. The implications for fiscal prudence and policy coherence are obvious. Not only will state governments spend more than they might have otherwise, but public policies in the states will become nothing more than a patchwork of particularized benefits aimed not at some larger policy vision but simply at satisfying the parochial needs of various groups within the states' political environments. An alternative, but equally dissatisfying, scenario is one in which as more groups representing more diverse and conflicting interests come to the table, elected officials will find it more difficult to forge the consensus necessary to fashion coherent policies. In some cases, conflict between competing interests will be so severe that stalemate will result, and state governments will simply fail to address pressing public problems. More likely, the need to accommodate competing interests will result in compromise and incrementalism, and state policies will be more politically expedient than policy wise.

Research reported by Gray and Lowery (1995) on the relationship between the character of the states' interest group systems and the activity levels of their legislatures provides evidence of both scenarios and, in doing so, offers confirmation for the conventional wisdom. According to their data, greater interest group density (i.e., more groups) was associated in the early 1990s with lower rates of bill introduction and enactment in the forty-six states included in their analysis, a finding consistent with the notion that greater interest group pluralism produces gridlock, stalemate, and inaction. At the same time, a greater diversity of interest groups, at least in terms of the presence of noneconomic interests, yields more enactments and a greater likelihood that legislation once introduced will be enacted. That finding, in turn, provides evidence of the first scenario, that is, that more diversity will produce more legislation as lawmakers find ways to accommodate the demands of various groups within a state. Based on these and additional findings Gray and Lowery imply that states in which the number of groups is relatively small but in which noneconomic groups are reasonably well-represented may be in a better position to make "effective policy in a timely, deliberate, and responsive manner" (p. 548).

Its obvious merits aside, Gray and Lowery's analysis only begins to get at the impacts of demand-side decentralization and fragmentation on state policymaking. In the final analysis, whether and to what extent the fears of those who subscribe to the conventional wisdom are realized in the American states depend in large part on what takes place on the supply side of government, in the governors' mansions, the legislatures, and the courts. Although the political environment in which those institutions operate conditions what governments do and how they do it, ultimately it is the men and women who serve in those institutions and the rules under which those institutions operate that determine how and how well state governments function. Accordingly, the next three chapters look at how governors, legislatures, and the states' highest courts have changed in recent decades and the implications of those changes for both representation and responsibility.

NOTES

1. This section is drawn primarily from Bibby and Holbrook (1996).

4

The Governors

The evolution of the American governorship over the past two decades mirrors that of state governments generally. As we have seen, state governments were rediscovered in the late 1970s and early 1980s, becoming for many the major source of political responsiveness and policy innovation. Yet, by the 1990s analysts were increasingly tempering their earlier optimism and pointing to a number of political and policy problems and limits. The experiences of the states' governors parallel those developments. Writing in 1978, political scientist Larry Sabato pointed to a new breed of American governor—younger, better educated, and more diverse—and bid "Goodbye to Good-Time Charlie." A decade later, David Osborne (1988) profiled six of the nation's most successful governors and credited their success to a new political paradigm that defied classification along the traditional liberal-conservative continuum. One need only look at the subsequent career paths of those individuals to appreciate their uniqueness and capabilities. Among the half dozen governors profiled in Osborne's now classic *Laboratories of Democracy* (1988), Dick Thornburgh of Pennsylvania would become the nation's attorney general; Arizona's Bruce Babbitt would serve as secretary of the interior; Michael Dukakis of Massachusetts would capture his party's nomination for the presidency in 1988; and Arkansas's Bill Clinton would win the nation's presidency just four years later. Although much of the success of governors in recent decades can be attributed to the personal characteristics of those individuals, governors today also enjoy more formal powers and institutional resources than their predecessors. As we shall see, governors now have greater tenure potential, more influence over their states' budgets, more institutional resources, and somewhat greater control over the executive branch. By the 1980s, it appeared that a new kind of American governor armed with new powers and resources and a new perspective on governing had emerged.

Yet, by the end of that decade analysts would begin painting a more problematic portrait of the American governor, one in which constraints often outweighed opportunities and achievements. One noted scholar, Thad Beyle, published an insightful text whose title, *Governors and Hard Times* (1992a), aptly captured the plight of being governor in the late

1980s and early 1990s. Faced with ailing economies, a seeming inability to deal with rising health, education, and welfare costs, mutinous legislatures, and heightened opposition to new taxes, governors like Douglas Wilder of Virginia, Lawton Chiles of Florida, Jim Florio of New Jersey, and Pete Wilson of California accomplished considerably less in their first years in office than their predecessors despite sharing many of their positive attributes (Beyle 1992a, 1993). Once again, the contours of the American governorship were changing.

Despite these apparent setbacks and limits, the states' chief executives are hardly in retreat. Both citizens and legislatures still look to the governor to set the state's political and policy agenda and as a source of new policy ideas. Governors in the 1990s enjoy considerable power and resources and are arguably the most important single actor in state government. Moreover, recent elections have ushered in a new cohort of successful Republican governors (and a few Democrats) who not only have overcome many of the obstacles alluded to earlier, but who are at the forefront of a new conservative policy agenda in both Washington and in the states. Today, several Republican governors, including John Engler of Michigan, Pete Wilson of California, Tommy Thompson of Wisconsin, George Bush of Texas, and Christine Todd Whitman of New Jersey, are reshaping their states' policy agenda and setting the tone for much of what is being considered in Washington. Writing shortly after the 1994 elections, a reporter for the *Washington Post* (January 29, 1995: A18) underscored the point by noting:

> Newly fortified by the November elections, Republican governors have outlined aggressive agendas for cutting taxes, shrinking government, reforming welfare and education, and rearranging the balance of power among Washington, the states, and local governments. Democratic governors, struggling to maintain their footing in the conservative currents running through the country, are promoting their own versions of this agenda for change. Like President Clinton, they are bent on reinventing government, restructuring welfare, fighting crime, and protecting the middle class.

In the pages that follow, I look more closely at how the office of governor has changed in recent decades and how those changes impact on the character of state politics and governing. The chapter begins by looking at two developments that have ostensibly produced a resurgence in the states' chief executives—increases in the formal authority and institutional resources afforded governors and the emergence of a new kind of American governor. Then I examine the evidence concerning the impact of those changes on individual gubernatorial success in the American states. That discussion naturally leads to a consideration of the constraints and obstacles that governors currently face. Finally, the chapter concludes by considering the broader implications of those developments for the quality of statehouse democracy and the ability of the states to govern in a responsible fashion.

Institutional Reforms

Over the past few decades, many of the formal powers and institutional resources of the American governor have been expanded. As a result, Larry Sabato (1978: 63) contends that "the governor is now truly master of his own house, not just the father figure." Governors today have a greater hold over the executive branch and are better able to exert themselves in dealing with the other branches of government. Two kinds of reforms have been enacted. Some, including the veto and enhanced gubernatorial budget authority, increase the governors' influence in dealing with the states' legislatures. Others—a shift to a "short ballot"; enhanced powers of appointment, removal, and reorganization; increased tenure; and increases in the staffing resources of the governor's office—aim at increasing the governors' analytic and management capabilities and yielding governors greater control over the executive branch of government.

The press for reform reflects a mix of motives and goals. Some contend that those who advocate reform do so simply to gain partisan political advantage. As Kenneth Meier (1980) notes, governors can use reorganization to achieve any number of political ends, including upgrading a program's importance, reorienting a program, or saving a failing program. Similarly, in discussing the timing of reform (in this case, the ability of governors to succeed themselves), Beyle (1990: 219) contends that "change in gubernatorial succession occurs when the incumbent governor wants the opportunity to serve a second term and puts his political muscle and organization behind the effort." Others view reforms as a means not only of enhancing the influence of individual governors, but promoting greater efficiency in state government. As Michael Baranowski (1995: 1) notes: "For much of the state government reform movement, it was simply assumed that extending terms, giving the governor greater control over the budget, expanding appointment power, and increasing veto power would naturally lead to a more influential governor, which would, in turn, lead to better, more efficient state government." Whatever the motivation, institutional reforms discussed in the following pages have frequently changed the nature of being governor.

Budget Authority

One of the most far-reaching and fundamental means of enhancing gubernatorial power has been the centralization of budget authority in the governor's office. By the mid-1990s, only a handful of states required the governor to share responsibility for developing the state budget (Beyle 1995a; Bowman and Kearney 1996). In the remaining states, an executive budget system, one in which the budget is initiated in the executive branch and then transmitted to the legislature, places the governor at the center of the budget process. In addition to initiating the budget, the line item veto, provided for in most states, gives the governor additional control over the budget. Table 4.1 provides additional insight into the governors' budget authority by looking at the power to cut spending in order to meet balanced budget requirements. As the table reveals, by the early 1990s eighteen states placed no limit on the governor's power to reduce spending. In an additional nine states that power is only limited in that governors must make uniform, across-the-board cuts. In thirteen states governors are allowed to make cuts, but must do so within predetermined limits on the amount. Nonetheless, only nine states require governors to receive formal legislative approval for any spending cuts.

Control over the budget process is important. The governor's budget authority and preeminence aids the governor in coordinating the activities of the executive branch, provides leverage over uncooperative agencies and departments, gives the chief executive control over the legislature's agenda, and provides a platform for presenting the governor's policy initiatives. As Sabato (1978: 84) notes, "The executive budget may well be the single most important tool possessed by the chief executive." Moreover, the importance of the budget and the centrality of the budget process have increased in the last two decades. According to Beyle (1996b: 81), during the 1980s and early 1990s "the governor's budgetary powers were the engines of gubernatorial policy politics. In almost every state, the impact of the recession, changes in the economy, and a declining federal government presence in domestic affairs caused severe budgetary turmoil as state revenues fell and a need for state governmental action rose." Given its importance, it is not surprising that considerable effort has been expended in reforming the budget process at the state level. One survey conducted in the 1970s indicated that thirty-three of the forty states responding had initiated major changes in the budget process over the previous decade (Ramsey and Hackbart 1979). Although the results have been mixed at best, several of these budget reforms, including initiatives such as zero-based budgeting and management-by-objective, have attempted to tie budget decisions more closely to measures of performance and to make state governments more accountable to their citizens.

The governors' budget authority is by no means unlimited, however. Most obviously, fiscal uncertainty facing the states places constraints on governors. Ambitious policy initiatives are often abandoned during re-

TABLE 4.1 Governor's Power to Reduce Expenditures to Balance the Budget After the Appropriations Bill Has Been Adopted, 1993

Very Strong (5 points)	Strong (4 points)	Moderate (3 points)	Weak (2 points)	Very Weak (1 point)
AK	AL	AZ	FL	AR
HI	GA	CO		CA
ID	IA	CT		IL
IN	ND	DE		KY
MA	OK	KS		ME
MD	SC	LA		MI
MO	UT	MN		NE
NC	WA	MS		NH
NJ	WV	MT		WI
NV		NM		
OH		NY		
OR		VT		
PA		VA		
RI				
SD				
TN				
TX				
WY				

NOTE: 5 points = There are no limitations on the governor's authority to reduce the budget

4 points = The governor can only make uniform, across-the-board reductions

3 points = The governor's authority to make reductions is limited to a predetermined amount, percentage, or by specific categories

2 points = The governor must consult with the state legislature before making any reductions

1 point = The governor lacks the authority to make any reductions without the approval of the state legislature or one of its committees

SOURCE: Robert Jay Dilger, "The Governor's Office: A Comparative Analysis," *West Virginia Public Affairs Reporter,* 10 (1993): 8. Reprinted by permission.

cessionary times as revenues decline and the demands for government relief in the areas of welfare, unemployment insurance, and health care increase. Even in less perilous economic times, many state revenues (gas taxes, for example) are earmarked for specific services (highway construction, for example). Federal mandates and programs of grants-in-aid further limit the governors' control over the budget. And, of course, in all but four states, legislatures have unlimited power to change the executive budget. As state legislatures come into their own and as members learn the virtues of pork barrel politics, governors may discover that even more of the budget is "uncontrollable."

The Veto

The ability to veto legislation is one of the oldest formal tools at the governors' disposal. Even during the 1800s when governors had few formal powers, most state constitutions provided the chief executive with at least some veto authority. That authority has been expanded in the last century and governors today have more authority and flexibility in the use of the veto (Beyle 1993).

Today governors can draw upon four kinds of vetoes (Dilger 1993). First, governors in every state can use a package veto, which rejects a bill in its entirety. Second, governors in all but a handful of states enjoy the line item veto. Under that kind of veto, the governor can veto a specific budget item without rejecting the whole appropriation. Needless to say, the line item veto gives the governor more flexibility and avoids the political costs of vetoing otherwise popular or necessary legislation. Third, in eleven states governors can target their disapproval through the reduction veto, which allows the governor to reduce a specific appropriation without eliminating the program completely. Finally, seven of the nation's governors can use an amendatory veto, which conditions acceptance of the bill upon the legislature making or accepting recommended changes.

Although the veto is largely a reactive device, its use forces legislators to take the governor's policy preferences into account in crafting legislation. Often just the mere threat of a veto can alter legislation (Bowman and Kearney 1986). Equally important, the use of the veto effectively changes the decision rules under which legislatures operate. Although it varies by state, override provisions usually require a "supermajority" of at least three-fifths of both houses to override the governor's veto. Not surprisingly, as legislative-gubernatorial conflict increases (more on this later), the governors' use of the veto has become a more visible and controversial part of the job. Over past twenty years, governors have increasingly used their veto powers and, for their part, legislatures are more frequently overriding those vetoes (Simon 1986; Beyle 1990). Nonetheless, the advantage still lies with the governors. In 1992–1993, only 3 percent of the governors' vetoes were overridden (Beyle 1996b).

That tendency aside, some would caution that the use of the veto can be a sign of weakness and not strength. According to this view, a strong governor can use his/her power of negotiation to avoid the confrontational politics that comes with the veto. In addition, although the risks are still small, as the prospect of a successful override grows, governors risk the embarrassment of losing. The prospect of a gubernatorial veto can also prompt legislators to be less responsible. Knowing that the governor will veto popular but unwise legislation allows lawmakers to symbolically placate important interests without having to live with unworkable or costly legislation.

The Short Ballot and the Fragmentation of Authority

One major way in which governors differ from the American president is that governors in most states share authority over administration with a host of separately elected executive branch officials, including lieutenant governors, attorney generals, state auditors, and the secretaries of state and treasury. Currently, over 500 separately elected officials head 260 state agencies (Beyle 1996b). Supposedly, electing executive branch officials separately provides a check on the governor. Most would agree, for example, that state auditors should be independent of those they audit (including the governor). Similarly, the value of having an independently elected attorney general has been underscored recently in those states where governors have faced prosecution for corruption. Yet having to contend with other elected executives has made the governors' job more problematic. Fragmented political authority makes it more difficult for governors to both formulate and carry out public policies as they find themselves dependent upon others over whom they have little formal influence. Moreover, as Sabato (1978) notes, all too often governors are held accountable by the public for the actions of others over whom they have no control. To add insult to injury, many of these separately elected officials enjoy unlimited tenure, something only a few governors possess. The problem is particularly onerous where it involves the lieutenant governor, a problem made worse if the lieutenant governor is of the other party. As Sabato (1978: 77) observes: "Even in the best of these situations, the trust necessary between governor and lieutenant is absent. . . . At the worst, split party control . . . can be chaotic, frustrating, and retarding to the governors' programs." Conversely, having governors and lieutenant governors elected together not only reduces potential tensions but also provides the governor additional resources and expertise, particularly as lieutenant governors become better trained, compensated, and utilized. In several states, lieutenant governors have been delegated major administrative responsibilities. In Florida, for example, during the early 1990s Lieutenant Governor Buddy McKay headed a major overhaul of the state's mammoth social services agency and oversaw a major restructuring and reform of the state's environmental agencies (Dunkelberger 1994).

Over the past few decades, there has been some movement to a shorter ballot as the number of separately elected officials has been reduced. Between 1956 and 1988, the number of separately elected executive branch officials fell by 28 percent, and the average fell from thirteen per state in 1950 to just six per state in 1996 (Beyle 1989; Council of State Governments 1996). On balance, however, the states have moved slowly in reducing electoral fragmentation; more than forty states still separately elect their attorney generals and nearly that many elect the state's treasurer and secretary of state. Currently, thirty-five states elect, in addition to their governors, at least five other statewide officials. Why are the states reluctant to reform on this score? The slow pace of reform reflects several factors including inertia, popular support for the long ballot, and the opposition of clientele groups that benefit from having particular offices free of gubernatorial control. In that kind of setting the political costs to a governor of abolishing particular offices is simply too great (Sabato 1978).

Appointment and Removal Powers

A closely related area of reform concerns the governors' appointment and removal powers. As was the case with *elected* executive officials, governors have historically been hampered by an inability to appoint and remove *administrative* officers. The issue is important. According to Ann Bowman and Richard Kearney (1986: 58), "The power of appointment and removal of the heads of state agencies, boards, and commissions is probably the most fundamental of all within the governor's managerial and policymaking command. Without that authority a governor holds little leverage to direct the actions of executive agencies." The importance of the issue notwithstanding, the available evidence indicates only modest reform of the governors' appointment powers in recent decades. Between 1960 and 1986, the number of states that afforded their governors strong or very strong appointment powers grew only slightly, from twenty-six to twenty-seven, while the number of chief executives with weak powers dropped from seventeen to fourteen. At the same time, governors enjoyed substantial increases in their appointment powers in a number of policy areas including corrections, welfare, highways, and health (Beyle 1989).

In addition to limits on their formal powers of appointment, governors are also constrained by practical, political restrictions (Beyle 1993). First, given the large number of appointments that typically have to be made within a relatively short period of time, governors may not pay sufficient attention to key appointments and suffer the consequences of a bad choice at some later date. Second, replacing large numbers of agency officials can create resentment within bureaucracies and engender a loss of support for gubernatorial initiatives within the bureaucracy. Third, Beyle (1993: 86) contends that "patronage appointments serve as rewards, but many individuals and groups feel they should be rewarded. Appointments are evaluated with a jealous eye, and jealousy is not a positive basis on which to build a working relationship." Finally, frequently governors and those around them have differing expectations about particular positions, and that can lead to power conflicts within the governor's coalition.

A similar picture emerges when it comes to the power to remove. Although eleven of the fourteen state constitutions revised following World War II include the power of removal, less than half the states' constitutions currently provide the governor with the power to remove individuals from executive branch positions, and most states place some restrictions on the governor's power of removal (Beyle 1996b). From a practical, political perspective, removal of agency officials too often entails political fallout and a loss of political support. A series of Supreme Court rulings have also placed limits on the governors' ability to fire patronage employees (Beyle 1993). In 1976, in *Elrod v. Burns*, the Court held that patronage firing violates an individual's first amendment rights of political belief and expression. While reaffirming its earlier decision, the court has relaxed that restriction somewhat in subsequent cases by providing that removal of patronage employees is allowable if the individual's political beliefs interfere with the performance or his or her job (see *Branti v. Finkel*, 1980). In addition, the court ruled in 1983 in *Connick v. Myers* that first amendment protections did not prohibit firing individuals for complaining about their jobs or supervisors. However, in 1990, in a case involving the office of Illinois governor James Thompson *(Rutan et al. v. Republican Party of Illinois)*, the U.S. Supreme Court reaffirmed its earlier rulings by maintaining that refusing to hire, promote, or transfer individuals on the basis of their political affiliation or party label violated first amendment rights.

The Power to Reorganize

Although some of the states reorganized their executive branches earlier in the century, the need to do so increased substantially following World War II. As the role of state governments grew, agencies and boards were created on an ad hoc basis with little thought given to efficiency or accountability. The result was frequently an organizational nightmare—dozens of agencies and boards with overlapping functions, with many answerable to independently selected boards, others to the legislature, and only some to the governor. Early in this period, governors lacked the authority to reorganize. In 1956, for instance, only two states allowed their governors to issue executive orders to reorganize, and even in those instances legislative confirmation was required. Over the next few decades the governors' power to reorganize was expanded, and by the late 1980s, two dozen states allowed their governors to reorganize through executive orders (Beyle 1989). Governors in nearly every state have taken advantage of the power to reorganize. Since the mid-1960s over twenty states have experienced comprehensive reorganizations and nearly every state has partially reorganized some part of the executive branch (Beyle 1992b; Conant 1992). According to the National Governors' Association (reported in Beyle 1992b: 59–60), since 1985 "14 states indicated some action in reorganization, 23 states established an external commission to review organization, productivity, or management, and 14 developed internal efficiency programs." Reorganization has been accomplished through a variety of means--the creation of new agencies and departments, the elimination of others, a reassignment of functions and responsibilities, and very frequently, the consolidation of several agencies into a single department or "superagency." What has been the effect of recent efforts at reorganization? Has restructuring the executive produced greater efficiency or is it merely a means by which governors extend their power? Analysis by Meier (1980) suggests that reorganization is more a political than an administrative tool. To demonstrate that, Meier examines the fiscal impact of executive reorganization in those sixteen states in which reorganization took place between 1965 and 1975. His findings reveal few reductions in either long- or short-run patterns of state spending and government employment. Two sets of explanations are offered to account for the failure of state reorganization to produce efficiency and costs savings. First, from an economic perspective, restructuring of state government may not yield greater efficiency because of the costs inherent in doing so. Agencies are likely to resist reorganization, thus raising the cost of implementing it. Moreover, if reorganization alters standard operating procedures within an organization, short-term start-up costs may be entailed, blunting any immediate efficiency gains. In addition, adopting many of the reforms advocated by classical administrative principles may actually impose new costs on agencies. Limiting the span of control, for example, requires new and costly supervisory personnel. A second explanation is more political. Given the political payoffs of reorganization, Meier submits that "perhaps the purpose of executive reorganization is to increase the control of the elected chief executive. After all, reorganization along A. E. Buck's (1938) principles simplifies administrative structure, places all agencies under the direct control of the chief executive, and allows the budget to be used to reward and punish agencies"(1980: 400).

Term of Office

Perhaps the simplest way of enhancing the power of the governor is to lengthen the amount of time the governor can serve in office. Most of the nation's first governors were limited to a single term in office. Even as late as the mid-1950s, governors in twenty-one states served two-year terms, and seventeen states did not allow governors the opportunity for succession. The problems with those kinds of term limits are obvious. Two-year terms require governors to spend an inordinate amount of time campaigning and seeking reelection and limiting a governor to a single term produces a "lame duck." Shortened terms of office also preclude a long-term perspective on policy development and implementation and threaten policy instability as new governors continually replace the policies of their predecessors. For these and other reasons, one major avenue for enhancing the governors' authority has been to increase the governors' tenure in office. Since 1955 the number of states that prohibit governors from succeeding themselves has shrunk to one (Virginia elects its governor to a single four-year term) and forty-eight states now provide for a four-year term. Not surprisingly, increased tenure potential has produced lower gubernatorial turnover. During the 1950s less than 30 percent of the states' governors served five years or longer. By the 1970s the comparable figure was 50 percent (Sabato 1978). More recent analyses reported by Beyle (1992c) also point to reduced turnover in the gubernatorial ranks. According to his data, the average number of governors per state fell from 2.3 in the 1960s to just 1.1 in the 1980s. Ideally, increased tenure has, in turn, allowed for more long-range policy planning and continuity in programming as governors are able to see their initiatives implemented.

Staffing

Efforts to increase gubernatorial authority are frequently efforts at increasing the resources available to the governor, what Robert Dilger has labeled enabling resources (1994). One major enabling resource is staff. As we have seen, the powers and responsibilities of state governments and their chief executives have grown substantially over the last forty to fifty years. As a result, the success of today's governor depends a great deal on the quality of people who work in the governor's office. The size of the governors' staff has increased from an average of 11 in 1956 to just under 50 in 1996 (Beyle 1993; Council of State Governments 1996). Altogether, governors in no less than thirty-eight states have at least 25 members on their personal staff, and of these, thirteen have 50 or more staff members. Equally important, key budgeting and planning personnel have been moved into the governor's office in many of the states. In 1960, for example, only 3 of the 37 state planning offices in existence were located in the governor's office. By 1988, 40 of the 45 planning divisions were either located in the governor's office or in a department of finance or budget (Beyle 1993). Those planning divisions perform a wide range of functions including policy initiation, budgeting, policy analysis, and interagency coordination. Increased planning and budgeting capabilities have been particularly critical in allowing governors to play the role of policy innovator (Beyle 1988).

Summary

Gubernatorial expert Thad Beyle (1996b) has looked at changes in the formal powers of the governors over the last four decades by comparing the governors' tenure potential, budget-making power, veto power, political

TABLE 4.2   Gubernatorial Powers, 1960–1994

Formal Powers (range)	Political Scientists				
	1960	*1968*	*1981*	*1989*	*1994*
Appointments (1–5)	2.9	3.0	3.2	3.2[a]	2.8
Budget making (1–5)	4.0	3.6	4.7	4.8	4.8
Tenure potential (1–5)	3.3	3.7	4.1	4.2	4.1
Veto (0–5)	2.8	2.6	4.1	4.4	4.4
Average score	13.0	12.9	16.1	16.6	16.15
Possible range	3–20	3–20	3–20	3–20	3–20
Actual range	7–19	8–20	10–20	12–20	12–19
Institutional Powers (range)	National Governors' Association				
		1965	*1985*	*1990[b]*	*1994[b]*
Appointments (0–7)		3.8 est.[c]	4.0 est.[c]	4.2	4.0
Budget making (1–5)		4.5 est.[c]	4.8 est.[c]	4.8	4.8
Tenure potential (1–5)		3.3	4.1	4.2	4.1
Veto (1–5)		4.2	3.6	4.4	4.4
Legislative budget-changing power (1–5)		1.3	1.2	1.3	1.3
Party control (1–5)		3.8	3.4	3.1	3.2
Average score		20.9	21.1	22.0	21.8
Possible range		5–32	5–32	5–32	5–32
Actual range		14–29	16–27	15–29	17–28

[a]Adjusted to make one-to-six point score into a one-to-five point score by dropping each state's score by one point.
[b]Updates of original NGA indices.
[c]Estimates based on information in NGA report.
SOURCE: Thad Beyk, "Being Governor," in Van Horn, ed., *The State of the States,* 3rd ed. (Washington, D.C.: CQ Press, 1996). Reprinted by permission.

strength in the legislature, and the legislature's ability to change gubernatorial budgets. A summary of his analysis and similar analysis by the National Governors' Association (NGA) is presented in Table 4.2. Although the NGA index shows little change over the thirty-five-year period, Beyle's index shows an increase of 24 percent in the formal powers of the states' governors between the 1960s and the 1990s. But, as the data reveal, the pattern is uneven. Although the governors' veto, budget-making, and tenure powers have increased over the last several decades, other institutional powers, including appointments, party control, and the legislatures' budget-changing powers have not. As Beyle (1996b: 85) concludes: "Reforms have been made on both sides of the separation-of-powers relationship, and while governors may now have more institutionalized powers at their disposal (budget-making, tenure potential, veto) state legislatures possess powers that are often used at the expense of the executive (budget-changing authority, party control)."

A New Kind of Governor

Institutional reforms are only one piece of the puzzle. Enhancing the formal powers and institutional resources of the governorship only begins to account for the kinds of changes in how the states' chief executives have performed in recent decades. The resurgence of the governors also reflects fundamental changes in the kinds of persons who seek the office, and perhaps more importantly, their approach to governing once they become governor. A review of the available evidence suggests there is, indeed, a new kind of American governor.

Demographically, an examination of the 312 governors who served between 1950 and 1975 demonstrates that governors in the post–World War II era are better educated, younger, and more diverse in terms of their religion. A comparison of the 1950–1975 cohort with those who served earlier in the century also indicates that more recent governors were more likely to have previously held elective office, particularly state legislative office. Nearly a quarter of those who served as governor over the 1950–1975 period had served in the legislature just prior to their election, a trend that accelerated somewhat in the 1970s. An additional 19 percent had held other statewide office and 10 percent had served in the Congress. Governors who served during this period were also more likely to be elected or appointed to a higher office after serving as governor, a finding that Sabato argues points to the enhanced prestige of the office (Sabato 1978).

Those trends continue in the 1990s. In 1992, the average age of America's governors was fifty-five and over a third were under fifty years of age. In addition, many brought considerable political experience to the job. In 1992, exactly half of the governors had served in their state legislatures and four-fifths had served in some capacity in state government.

Evidence suggests that these changing demographic and career patterns are an important influence on gubernatorial performance. In looking at the "outstanding governors" in his cohort, Sabato found that the more successful chief executives were in fact better educated and younger and were more likely to have come to the governorship from the state legislature or the Congress. Those governors were also more likely to subsequently serve in higher appointive or elective office. A reanalysis of Sabato's data indicates that the single most important predictor of gubernatorial success is the age at which individuals first held the governorship. Individuals who began their gubernatorial careers earlier proved, on balance, to be more effective governors (Sigelman and Smith 1981).

In the final analysis, what may set the new kind of governor apart is the approach to governance they bring to state government. In one of the more influential books of the 1980s, *Laboratories of Democracy*, David Osborne (1988) maintains that the nation's more successful and innovative governors have adopted a new political paradigm that defies placement along the traditional liberal-conservative continuum. Having found both New Deal liberalism and Reagan conservatism unworkable in a global economy, Osborne contends that the new breed of governor embraces a post–New Deal political paradigm that envisions an active public role that aims to promote economic development and reshape the economic marketplace. According to Osborne (p. 330), the new political paradigm rests on a number of fundamental principles: "growth with equity, a focus on market solutions, a search for nonbureaucratic methods, fiscal moderation, investment rather than spending, redistribution of opportunity rather than outcomes, and a new federalism." For those who share these principles, the proper role of government entails taking the lead in reshaping the economic marketplace, but relying on market solutions to do so. As Osborne notes (p. 5):

> Government's primary role is to nourish the elements that make innovation possible: a vibrant intellectual infrastructure; a skilled, educated workforce; an attractive quality of life; an entrepreneurial climate; a sufficient supply of risk capital; a healthy market for new products and processes; a commitment to industrial modernization; an industrial culture built on cooperation and flexibility; and a social system that supports innovation and change.

In more concrete terms, this new approach to governing entails the kinds of initiatives that many states, including Arkansas, Michigan, Pennsylvania, and Massachusetts, undertook in the early and mid-1980s to promote their states' economies, including, among other things, education and welfare reform and the creation of mechanisms such as small-business incubators, financing programs for new and small businesses, venture capital pools, and procurement assistance programs that represent an alternative to traditional "smokestack chasing" efforts.

Governors in the 1990s seem to share a number of their predecessors' attributes including pragmatism, a willingness to innovate, fiscal conservatism, and the perceived need for a new partnership between the public and private sectors. Pete Wilson of California is a good example of a pragmatic governor. Unlike fellow Republicans who preceded him, Wilson initially ran as pro-gay, pro-choice, and pro-environment. During his first term, he proposed a series of social service programs (family planning, prenatal care, and school-based health clinics, for example) aimed at preventing rather than ameliorating social problems and an ambitious program of wetland, wildlife, and forest protection. At the same time, early in his first term Wilson proposed cuts in the average monthly welfare payment and took a hard line on crime. Bowing to conservative pressures later in his term, the governor vetoed legislation adding sexual orientation to antidiscrimination legislation. Soon thereafter, he vetoed legislation extending unemployment benefits for an additional thirteen weeks (Gable 1992). Wilson's swing to the right continued into his successful reelection bid in 1994. Running well behind his Democratic challenger, Wilson announced his support for Proposition 187, a controversial but ultimately successful statewide ballot measure that denies government services to illegal immigrants. Wilson's conservative tilt continued following his reelection and as he sought, unsuccessfully, the Republican nomination for the presidency. In 1995, Wilson announced his opposition to affirmative action and convinced the California Board of Regents to eliminate affirmative action programs in the state's university system.

Massachusetts's former Republican governor William F. Weld provides another example of the new kind of governor and illustrates the problems those individuals face in the 1990s. Elected in 1990 in one of the most unusual races in Massachusetts history, Weld came into office trumpeting many of the principles promoted by Osborne and others. In describing Weld's approach to governing during his first term in office, Boston College political scientist Dennis Hale (1992: 132–133) notes:

> Governor Weld's inaugural address established the main theme, a Reaganesque assault on government. Government is the problem, not the solution. Government is too big, too clumsy, and too greedy; tax increases only feed its worst appetites and vices. The only way around the problem of government is to have less of it. . . . Weld offered a vision of a stripped down state government that would tailor its benefits first to its revenues and second to need. Instead of placating interest groups with "pilot programs" that quickly became entitlements, the government would encourage competition and entrepreneurship, even to the extent of turning the management of public programs and institutions over to private contractors. We will not abandon the safety net, he promised. But we will abandon nearly everything else. And there will be no new taxes, period.

For all his fiscal conservatism, Weld takes a more liberal, and at times, libertarian approach on environmental issues and matters of private conduct. Weld supports gay rights and, surprisingly given Massachusetts strong Catholic tradition, the complete deregulation of abortions. In assessing Weld's approach to governing, Kathleen Sylvester (1992: 36) contends that the governor "doesn't like government intervening in the marketplace, and he doesn't like it intervening in the lives and decisions of individuals." That faith in the private sector is seen in the governor's support of privatization as an alternative means of delivering state services.

By 1992, five of the state's thirty-four hospitals had been closed, health care for prisoners had been shifted to private companies, and the governor had proposed turning the Massachusetts Turnpike over to private interests (Sylvester 1992).

The severity of the state's fiscal crisis provided an early opportunity for Weld to act on his larger principles of government. When Weld took office in 1990, state unemployment stood at 8.5 percent, Standard and Poors had just dropped the state's bond rating to BBB (essentially "junk bond" status), and the state still had a $850 million deficit despite two years of billion dollar tax increases. Working with the legislative leadership, a series of compromises and agreements were eventually reached on a 1991 budget that shrank total state spending by $800 million. Altogether, expenditures on three hundred social and educational programs were cut, aid to local governments was reduced by nearly 13 percent, and state employees were furloughed for two weeks without pay (Hale 1992). According to one estimate, Weld's administration cut the number of state employees by 14 percent in his first two years of office (Eggers and O'Leary 1994a). Equally important, Weld was able to avoid any major tax increase and cut the state's income tax from 6.25 to 5.95 percent. However, although Weld was able to reach agreement on pressing budget matters, other elements of his first-term agenda, including bills dealing with the death penalty, police consolidation, court reform, and abortion, received little legislative attention. Those setbacks aside, Weld nonetheless easily won reelection in 1994 with 71 percent of the vote. Following his reelection, Weld continued his efforts to shrink the state's budget by giving his legislature an ultimatum on welfare—either produce major welfare reform by February 1995 or face a reduction in welfare benefits. Both the state senate and house came up with plans that would, among other things, require all able-bodied welfare recipients with children over the age of six to work, cut benefits by nearly 3 percent, set limits on the length of time individuals can receive welfare (24 months in any five-year period), and require teenage mothers to live with their parents.

Gubernatorial Change: An Initial Assessment

The office of governor has undergone considerable change over the last several decades. As we have seen, there is a new kind of governor—younger, more experienced in state government, and more assertive—armed with greater institutional powers and authority. The question remains, however, as to whether these developments have actually produced more effective governors. Evidence from a number of quarters suggests they have, but only up to a point. There is, for example, some evidence that governors who enjoy more formal authority and power are better able to influence the decisions and actions of administrative agencies (see, e.g., Dometrius 1979 and Hebert, Brudney, and Wright 1983). Similarly, a survey of state senators in the mid-1970s found that three of the governors' formal powers—budget authority, administrative controls, and the legislative veto—were perceived by legislators as important gubernatorial tools (Bernick 1979). More recent evidence indicates that governors who possess more institutional authority, including greater tenure potential, appointment powers, budget authority and veto power, were given more favorable evaluations by their fellow governors (Dilger, Krause, and Moffett 1995).

At the same time, the available research suggests that the formal powers and authority of the governors only go so far in ensuring gubernatorial success. In the first instance, the governors' influence is also conditioned by the political context in which governors operate. One study suggests, for example, that gubernatorial influence is greater in those states in which the legislature is dependent on the executive budget for data and analysis (Abney and Lauth 1987). Other studies suggest that the ability of governors to achieve their political and policy goals depends upon their popular support (Bernick 1979) and the size of the governors' election margin and the governors' partisan majority in the legislature (Sigelman and Dometrius 1988). The analysis of Lee Sigelman and Nelson Dometrius indicates that the formal powers of the governors both condition and are conditioned by their informal political resources. They conclude: "The more extensive the formal powers of the governorship, the more pronounced the effect of informal power resources on the governor's administrative influence. More importantly, although formal powers do not make a major contribution to gubernatorial influence where informal political clout is lacking, the combination of informal political resources and a wide range of formal powers greatly enhances the governor's influence" (1988: 167).

The personal attributes of the governors matter as well. As we have seen, there is some evidence to suggest that younger governors are more effective (Sabato 1978; Sigelman and Smith 1981). Other studies have found that the governors' ability to interact with the media and other state officials is as important, perhaps more important, than their formal powers or institutional resources (Bernick 1979; Beyle 1995a). Beyle, for example, discovered that governors who interacted well with other political actors were given higher marks on their performance by the public in the early 1990s.

To further illustrate the impact of the personal attributes and formal powers and resources of the governors on their performance, Table 4.3 reports a series of findings that summarize the relationship between measures of those concepts and an increasingly important aspect of the governors' day-to-day job—the use of the gubernatorial veto. Two measures of gubernatorial veto behavior are referenced in the table. The first, the number of vetoes in 1991, provides a measure of gubernatorial assertiveness and the extent of legislative-executive conflict. The second, the percentage of times the governors' veto was upheld is a rough indicator of how governors are faring with their legislatures.

In measuring the formal powers of the governors, Robert Dilger's (1993) estimates of the governors' formal powers as of 1990 in five areas—appointment powers, tenure potential, veto authority, budget-making powers, budget-cutting authority—are used. The measures are identical to those used previously by Beyle with two major exceptions. First, Dilger substitutes a measure of the governor's authority to balance the budget after the state legislature has passed its appropriations bills for Beyle's budget-changing index. In doing that, Dilger captures much more variability in the concept. Second, Dilger extends his measure of veto authority to include the reduction veto. Each of the five indices ranges from 1 to 5, where a higher value indicates more gubernatorial power. Dilger's (1994) index of gubernatorial staff is used as an index of the institutional resources of the states' governors. Based on 1992 staffing data, Dilger assigns each state a value ranging from 2 (less than 2 staff members) to 10 (over 60 staff).

A series of measures are used to get at the informal powers of the governors. First, the governor's age when first elected is used as a proxy for the new kind of governor that Sabato, Osborne, and others describe. Second, two indicators—the number of years the governor served in state government and years of service in the state legislature—are used to get at individual governor's experience in state government. Here the assumption is that governors with more experience in state government, particularly in the legislature, will have better-honed political instincts and connections. Sigelman and Dometrius's (1988) analysis of gubernatorial influence suggests two additional measures of the governors' informal powers—the governor's margin of victory in his/her last election and the proportion of the legislature's membership from the governor's party.

Although the evidence in Table 4.3 represents only a small slice of gubernatorial-legislative dynamics, it does confirm earlier analyses. More particularly, the data demonstrate that at least some of the formal and informal powers of the office shape gubernatorial assertiveness and success. In terms of assertiveness, the evidence indicates that two aspects of the governors' formal authority condition their subsequent willingness to wield the veto. The first, the governors' formal veto authority, is hardly surprising. One would expect an increase in veto powers to produce an increase in the actual number of vetoes. Indeed, a high level of vetoes typically reflects the availability of a line item veto. The more intriguing finding is the negative relationship between the governor's use of the veto

TABLE 4.3 Gubernatorial Power and Legislative-Executive Conflict, 1991 (entries are standardized regression coefficients, t-ratios in parentheses)

	# of Vetoes 1991 (n = 49)	% Vetoes Sustained (n = 47)
Informal Powers/Resources		
Number of years legislative service	−.23 (−1.65)*	.22 (1.52)+
Number of years in state government		
Age when first elected	.21 (1.44)+	
Margin of victory		
Party margin in legislature		.24 (1.68)*
Formal Powers/Resources		
Appointment		
Tenure potential		
Budget-making authority		.28 (2.02)*
Budget-cutting authority	−.44 (−3.15)**	
Veto	.33 (2.23)*	
Staff		
Adjusted R^2	.19	.12
F	3.82**	3.12*

+ significant at .10 level
* significant at .05 level
** significant at .01 level

and his/her ability to cut the state's budget after it has been enacted to achieve a balanced budget. Apparently, where governors are able to make those cuts and to make them with few limits, there is less of a need to veto legislation or to confront the legislature on budget matters.

The evidence in Table 4.3 also illustrates the importance of the informal attributes of the office. Older governors, for example, use the veto more often, suggesting perhaps that younger governors, representing the new kind of governor alluded to earlier, are better at working out differences with their legislatures and avoiding the confrontation that a veto often yields. Alternatively, that finding may indicate that more seasoned governors are more willing to assert their authority. Equally important, the data indicate that governors who have served in their legislatures are less likely to veto legislation, suggesting, once again, an ability to work more cooperatively with members of the legislature.

Looking next at the rate at which the governors' vetoes were sustained, the evidence seems to suggest that increasing the governors' formal powers has not worked to their advantage in dealing with their state legislatures. Although governors with greater budget-making authority enjoy a higher success rate in terms of their vetoes, the remaining measures of the governors' formal authority prove unrelated to the rate at which the governors' vetoes are sustained.

Two of the informal attributes of the nation's governors are related to veto success, however. First, governors with prior service in the state legislature enjoy a higher success rate. Once again, serving in the legislature appears to be a valuable training ground for future governors. Second, and not surprisingly, increases in the governors' partisan percentage in the legislature are associated with increases in veto success (see Wiggins [1980] for similar findings). That finding takes on particular significance as the rate of divided government increases across the American states.

Constraints

As we have seen, the exercise of gubernatorial power is constrained by the larger context within which governors operate. The character of a state's legislature and courts and the economic and political culture within which a governor operates necessarily limit the advantages that formal grants of authority or the personal attributes of an individual governor might provide. More broadly, the experiences of many of America's governors in the late 1980s and the 1990s suggest that a number of factors have limited and will continue to limit their ability to achieve their policy and political aspirations. Scandals, limits on the formal powers of the governorship, federal actions, conflicts within and across political institutions, volatile economies, and a restless and angry public place major constraints on today governors. Two factors have been particularly troublesome in recent years. First and foremost, today's governors face fiscal constraints that, while not of their own making, nonetheless handcuff even the most innovative and active chief executive. Although the states are in the best fiscal shape they have been in in over a decade, state officials remember how devastating the recession of the late 1980s and early 1990s was and analysts are fearful of the next recession. Moreover, the states' electorates continue to oppose new taxes while resisting cuts in public services. Ironically, the states' fiscal concerns are increasingly emanating from Washington, D.C. As Henry Raimondo (1996: 49) notes: "In the 1980s, the federal government gave the states the cold shoulder. Instead of a policy dialogue, it took unilateral policy actions. The signals were unmistakable: a cut in federal grants, an increase in the unfunded federal mandates (for example, the Americans with Disabilities Act and the Clean Air Act, among others), the serious consideration of a balanced budget amendment, and proposed cuts in federal social programs such as welfare and health care."

Although the federal government in the 1990s is likely to impose far fewer mandates, the continuing pressures to balance the federal budget and the corresponding desire to shift more authority for programming to the states mean that governors will continue to spend much of their time dealing with budget issues. And, as prior research has demonstrated, fiscal difficulties often produce political troubles. Sabato's (1983) analysis of gubernatorial defeats between 1950 and 1980, for example, illustrates the dangers that fiscal matters, in particular taxes, pose. Although the defeat of incumbent governors reflected a wide variety of issues, including scandal, party competition, and intraparty politics, after the 1960s, taxes emerged as a major contributor to gubernatorial losses. According to Sabato, taxes accounted for nearly 30 percent of all incumbent losses in the 1960s and 19 percent in the 1970s. Governors in the late 1980s and early 1990s faced a similar dilemma. Faced with increasing demands on state services, stagnant economies, and unable to reach agreement with legislators and interest groups over budget cuts, governors reluctantly offered new taxes and, in many cases, suffered the electoral consequences of doing so. In 1990, for example, of the six incumbent governors eligible for reelection in New England, three chose not to run, in part, because of the loss of popular support over taxation. That same year, the defeat of two other incumbent governors, Mike Hayden of Kansas and Bob Martinez of Florida, can also be traced to some degree to how they handled tax issues (Beyle 1990). More recently, Governor Jim Florio's defeat in New Jersey in 1993 can be attributed in large part to his earlier support for a tax increase in that state. Although governors in the mid-1990s have successfully avoided tax increases and cut spending, the specter of the next recession looms over many of the states' capitals, and many worry that continued federal "defunding" and devolution will further diminish the states' abilities to deal effectively with pressing policy problems in education, health, and welfare.

There is also reason to believe that governors in the 1990s are increasingly being held accountable for the condition of their states' economies. Early research on gubernatorial elections generally concluded that those contests were affected more by national economic conditions and presidential performance than by the states' economies or the governors' economic policy performance (see, most notably, Holbrook-Provow 1987 and Chubb 1988). More recent analyses (see Svoboda 1995; Partin 1995; and Salmore and Salmore 1996) suggest, however, that as result of (a) the growing visibility, powers, and activity of the nation's governors, particularly with respect to economic development, and (b) the movement of gubernatorial elections in all but a handful of states to nonpresidential years, presidential-gubernatorial politics have become "decoupled" and the states' voters are more likely to engage in retrospective voting on the states' economies. Analysis of the 1990 gubernatorial elections, for example, indicates that in the thirty-six gubernatorial races taking place that year, incumbent governors were often held accountable for the economic conditions of their state. Voters who perceived that the state's economy had grown worse were more likely to vote against the incumbent, whereas voters who perceived that the state's economy had improved tended to vote for the sitting governor. In addition, there was little evidence in the 1990 race that gubernatorial voting was influenced by presidential approval or national economic conditions (Partin 1995).

Second, governors face an increasing amount of competition and conflict with the judicial and legislative branches of government. For their part, the states' courts have, in many instances, chosen to become more actively involved in state policy. Active judiciaries have declared school systems, health care facilities, and state prisons unconstitutional and forced legislatures and governors to deal with issues they have neither the time nor the resources to address. Ironically, some of the growth in judicial activism in recent years has been prompted by the inability of governors and legislatures to resolve their differences. In a number of states, for example, the courts have had to adjudicate conflicts between governors and legislators over a variety of budget issues, including the transfer of funds from one program to another, the use of emergency funds, and midyear budget cuts (Simon 1986). State courts have also been asked to rule on the constitutionality of recent attempts by state legislatures to increase their influence over the executive branch. Several legislatures, for instance, adopted legislative veto provisions in the 1970s and 1980s, only to have them overturned in federal and state courts. Similarly, the placement of state legislatures on executive branch boards and commissions has been challenged on the grounds that it violates the doctrine of separation of powers (Beyle 1993).

Relations between governors and their legislatures are even more precarious. Although legislative-gubernatorial conflict is hardly new, it seems to be occurring more frequently and with more intensity. Analyst Lucinda Simon (1986: 1) writes:

> To read the headlines of capital city newspapers and political science literature, one might conclude that legislatures and governors are wrestling daily for control of the statehouse and the levers of government. First one branch is described as dominant, then the other seizes the upper hand, and the role reverses again. Legislative-executive differences are nothing new, but of late the conflicts are intense, acrimonious, and, at times, fought along the constitutional boundaries of our tripartite system of government.

That conflict results from a number of developments. Much of the conflict in recent years reflects the professionalization of many state legislatures. As legislatures increase their institutional capacity and as a new kind of lawmaker appears on the scene, legislators and their leaders are no longer willing to defer to governors and executive branch agencies. Recent efforts to reassert legislative authority pit lawmakers against governors and agencies across a variety of arenas including budget matters, administrative rule making, policy development and innovation, and, increasingly, the day-to-day operations of executive branch agencies.

Increased legislative-executive conflict also mirrors an increase in partisan competition and divided government. As Robert Dilger (1993: 9) notes:

> Partisanship is an important variable in the relationship between the governor's office and the state legislature. If the governor's political party controls the state legislature, partisan conflicts can be minimized and the governor's ability to achieve his or her goals is enhanced. However, if the governor's party does not control the state legislature, partisan conflicts are more likely to arise and the governor's ability to achieve his or her policy goals is reduced.

Unfortunately, fewer and fewer governors enjoy a partisan majority in one or both state legislative chambers, a contrast to earlier years. In 1954, only nine of the forty-eight states had a politically divided state government (Beyle 1993). By 1996, in contrast, Republicans and Democrats shared political control in thirty-one states. The increase in the rate of divided government reflects increased partisan competition within the electorate, which, in turn, reflects a number of recent developments including a strengthening of the state's political party organizations, more split-ticket voting, increasing social and economic heterogeneity within the American states, and an increase in candidate-centered campaigns. Whatever its causes, heightened partisanship and divided government make it much more difficult for governors to find politically acceptable solutions to increasingly contentious problems.

Conflict and stalemate also result from changes in the states' policy agendas. Thirty to forty years ago, the states addressed fewer and much simpler issues, issues on which there was more agreement and less technical uncertainty. At the risk of oversimplifying, in the years following World War II, the states built highways, hospitals, and schools and left more contentious issues such as civil rights, the environment, and urban problems for others to deal with. Today in contrast, state governments are being called upon to deal with difficult and seemingly intractable social and economic problems ranging from AIDS to doctor-assisted suicide to violence in the schools to gay rights. Each of those issues and scores of others entail difficult choices, require major remediation, and tax already scarce revenue sources. In that kind of problem setting, conflict between and within branches is perhaps unavoidable.

Recent developments aside, conflict between the two branches may be inescapable because of the uncertainty and tension occasioned by constitutional provisions for a separation of powers and checks and balances and, equally important, because of the fact that governors and legislators approach issues from much different perspectives. Governors after all, represent statewide interests, whereas legislators represent districts. Governors also are more likely to take a short-term perspective. Most governors realize that their greatest accomplishments will have to occur in the first year in office, in the glow of their honeymoon period and before the legislature's midterm election. Legislators, in contrast, often are able to take a more long-term perspective, particularly in those states with greater careerism (although that may be changing in the face of term limits). Moreover, individual legislators do not have to point to major legislative accomplishments as a measure of their job performance in the eyes of their constituents. Governors do. Finally, there are structural differences between the legislative and executive branches of state government that shape how lawmakers view and deal with policy issues. Typically, the executive branch is much more centralized and hierarchical, whereas state legislatures are becoming increasingly decentralized.

Implications for Governing

The American governorship is much changed in the 1990s. The questions that remain concern how those developments have impacted on the quality of governing in the American states. Unfortunately, few studies look at the implications of gubernatorial change for statehouse democracy or policy responsibility. Nonetheless, there are good reasons for believing that changes in the American governorship have conditioned the quality and character of state governing, and, on balance, done so in a positive fashion.

In the first instance, governors have frequently been at the center of many of the policy innovations that have emerged from the states in recent years. In the 1980s, it was the governors that provided much of the leadership for educational reform and efforts to improve the states' business climates. In the 1990s, governors have often been at the forefront of policy innovations in health care and welfare. Although individual governors are usually not the source of innovative policy solutions at the state level, they are often the ones able to generate the public support and the political coalitions necessary to translate innovative policy ideas into actual legislation. Research by Robert Crew and Marjorie Hill (1995) underscores the importance of gubernatorial leadership. Looking at the fate of "important and significant" legislation in the state of Florida between 1965 and 1995, Crew and Hill report that the likelihood that key legislation would actually pass was greater where individual governors had made that legislation part of their own priorities (measured in terms of whether the initiative was included in the governor's state of the state address). Interestingly enough, they note that major legislation was more likely to be passed later, rather than earlier, in a governor's term, a finding that challenges the conventional wisdom that chief executives need to win their legislative victories in the earliest months of their term.

Second, the available evidence suggests that increases in the formal powers and institutional resources of the states' governors have contributed to the quality of governing as well. As we have seen, governors with more formal powers and greater resources are given higher marks by their peers, are more likely to win veto confrontations with their legislatures, and exert more influence over administrative agencies. Although the ability to sustain vetoes or control administrative agencies hardly ensures that coherent and effective policies will be passed and implemented, the ability of governors to assert their authority is frequently a prerequisite to effective governing. As Lawrence Dodd (1981) and others have argued, the viability of Madisonian democracy and a separation of powers depends in large part on the ability of each branch to assert its institutional will. Moreover, most analysts agree that gubernatorial (as well as legislative) control of public bureaucracies is a necessary if not sufficient condition for effective implementation. More broadly, as I note in the first chapter, political reforms that centralize authority (e.g., movement to the short ballot or increases in the powers of appointment or removal) make it more likely that state governments and their governors will be able to act decisively and uniformly.

There is also some, albeit limited, empirical evidence that institutional changes that increase either the capacity of the executive branch or centralize executive branch authority impact on the character and quality of state policy. States that afford their governors more formal power and resources are more likely to enact liberal policies (Barrilleaux and Crew 1991) and to be cited by officials in other states as innovative (Hedge 1997). Similarly, states with more centralized executive branches are more likely to enact legislation (Gray and Lowery 1995). Finally, there is evidence that increasing the institutional power and resources of the governors' offices has contributed to the quality and effectiveness of state economic policies, something much on the minds of state officials in recent decades (Brace 1993; Hedge 1997).

Although changes in the character of those who serve as governor together with increases in the institutional resources they have at their disposal have contributed to the quality of governing, many fear that a third aspect of an evolving American governorship—the increase in the rate of divided government—will make governing more problematic. Based largely on an analysis of the national government, a number of scholars have argued that divided government undercuts policy coherence by exacerbating the conflict between the legislature and chief executive (see, e.g., Sundquist 1992; Ginsberg and Shefter 1991; Schick 1993). In some instances, that conflict is likely to produce stalemate and inaction as governors and legislators are unable to reach agreement on the more contentious issues facing their states. In other instances, divided government is likely to yield both excessive spending as partisans on each side of the aisle find themselves providing distributive benefits to their respective constituencies and unwise tax cuts as the parties seek to outdo each other in demonstrating to the voters their ability to cut taxes. There is also a concern that divided control of government undercuts the ability of administrative agencies to effectively implement public policies as unresolved conflict carries over into the implementation phase of governing (see Moe 1989).

What little evidence there is at the state level both supports and refutes the notion that divided government produces policy irresponsibility. Research by James Alt and Robert Lowery (1994) and James Poterba (1994) indicates that divided government, including split legislatures, detracts from the ability of the states to keep their fiscal houses in order. Looking at the states' responses to revenue shocks over the period 1968–1987, Alt and Lowery discover that unified governments are more likely to respond to revenue shortfalls than are states with either split branches or split legislatures. In particular, their analysis indicates that unified governments were much more likely to raise revenues in response to deficits but, interestingly enough, were less likely to cut spending. On balance, for each dollar of deficit, unified governments were able on average to offset the revenue shortfall by 45 cents compared to 25 cents among states with split branches and 11 cents in those states with split control of the legislature.

At the same time, research reported by Virginia Gray and David Lowery (1995) and Hedge (1997) provides little evidence that divided government yields political stalemate and inaction or detracts from the quality of state policies. Both studies fail to uncover a linkage between divided government and the ability of state governments to enact legislation. In each case, states with unified governments were no more likely to propose or enact legislation in the early 1990s. The reader should keep in mind, however, that those studies looked at the total volume of legislation within the states. Had they looked only at major pieces of legislation it is entirely possible that differences between divided and unified governments would have appeared. However, Crew and Hill's (1995) analysis of "major," "significant," or "important and timely" legislation in Florida between 1965–1995 found similar tendencies—divided government did not slow down the rate of important legislation. In addition to looking at the impact of divided government on the rate of legislative activity, Hedge's analysis also considers the impact of both divided government and divided legislatures on the quality of state policy but finds that split control does not detract from the ability of the states to innovate or to produce quality environmental or economic development programming.

Finally, although most of the effects of gubernatorial change fall on the responsibility side of governing, there is at least one way in which those developments have strengthened statehouse democracy. In particular, two developments have probably contributed to the ability to hold the states' governors accountable. First, shortening the ballot and increasing the governors' power to appoint and remove executive branch officials promotes accountability by reducing the fragmentation of executive branch authority and thereby making it easier for voters to assign responsibility, credit, and blame for the actions of state government. Second, as Stephen Salmore and Barbara Salmore (1996) note, gubernatorial elections in recent decades have been characterized by both a decoupling of national and state elections (due, in large part, to simply moving elections for governors to nonpresidential election years) and an increase in candidate-centered campaigns. Each of those developments contributes to accountability by increasing the likelihood that incumbent and nonincumbent candidates for governor will be judged on their personal merits and not on presidential politics or party loyalties. Of course, as we saw in 1994, holding gubernatorial elections at the midterm does not always insulate those races from national politics. Similarly, candidate-centered races hardly guarantee that campaigns will entail a serious or accurate discussions of the issues. Nonetheless, changes in gubernatorial electoral politics increase the chances that elections for governor will be about what governors do or do not do. And that bodes well for statehouse democracy.

Conclusions

As state governments assume a greater role in American governance, it is to the states' governors that Americans increasingly look for leadership. In many ways, today's governors are ready and willing to take on the challenge as the century ends. As we have seen, many of the governors' formal powers and institutional resources have been increased. And the informal resources at their disposal, including their vigor and new approaches to governing, also enhance their ability to govern. But the nation's governors also face more constraints than ever before. Competition with other branches of government, a new system of interest group politics, unpredictable economies, and skeptical publics have made the job of being governor more difficult.

Yet there are reasons for being optimistic in the years ahead. The economy is healthy, governors and legislatures are finding common ground, and the president and Congress seem more than willing to let the states assume a larger share of the responsibility for governing America. All of these things make the job of being governor more manageable. Nonetheless, whether it remains manageable depends on things outside of most governors' control, including the subjects of the next two chapters—the legislatures and the courts.

5

The Legislatures

Few political institutions have experienced as much fundamental and far-reaching change in such a short period of time as have state legislatures. Just three decades ago many state legislatures were sadly malapportioned, unrepresentative, dominated by their governors and/or special interests, and unable and unwilling to deal with the pressing issues of the day. As one commentator (Heard, reported in ACIR 1982: 75) noted in 1966, "State legislatures may be our most extreme example of institutional lag. In their formal qualities they are largely 19th-Century organizations." Most state legislatures truly were "sometimes governments" and not very good at that. Nonetheless, within a very short time many legislatures transformed themselves into effective and representative lawmaking institutions. As Alan Rosenthal (1989: 69) notes: "Within a decade legislatures had been rebuilt. They increased the time they spent on their tasks; they established or increased their professional staffs; and they streamlined their procedures, enlarged their facilities, invigorated their processes, attended to their ethics, disclosed their finances, and reduced their conflicts of interest." In addition, legislatures across the country experienced a dramatic increase in the number of careerists, minorities, and women serving as lawmakers and successfully reasserted their authority vis-à-vis their governors.

What accounted for all that change? Some of the pressures for reform came from within as a new breed of legislator joined forces with progressive leadership in many states to reshape legislatures. Much of the impetus for change, however, came from outside the institution and included the Supreme Court's reapportionment rulings, the challenge of gubernatorial reforms that threatened to further usurp legislative prerogatives, the growing demands placed on governments at all levels, and pressures from various reform groups, most notably the Citizens Conference on State Legislatures (CCSL). During 1969–1970, the CCSL, with support from the Ford Foundation, undertook a major study of the legislatures in each of the fifty states in an attempt to assess their "technical" or decisionmaking capabilities. State legislatures were evaluated in

TABLE 5.1   CCSL Criteria and General Recommendations for State Legislative Reform

Criteria	Recommendations
Functional	Remove restrictions on session length, frequency, and agenda. Provide more staff to leadership, committees, and members. Provide adequate office facilities for leadership, staff, committees, and members. Use deadlines and rules to regulate flow of legislation. Reduce the number of committees and individual committee assignments.
Accountable	Use single-member districts to elect members. Election of legislative leaders by full membership or party caucus. Increase public access to legislative actions and decisions. Provide greater access to the press and news media.
Informed	Use pre- and interim session periods to draft and consider legislation. Increase the number and kinds of legislative staff and services. Reduce the number of standing committees. Upgrade bill-drafting capability.
Independent	Remove restrictions on session length, frequency, and agenda. Provide legislative control over its budget and salaries. Increase the legislature's budget authority and role. Increase legislative oversight capability. Regulate lobbyists. Adopt conflict of interest provisions.
Representative	Use single-member districts to elect members. Provide resources for district offices. Keep restrictions on holding office to a minimum. Provide adequate compensation to members. Diffuse legislative leadership and authority. Guarantee minority membership office and staff resources and committee assignments.

SOURCE: Compiled from Citizens Conference on State Legislatures, *State Legislatures: An Evaluation of Their Effectiveness* (New York: Praeger Publishers, 1971).

terms of the five criteria listed in Table 5.1. One important result of that effort was a series of recommendations, many of which are listed in the table, that called on the states to recast their legislative institutions. And recast them they did. By the end of the 1970s many of the states had put into place several of the reforms that the CCSL and others had prescribed.

America's state legislatures were, to use the benchmarks provided by the CCSL, much more functional, accountable, informed, independent, and representative (see ACIR 1982 and Bowman and Kearney 1986).

Yet by the 1990s, state legislatures had become what one analyst (Ehrenhalt 1992) refers to as "embattled institutions." Public support for state legislatures had hit an all-time low. Surveys from a handful of states reported by the National Conference of State Legislatures (reported in Jones 1992), for example, indicated that the percentage of citizens giving their legislature a positive rating fell from 50 percent in 1968 to just 30 percent in 1990. The public's dissatisfaction with their legislatures is most clearly seen in the imposition of term limits in twenty-one of the twenty-four states with initiatives during the 1990s. The irony, of course, is that most legislatures are substantially more viable today than they were in 1968. Much of the public's disenchantment seems to reflect an increase in the public's awareness of and expectations for their lawmaking institutions as well as a more general dissatisfaction with governments at all levels.

But the problem of state legislatures is not simply one of public perceptions or misperceptions. Increasingly, conflict both from within the legislature and with the other branches of state government have produced stalemate and delay, and state governments, for all their reforms, frequently appear unable to govern. Part of the problem stems from a number of developments over which legislatures have little control. Stronger governors and more active courts, for example, make interinstitutional conflict more likely and perhaps inevitable. Greater interparty competition and an increase in divided government also ensure that greater conflict will occur. In addition, cutbacks in federal aid and continuing efforts to devolve additional responsibility to the states by the federal government have meant that state governments are called upon to do more governing with fewer resources.

Some of the problem lies within legislatures themselves, however, and flows from the reforms of the past three decades. In many ways, the states and their legislatures are the victims of their own success. As legislatures take on a wider range of difficult and complex policy issues and as they produce innovative policies that challenge the status quo, the political and economic stakes of state government increase, together with the potential for conflict. Moreover, scholars and practitioners alike are increasingly aware that many institutional reforms, particularly in recent years, have "congressionalized" state legislatures by promoting greater careerism, institutional assertiveness, partisanship, and legislative fragmentation—all of which threaten the ability of state legislatures to fashion coherent and acceptable legislation. For those familiar with the U.S. Congress's evolution, none of this should come as a surprise. Congressional scholars have long understood that fragmented and decentralized legislatures can be wonderfully responsive, particularly to well-organized groups (see most notably, Rieselbach 1977). However, greater responsiveness often undercuts legislative responsibility and the ability to govern wisely.

To better understand the current condition of America's constantly evolving legislatures, the major developments of the past few decades are discussed in the pages that follow. Five sets of changes seem particularly important—institutional reforms, the emergence of a new legislative career, term limits, an increase in the number of women and minorities serving in state legislatures, and greater legislative assertiveness. The chapter ends by looking at the broader consequences of these and other changes on the ability of the states to govern.

Institutional Reforms

Reformers generally agree that a viable legislature requires, at a minimum, the requisite organizational resources and procedures that allow legislators to perform their lawmaking, oversight, and representation tasks in a timely, coherent, and ethical fashion. Over the past several decades, reformers have put into place a number of structural reforms that attempt to streamline and rationalize legislative decisionmaking, including increased staffing, procedural reforms, and committee reforms. In addition, a number of states have wrestled with the difficult issue of regulating member ethics. Each of these changes in discussed in the following pages.

Increased Staffing

State legislative staff, both housekeeping and professional, has grown steadily throughout the last century. Early in the 1900s, many states established permanent legislative research, bill-drafting, and legal offices. By the 1950s, a number of states had created fiscal and budget offices in an effort to assert their independence on budget matters from their governor (Pound 1986). In more recent years, the number of staff has continued to grow and, equally important, new kinds of staff now serve the nation's legislatures. Between 1979 and 1988, legislative staff grew by 24 percent to a total of 33,000 staff (Jones 1994). Much of that increase was among professional staff including computer specialists, program evaluators, auditors, technical and scientific staff, and other specialists. By the late 1980s, professional staff represented nearly half of state legislative personnel (Weberg 1988).

Two other developments concerning staff are worth noting. First, staffing has become more decentralized as more and more staff are allocated to individual members, legislative committees, and party leadership. By the mid-1990s, for instance, legislators in over half the states had personal staff and in about two-thirds of those states, staff served year round (Council of State Governments 1996). There has also been a corresponding increase in the allowances provided members to fund their district offices. In New Jersey, for example, the members' district staff allowance increased from $22,000 to $60,000 between 1982 and 1988. During that same period, Illinois lawmakers saw their district budgets double in size (Weberg 1988). Staff are also increasingly being assigned on a permanent basis to legislative committees, particularly in larger states such as California, Florida, New York, and Pennsylvania (Pound 1992). Second, a growing number of staff are explicitly partisan. By the late 1980s a dozen or so states were providing the legislative parties with their own staff (Rosenthal 1989). Not only does the addition of more full-time staff aid party officials in carrying out their leadership duties, but an increase in partisan staff has allowed party leaders to play a larger role in the election and reelection of their colleagues.

The importance of staff can hardly be overstated. Legislative staff perform a number of vital functions for their legislatures. Professional staff improve the overall quality of information that reaches lawmakers. Specialized staff bring specialized knowledge to bear on issues and serve as a filter through which policy proposals are assessed. Increased staffing has been especially crucial in allowing legislators to attend to their casework and constituent service functions. Taking care of the folks back in the district is a labor-intensive activity and staff provide that labor. Legislative staff have also been particularly crucial in helping legislatures assert their authority vis-à-vis the governor. As Ann Bowman and Richard Kearney (1986: 87) note, "In the absence of competent budgetary assistance for the legislators, the governor dominates the process." Given the central importance of budgets, it is no wonder that nearly every state legislature has created some kind of staff unit that is devoted to analyzing the budget.

The importance of staff is particularly important in those states which have shorter sessions and part-time lawmakers. In those instances, full-time professional staff can compensate for part-time members who are able to devote only a relatively small amount of time to legislative issues. But therein lies a danger. When part-time (or for that matter full-time) legislators become too dependent on staff for information and ideas, the possibility arises that staff and not elected officials will set the legislative agenda and control the range of options considered, and conceivably selected, by the members.

The role of staff in the next few decades will continue to evolve in response to the kinds of changes we document throughout this chapter. In the wake of term limits, greater partisanship, and other developments, legislative staff will need to become more politically sensitive and increasingly responsible for teaching members about the legislature and the legislative process and serving as the repository of institutional memory (Weberg 1997).

Procedural Reforms

As the workloads of the states' legislatures increase, there is a heightened need to increase the amount of time legislatures are in session and the efficiency with which that time is used. Recent reforms have attempted to achieve both ends. First, there has been a steady increase in the length of the states' legislative sessions, despite recent attempts by some citizen groups to shorten the time their legislatures meet. Following World War II, only four states met annually. Today all but seven (Arkansas, Kentucky, Montana, Nevada, North Dakota, Oregon, and Texas) do. And in many cases, special sessions in the off year have become the rule rather than the exception. In Texas, for example, state lawmakers met for 270 days in 1989–1990 despite the constitutional provision that the legislature meet for only 140 days in 1989. In 1993, no less than twenty-two states called their lawmakers back forty times for additional deliberation. For its part, Arizona held twelve special sessions in the 1992–1993 biennium (Jones 1994). Second, several states have adopted legislative rules that, ideally at least, attempt to ensure that legislative time is used wisely. In any given legislative cycle, over 200,000 bills are introduced in America's legislatures and roughly one-fifth of those become law (Patterson 1990). Obviously, that volume of legislation raises concerns that important policy decisions will be rushed and only perfunctorily weighed. In order to streamline the process by which legislation is considered, a series of limits have been put into place that either make it more difficult to introduce legislation or seek to ensure that the full chamber has sufficient time to review proposed laws. A number of states have tried to set numerical limits on the number of bills that can be introduced. In Colorado, for example, individual lawmakers are limited to introducing five bills per session. More frequently the states have set deadlines on how late in the session bills can be introduced. Forty-seven states have such deadlines. In addition, an equal number of states allow members to introduce legislation before the session begins, an attempt to give legislators more time to consider proposed bills (Jones 1994).

Committee Reforms

Committee reform has also received a great deal of attention in recent years. First, over the past several decades, the states have reorganized their legislatures' committee systems. State legislatures have long been criticized for having too many committees. Critics maintain that a large number of committees fragments the legislature, spreads the members' time too thin as individuals serve on an excessive number of committees, and produces unnecessary duplication and overlap. The CCSL recommended that the number of committees in each statehouse be limited to just ten to fifteen. The change in this regard has been dramatic. In the 1980s there were fewer than half the number of committees as there were fifty years earlier. By the end of the 1980s the average number of house and senate committees was 20 and 15, respectively.

Second, and equally important, the last few decades have seen an increase in the role of legislative committees. As committees gain more resources, including permanent professional staff, and as the complexity of the legislation they consider grows, committees have seen an increase in their power and autonomy. Recent evidence underscores the growing importance of committees. Based on interviews with over 2,000 legislators during the early 1980s, Wayne Francis (1989) developed the classification scheme of the respective decisionmaking roles of committees, party caucuses, and party leaders that is presented in Figure 5.1. As the figure indicates, legislative committees play a prominent role in the decisionmaking of many state legislatures. In fifteen instances, committees are perceived as dominating decisionmaking in either the house or the senate. In an additional sixty-six chambers, committees share that influence with party leaders, the party caucus, or both.

Growth in the role of committees promises to add to the quality of decisions as legislatures take advantage of a division of labor and specialization. The likelihood of that occurring is enhanced where committees enjoy professional staff. In addition, a greater role for committees makes legislatures more democratic as power and responsibility are distributed to more members and open to a wider range of interests. At the same time, a strengthened committee system can have negative consequences as well. First, as we have seen in the U.S. Congress, greater committee autonomy can add to the fragmentation and decentralization of state legislatures and undercut the ability of the legislative leadership to form workable coalitions. As Rosenthal notes (1993: 137), "Ten or twenty standing committees, each in its own domain doing its own thing, constitute a formidable centrifugal force in a legislative body." Second, to the extent that autonomous committees are not representative of the larger membership there is a threat that policies will represent narrow interests. Research on the Nebraska legislature suggests that may well be occurring. Based on his analysis in the mid-1980s, Keith Hamm (1986) discovered that "interesteds," those members who have a direct interest in the committee's jurisdiction, tended, not surprisingly, to make up a majority

118

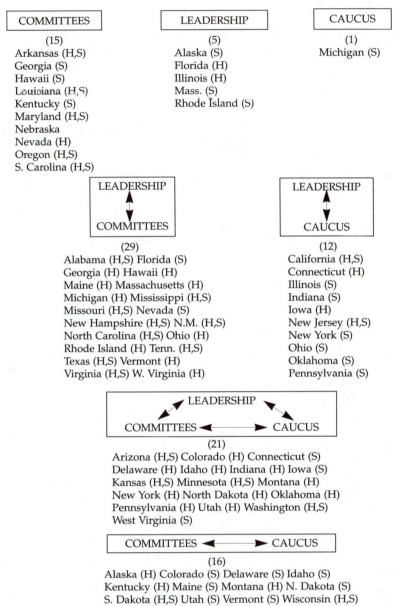

COMMITTEES

(15)
Arkansas (H,S)
Georgia (S)
Hawaii (S)
Louisiana (H,S)
Kentucky (S)
Maryland (H,S)
Nebraska
Nevada (H)
Oregon (H,S)
S. Carolina (H,S)

LEADERSHIP

(5)
Alaska (S)
Florida (H)
Illinois (H)
Mass. (S)
Rhode Island (S)

CAUCUS

(1)
Michigan (S)

LEADERSHIP ↕ COMMITTEES

(29)
Alabama (H,S) Florida (S)
Georgia (H) Hawaii (H)
Maine (H) Massachusetts (H)
Michigan (H) Mississippi (H,S)
Missouri (H,S) Nevada (S)
New Hampshire (H,S) N.M. (H,S)
North Carolina (H,S) Ohio (H)
Rhode Island (H) Tenn. (H,S)
Texas (H,S) Vermont (H)
Virginia (H,S) W. Virginia (H)

LEADERSHIP ↕ CAUCUS

(12)
California (H,S)
Connecticut (H)
Illinois (S)
Indiana (S)
Iowa (H)
New Jersey (H,S)
New York (S)
Ohio (S)
Oklahoma (S)
Pennsylvania (S)

LEADERSHIP ↔ COMMITTEES ↔ CAUCUS

(21)
Arizona (H,S) Colorado (H) Connecticut (S)
Delaware (H) Idaho (H) Indiana (H) Iowa (S)
Kansas (H,S) Minnesota (H,S) Montana (H)
New York (H) North Dakota (H) Oklahoma (H)
Pennsylvania (H) Utah (H) Washington (H,S)
West Virginia (S)

COMMITTEES ↔ CAUCUS

(16)
Alaska (H) Colorado (S) Delaware (S) Idaho (S)
Kentucky (H) Maine (S) Montana (H) N. Dakota (S)
S. Dakota (H,S) Utah (S) Vermont (S) Wisconsin (H,S)
Wyoming (H,S)

FIGURE 5.1   Classification of State Chambers According to Importance of Party and Committee Decisionmaking (criterion: 50% of majority party respondents selected survey item)

SOURCE: Wayne Francis, *The Legislative Committee Game* (Columbus, Ohio: Ohio State University Press), 1989, p. 44. Reprinted by permission.

of the membership on nine of twelve committees analyzed. At the same time, there was only limited evidence that "interesteds" dominated committee agenda setting.

Ethics Reform

While much of legislative reform focuses on upgrading institutional capacity, other reforms are concerned with issues of institutional *integrity*. In the wake of scandals in a number of states, state lawmakers have increasingly turned their attention to legislation concerning the personal ethics of their members. The record to date has been mixed. Reviewing state efforts through the 1980s, Bowman and Kearney (1986: 89) conclude that "most legislatures have prohibited the more blatant conflicts of interests such as serving as paid lobbyists for corporations, public utilities, or other interests, or accepting retainers from interests with legislative concerns over which the lawmaker has potential influence." Yet, a content analysis of state ethics rules in thirty-seven states suggests that by the early 1990s a sizable number of states still lacked any meaningful controls over the ethics-related actions of their members (Goodman, Holp, and Rademacher 1994a, 1994b). Five areas of restricted activity were included in that analysis: (1) the use of the member's office for personal gain; (2) conflict of interest restrictions (both disclosure requirements and limits on member actions when there was an apparent conflict of interest); (3) the use of public resources for personal gain; (4) the receipt of gifts from individuals, lobbyists, and firms; and (5) restrictions on legislators representing private interests before state or local agencies or the legislature itself. Although a majority of the states included in the analysis had restrictions in terms of potential conflicts of interests, the use of public office for personal use, and the receipt of gifts by legislators, several states did not. Seven of the thirty-seven states had no rules prohibiting elected officials from using their official position to secure contracts, employment, or favored treatment. Only a third of the states required members to disclose business interests that might reflect a conflict of interest. Similarly, thirteen states did not set limits on member voting or otherwise taking action on issues in which the member has a conflict of interest. Seventeen states did not prohibit their members from using public resources for the private use of the members or their families. And surprisingly, only eight states had rules restricting legislators in terms of representing private interests before state or local governments. More recently, Marshall Goodman, Timothy Holp, and Karen Ludwig (1996) have used the responses of the forty or so states that subsequently responded to their request for information to construct an index of the strength of state ethics legislation. Those scores are reported in Table 5.2 and reflect the

TABLE 5.2   Strength of States' Ethics Legislation

Low (n = 16)	Moderate (n = 15)	Moderately High (n = 8)	High (n = 4)
Arizona (9)	Alabama (13)	Connecticut (30)	Hawaii (34)
Arkansas (2)	Alaska (16)	Florida (21)	Kentucky (34)
California (9)	Colorado (14)	Iowa (24)	Tennessee (40)
Delaware (0)	Kansas (16)	Maryland (21)	West Virginia (33)
Georgia (0)	Louisiana (14)	Massachusetts (24)	
Idaho (7)	Maine (17)	New York (21)	
Illinois (7)	Nebraska (11)	Pennsylvania (23)	
Indiana (0)	New Mexico (11)	Rhode Island (22)	
Mississippi (8)	Ohio (16)		
Montana (7)	Oklahoma (15)		
New Hampshire (0)	Texas (13)		
Nevada (9)	Utah (18)		
North Carolina (2)	Virginia (11)		
North Dakota (4)	Washington (12)		
Oregon (9)	Wisconsin (14)		
South Dakota (0)			

NOTE: The number in parentheses represents the state's total score regarding the comprehensiveness of their ethics legislation. No data were received from Michigan, Minnesota, Missouri, New Jersey, South Carolina, Vermont, Wyoming.

SOURCE: Marshall Goodman, Timothy Holp, and Karen Ludwig, 1996, "Understanding State Legislative Ethics Reform: The Importance of Political and Institutional Culture," in James S. Bowman, ed., *Public Integrity Annual* (Lexington, KY: Council of State Governments), p. 53.

number of restrictions in place in each of the states across the five categories of restricted activity noted previously. Possible scores range from 0 to 61. As the table indicates, a substantial majority of the states fall into the low to moderate category and only four states—Hawaii, Kentucky, Tennessee, and West Virginia—are rated in the high category.

Information provided by the National Conference of State Legislators (Prochnow 1994; Neal 1995, 1996) indicates that a number of the states have moved to strengthen legislative ethics in the years following Goodman and his colleagues' research. Altogether, thirty states passed some form of ethics legislation in 1994, as did eighteen states in 1995. Several states addressed the issue of members receiving gifts from lobbyists and others. In 1994, for example, Minnesota joined Wisconsin and South Carolina in adopting a "no-cup-of-coffee" rule for its legislators and lobbyists. Others states have set limits on gift giving. In 1995, for example, Tennessee prohibited legislators from accepting gifts from lobbyists with one exception—tickets to college athletic events. In addition, a number of states passed legislation requiring members and interest groups to report gifts to members. At least four states, Ohio, Illinois, California, and Michigan, banned honoraria in 1994 or 1995. State legislatures are also attending to the problem of conflict of interest and the use of office for personal gain. As a result of legislation passed in Louisiana in 1995, for instance, firms in which members have an economic interest are prohibited from securing state contracts if there is no competitive bidding. In a related fashion, Alabama, Ohio, and Maryland passed legislation limiting the ability of former and current members from representing private interests before state governments. Those changes, notwithstanding, many of the gaps in the states' ethics legislation that Goodman and his colleagues noted earlier still exist.

The New Legislative Career

The emergence of a new legislative career has provided much of the impetus for the institutional change that has occurred over the past three decades. More so than ever before, today's lawmaker arrives at the statehouse earlier, leaves later, and makes more noise and demands more attention in the interim. As a leading legislative scholar (Rosenthal 1981: 57) notes, "The people who serve as state legislators are not what they used to be. There is a new breed, unlike the old timers—the court house politicians, the representatives of malapportionment, the old county board members, the slow-witted and cigar-smoking politicians. The new breed is young, well educated, bright, hardworking, aggressive, and sometimes zealous." Increasingly, the very character of legislative institutions themselves are being reshaped to accommodate and promote member ambitions and goals. Indeed, to the extent that there has been a "congressionalization" of the states' legislatures it is because the new crop of state lawmakers looks suspiciously like its counterpart in the U.S. House and Senate.

Evidence of a new legislative career can be found in a number of quarters. In the first instance, the new legislative career is seen in patterns of member turnover. Over the course of the twentieth century, the rate of turnover has declined dramatically. Between the 1930s and the 1980s, the average rate at which new members entered their states' upper and lower chambers fell from 51 and 59 percent to just 24 and 28 percent, respectively (Niemi and Winsky 1987). Lower turnover, in turn, is reflected in two other patterns—a decline in the rate of voluntary turnover and a high incumbent electoral success rate. Between 1966 and 1976 the rate at which members voluntarily left their legislatures fell from nearly 40 percent to just under a quarter (Rosenthal 1981). In several states the number of members seeking reelection is even higher. Of the 119 legislators eligible for reelection in New Jersey in 1983, for example, 114 sought reelection. In 1985, all but 2 of the state's 80 assembly members chose to seek yet another term. Although the New Jersey rates are unusually low, in a number of states, including California, Connecticut, Florida, Illinois, Indiana, Kentucky, Michigan, Ohio, and Wisconsin, the rate of voluntary retirement is typically less than 10 percent (Rosenthal 1989). Moreover, as members increasingly seek subsequent terms, they are reassured by the fact that they will continue to do so successfully. Between 1978 and 1986 incumbents enjoyed at least a 90 percent success rate in twenty-six of the thirty-six legislative chambers included in an analysis reported by David Breaux and Malcolm Jewell (1992). And incumbents are apparently winning more handily. In 1986, the average winning percentage of incumbents in each of the states included in Breaux and Jewell's analysis ranged from 65 to 90 percent, and in thirteen of the thirty-four chambers for which data were available, incumbents sailed into office with, on average, at least 80 percent of the vote.

Perhaps the best indication of the new legislative career is found in the self-perceptions of members. Research from a number of quarters indicates that members increasingly view themselves as full-time lawmakers. A study conducted by the National Conference of State Legislatures in 1993 (reported in Jones 1994) found that 15 percent of all legislators reported that their legislative career was their sole occupation. The same study found even higher rates in a number of states. Over half of those serving in Massachusetts, Michigan, New York, Pennsylvania, and Wisconsin viewed themselves as full-time legislators.

Other attitudes and values seem to be changing as well. A survey of veteran legislators conducted in 1993 suggests that how members view their jobs and the institution may be undergoing fundamental change (Moncrief, Thompson, and Kurtz 1993). First, senior legislators contended that members today are more concerned with gaining reelection and attending to constituents. Approximately two-thirds of those responding agreed that members currently give a higher priority to reelection and are more concerned with district affairs. Nearly 80 percent reported that members now spend more time on fund-raising than they did in the past. Second, veteran legislators maintained that members are more independent and less likely to adhere to the informal norms of apprenticeship and institutional loyalty. In particular, those members reported that individual members are much more likely to seek publicity on their own and to campaign against the legislature while less likely to learn legislative norms.

Finally, a new legislative career is evident in member behavior. As members more frequently seek and realize reelection, increasing attention is turned toward those activities that promote reelection, including fund-raising, constituent service, and pork barrel politics. Although none of these activities is new to the legislative scene, both the need to attend to these endeavors and the ability of individual members to do so have increased in recent years. For instance, the cost of running a successful campaign has grown dramatically in many states in the past few years. In Oregon, one source estimates that the average cost of running for the state senate increased by 384 percent (adjusted for inflation) between 1980 and 1988 (Moncrief, reported in Neal 1992). In the 1994 elections in California, candidates in nine of twenty senate and nine of eighty assembly races together raised over a million dollars (Rosenthal 1996). Although California is obviously an extreme case, campaign costs elsewhere are frequently substantial, particularly in large states such as Florida, Michigan, Ohio, Pennsylvania, New York, and New Jersey. In many states campaign costs continue to grow. To meet the rising costs of campaigns in the 1990s, more and more effort has to be devoted to fund-raising both by the political parties and individual members. As we saw in Chapter 2, party leaders in a substantial number of states expend considerable time and energy raising sizable amounts of money for their colleagues' races. Increasingly members themselves are assuming the responsibility for fund-raising and the number of fund-raisers has increased dramatically in many states. The frequency and intensity of fund-raising has grown to the point where, as Rosenthal (1989: 86) puts it, "If lobbyists used to prey on legislators, the tables have turned; now legislators seem to be preying on lobbyists." It is not uncommon, for instance, for legislators in some states to hold fund-raising events during the session when legislation important to various interest groups and lobbyists is being considered. Lobbyists and others frequently receive numerous requests for donations. Rosenthal (1989) reports that one contract lobbyist in California received fifty such solicitations in just two months in 1987.

The increased attention to fund-raising is matched with a renewed emphasis on constituent service. Members spend an appreciable, and increasing, amount of time and institutional resources attending to the folks back home. In talking about changes in their jobs, a substantial majority (well over 80 percent) of those responding to Gary Moncrief, Joel Thompson, and Karl Kurtz's survey indicated that attending to constituent demands and doing casework consumed an increasing amount of their and their staff's time. That service takes one of two forms—communicating with constituents and casework (Rosenthal 1986). Although members continue to perform each kind of service, increasingly members are shifting their focus to casework, presumably on the assumption that casework is a safe and effective means of maintaining political support. As structural reforms are put into place, members are better able to perform that service. Increases in the staff available to the individual member make it easier to keep up with and respond to constituent demands. The computerization of state legislatures has made service easier as well. State of the art computing systems now allow members to more effectively track constituent requests and when combined with census and electoral data to build sophisticated voter data bases (Jones 1992).

Today's new kind of legislator pursues one old-fashioned legislative activity—bringing home the bacon to his or her constituents. In a number of states allocating pork to individual members has become routinized. The pork barrel process in North Carolina during the early 1980s is a case in point. During that period, legislative leaders in both the house and the senate would decide at the end of each session how much money was left in the budget and allocate that amount to so-called special appropriations that were subsequently folded into a single omnibus bill approved near the end of the session. Although the amount of special appropriations still constituted a small fraction of the state's budget (less than 1 percent) the amount of pork grew substantially in the early 1980s. Between 1981 and 1984, overall state spending grew by just 11 percent while pork barrel spending increased by 132 percent. In allocating pork among the membership, not surprisingly members of the majority party, those from rural districts and those who chaired so-called money committees fared better than others (Thompson 1986a).

Not every lawmaker is concerned solely with reelection, however. At least some of the new generation of members are as concerned with public policy as they are with reelection. For example, Carol Weissert (1991) discovered a sizable number of policy entrepreneurs serving in the North Carolina legislature. These entrepreneurs were characterized by their expertise and long-term involvement with an issue and their "desire to become the leading spokesman on a particular, if relatively narrow, area" (p. 264). Policy entrepreneurs perform a number of functions for legislatures, including (1) serving as middlemen between professional experts and the larger political community; (2) providing sources of reliable information; and (3) through their persistent and overtime support of certain policy stands, "softening up" the political system for policy proposals while waiting for a policy window to open. Not surprisingly perhaps, the entrepreneurs in North Carolina were more likely to be identified by their colleagues, lobbyists, and the press as effective legislators.

The emergence of the new legislative career reflects a number of developments. The Supreme Court's reapportionment mandate in *Baker v. Carr* (1962) and *Reynolds v. Sims* (1964) not only loosened rural legislators' stranglehold over their legislatures, but by creating new districts in urban areas, provided new opportunities for a larger number of candidates to be elected. The increasing responsibilities of state governments have also contributed to a rise in legislative careerism. As state governments address the important policy issues of the day, their legislatures become more interesting and more attractive places to work. Ironically, state legislative careerism is also promoted by the absence of political opportunities beyond the legislature. Put simply, where there is a dearth of higher offices for members to seek, membership turnover is likely to be lower as fewer individuals are able to use the state legislature as a springboard to higher office (Squire 1988).

Perhaps nothing has promoted careerism as have the legislative reforms of the past few decades. Taken together, various structural reforms have provided members with both the means and opportunities to pursue full-time, long-term legislative careers. A number of reforms have been particularly important.

First, the movement to longer and more frequent sessions has produced more full-time lawmakers. Following World War II, only four state legislatures met annually. Today, forty-three meet on an annual basis and the remainder are often called into special session in those years when they are ostensibly in recess. Moreover, members increasingly remain active during the interim between sessions. In several states, committees meet monthly during the legislature's recess, and members spend an increasing amount of their time between sessions attending to district interests. The result is that the part-time legislator and those occupations that historically were overrepresented in part-time legislatures (business and the law) are increasingly being crowded out by individuals who are willing and able to pursue full-time legislative careers. That tendency is particularly evident in the decline in the rate at which attorneys serve in their state capitols. In the 1960s nearly one legislator in three was an attorney. By the mid-1980s that figure had dropped to just 16 percent (Jones 1992).

Second, in several states the rise of legislative careerism reflects increased compensation. Although legislative salaries are still quite low in most states (in only eleven states are members paid more than $30,000 in salary), compensation has increased over the past several years in terms of base salary, fringe benefits, and per diem reimbursement. In addition, in some states members are given free rein to use excess campaign funds for their "official use." And several states provide extra compensation to party leaders and committee chairs. The result of all this is that in a growing number of states individuals can afford to be full-time lawmakers. Recent research confirms that there is a direct and positive relationship between legislative salary and legislative careerism; available estimates indicate that each $10,000 increase in legislative salary reduces member turnover by 3 percent (Luttbeg 1992) and increases the average amount of legislative service by a little over a year (Squire 1988).

Third, the increase in legislative staff noted earlier has also promoted careerism, particularly as a larger proportion of staff resources have been allocated to individual members. Staff resources, both personal and institutional, are increasingly being used to perform constituent service and help individual members win reelection. Not only does the growth of personal staff allow members to respond to existing demands for constituent service, but that growth may generate *additional* demand. As one state legislator put it (reported in Kurtz 1993: 9):

> I think the growth of personal staff has generated more constituent business. Initially people wanted staff to respond to constituent questions but once you have more personal staff involved, the staff wants to do more, the legislators want to do more and they solicit constituent business. Word gets around and people start thinking more about using their legislators to try to solve problems with executive branch agencies. So it's a kind of a self-generating business.

Members have also benefited from the growth of partisan staff in several states. And as the number of staff assigned to the party leadership or caucus increases, so too does its use for electoral purposes. As Rosenthal (1989: 81) notes, "wherever partisan staffs are of sufficient size, their overriding objective appears to be elective rather than legislative."

Whatever its causes, the new legislative career has had consequences that go well beyond the individual member. The emergence of a new legislative career has undoubtedly increased the collective capability of most state legislatures. Although it is difficult to prove, many analysts would contend that the new kind of legislator is brighter, interested in a wider range of issues, and more involved in those issues. The result is that legislators are better able to deal with complex issues in a more innovative and effective manner. A new cohort of legislators has also democratized many legislatures as individual members seek a greater role in the institution's deliberations.

On a less positive note, the new legislative career has meant that a greater share of institutional resources, including the members' time, is devoted to satisfying individual members' personal goals, including reelection. As we have seen, increases in legislative staff have frequently been channeled to district offices and constituent service activities, party leaders have become fund-raising arms of the membership, and expensive computer systems allow members to perform constituent service more quickly and with better results. In addition, the rise of the individual legislative entrepreneur has promoted greater localism and, ultimately, legislative fragmentation. As Rosenthal (1986: 29) notes, "the closer legislators are tied to their district, the more difficult it may be for them to consider statewide interests or institutional concerns." That fragmentation is likely to increase as individuals seek and acquire more institutional power through committee reforms that promote a greater decentralization of authority. And of course, greater parochialism and fragmentation are likely to undercut policy coherence. The new legislative career, with its emphasis on reelection and constituent service, is also likely to promote greater favoritism in state policy and, in doing so, detract from the quality of legislative oversight. If Thompson's analysis of the pork barrel process in North Carolina is any guide to what occurs in other states, the decision rules that guide pork barrel allocations frequently reward partisanship and reduce the likelihood that the allocation of public policies will reflect the need for government services and benefits. There is also little reason to believe that member intervention on behalf of individual constituents constitutes effective legislative oversight. Although some argue that constituent service can serve as a viable means of oversight (see, e.g., McCubbins and Schwartz 1984), it rarely does so because of its focus on the particular case. Indeed just the opposite may occur. As long as the needs of individual members and their constituents are attended to by executive agencies, there is little incentive for members to inquire into the overall administration of public policies or to correct larger problems that might arise.

Term Limits

Whether the positive and negative impacts of careerism will continue depends on whether the trend toward longer legislative service persists. Voter initiatives in twenty-one states in recent years have attempted to ensure that they will not. In 1990, voters in California, Colorado, and Oklahoma enacted term limits for their state legislators and in 1992, 1994, and 1995 were joined by voters in eighteen additional states. Those limits, ranging from 6 to 12 years, hold out the potential for substantially affecting not only the degree of legislative careerism but the larger fabric of legislative life in the United States, in both the short and long term.

Although term limits are only now beginning to go into effect,[1] it is possible to estimate the career impacts of limits by looking at current rates of turnover. In the early 1990s, Gary Moncrief and his colleagues (1992) looked at the retention rates over a 12-year period for the cohort of state legislators first elected in 1979–1980 to estimate the likely impacts of term limits. Based on their analysis of all fifty states they conclude, among other things, that the impact of term limits on member turnover will depend on the length of the term limit, the degree of legislative professionalism, and the political opportunity structure for members. According to their data, term limits will have their greatest impacts in professional legislatures, where members are limited to fewer years of service, and in those legislatures that provide members with sufficient compensation to make service in that body a career but fail to provide the member sufficient opportunities to advance to "better" political offices (Opheim 1994 reports similar findings).

Table 5.3 reports Moncrief et al.'s data for those twenty states that had term limits in place in 1996.[2] As the table indicates, a reanalysis supports similar conclusions. If the retention rates in the 1980s are any guide, for a significant number of legislative chambers, particularly the so-called citizen legislatures, the impacts of term limits on careerism are likely to be negligible. Less than half of the class of 1979–1980 were still in office by 1983–1984 in sixteen of the forty chambers referenced in the table and less than a third were still serving after 12 years in two-thirds of the chambers. At the same time, the fact that a majority of those elected in 1979–1980 in a majority of legislatures were still in office 6 years later suggests that limits will shave at least some time off the natural career span of members in those states. And in those handful of chambers in which a sizable majority of members were still serving after 12 years, the subsequent career impacts of term limits are likely to be dramatic. Not surprisingly, the impacts of term limits are most likely to be felt in the so-called professional legislatures; in only one instance, the Ohio Senate, did a majority of members fail to serve for 6 years, and in five of the eight professional chambers, a majority were still serving after 12 years. Interestingly, hybrid legislatures, legislatures that share many but not all of the attributes of professional legislatures, also enjoyed a fair amount of member continuity (at least in the intermediate term).

The more important impacts of term limits will be felt at the institutional level. The effects will not be known for years, but scholars generally take the position that, on balance, limiting members' terms will bode ill for state legislatures by making legislative leadership more difficult, contributing to policy incoherence, and reducing the power of legislatures relative to governors, interest groups, and the state bureaucracy. At the same time, many hold out the possibility that state legislatures will adapt to term limits much as they have adapted to other changes, blunt-

TABLE 5.3 Return Rates for State Legislative Class of 1979–1980 Among States with Term Limits (as of 1996)

	Lower Chamber			Upper Chamber		
	Term Limit	% Still in Office 83–84	% Still in Office 89–90	Term Limit	% Still in Office 83–84	% Still in Office 89–90
Professional						
California	6	84%	64%	8	63%	63%
Massachusetts	8	82	48	8	75	75
Michigan	6	57	43	8	65	65
Ohio	8	69	50	8	40	20
State Average		73	51		61	56
Hybrid						
Arizona	8	63%	25%	8	86%	57%
Colorado	8	33	17	8	44	0
Florida	8	62	31	8	62	15
Missouri	8	72	42	8	40	40
Oklahoma	12	70	30	12	56	22
Oregon	6	67	27	8	17	0
Washington	6	42	8	8	82	64
State Average		58	26		55	28
Citizen Legislatures						
Arkansas	6	83%	61%	8	50%	25%
Idaho	8	50	21	8	14	14
Louisiana	12	68	32	12	81	50
Maine	8	49	18	8	57	29
Montana	6	46	14	8	36	27
Nevada	12	36	7	12	17	17
South Dakota	8	42	12	8	36	21
Utah	12	38	15	12	75	25
Wyoming	6	40	28	12	60	20
State Average		50	23		47	25

NOTE: The classification of legislatures is taken from Kurtz (1990). Professional legislatures are characterized by full-time members, large staff, and higher pay. Citizen legislatures are those with low pay, small staff, and part-time members. Hybrid legislatures fall in between.

SOURCE: Compiled from Gary Moncrief et al., "For Whom the Bell Tolls: Term Limits and State Legislatures," *Legislative Studies Quarterly* 17 (1992): 37–47.

ing the negative consequences of limiting legislative careers. Each of these points is elaborated in the following discussion.

Many fear that term limits will undercut legislative leadership by either producing leaders who are less able to lead or members who are less willing to be led (or both). One concern, for example, is that where members are able to serve only 6–8 years, individuals will assume leadership roles much earlier in their careers and with much less expertise and experience. A number of scholars (see, e.g., Squire 1992 and Hodson et al. 1995) have noted the tendency in recent years for legislative leaders to serve longer terms and to have served an extended apprenticeship before assuming a key leadership post. Obviously that will change as individuals move into leadership positions more quickly and without the benefits of lengthy periods of seasoning. The result could be leaders who lack the political skills, acumen, and chits necessary to manage conflict, build coalitions, and effectively represent the institution to others. Term limits are also likely to produce more turnover in leadership and a situation where leaders, serving a fixed, shorter term, will be regarded during much of their tenure as "lame ducks" (see, e.g., Jewell and Whicker 1994). Relatedly, Rosenthal (1992: 207) contends that term limits will promote higher turnover because "members are not going to tolerate anyone serving six, eight, ten, or twelve years as leader. The rest of the members will have very little time to wait for their own chances." There is also the fear that term limits will make members more difficult to lead by promoting greater individualism and less loyalty to the institution or to the party. As Michael Malbin and Gerald Benjamin (1992: 213) note:

> If the term limits produce amateur legislators, the amateurs might be more inclined than contemporary careerists to follow their personal convictions. On the other hand, if the limits merely encourage professionals to run for new offices periodically, the professionals would become more entrepreneurial. In neither case would most members be likely to feel a long-term, institutionally based incentive for following a collective institutional leadership.

Another concern is that term limits will detract from the quality of legislative policymaking. Advocates of terms limits have argued that limits will promote better governing by not only bringing new members with fresh ideas to state legislatures, but also by bringing in members who are more willing to make the difficult, but often unpopular decisions that today's changing political and economic environment requires. A number of scholars, however, challenge that view by contending that term limits will undermine the ability of legislatures to fashion public policy in a coherent manner. First, critics of limits maintain that by promoting greater turnover and a more inexperienced membership, term limits will rob legislatures of members who have sufficient knowledge of policy issues or the political process to build the coalitions necessary to pass legislation. As one veteran staffer (reported in Gurwitt 1996: 17) from a state that will soon be facing the results of term limits lamented: "People are making very important policy decisions with very little knowledge of what they're deciding. Some of the questions that we've heard, and the lack of knowledge behind them, have been staggering." That inexperience carries over to the problems of leadership and coalition building. Acknowledging the problems inexperienced committee chairs have had in Maine as term limits take effect in that state, Gurwitt (1996: 18) notes:

Many of the other new committee chairs in Maine proved unable to move anything out of their bailiwicks, in large part because they either did not know how to get beyond partisan bickering or could not subsume their personal missions for the purpose of forging compromise. Those skills tend to come with legislative maturity; term limits, on the other hand, turn legislatures into political hothouses, in which newcomers undergo a sort of forced growth as they take on responsibilities before they may, in fact, be ready.

There is also a concern that term limits, at least in those instances in which members are both motivated and allowed to seek other office, will make legislators more risk averse as members, including the leadership, position themselves for other races (see, e.g., Malbin and Benjamin 1992). The result is that legislators and their leaders will become less willing to tackle difficult policy issues or make choices that are policy wise but politically foolish. Relatedly, as members see their futures lying elsewhere, fewer incentives will exist for members to attend to institutional needs and maintenance. Where members are able to make a career of the legislature, there are incentives, including internal power, perks, and prestige, for performing tasks, such as service on an ethics committee or within the party leadership, which contribute to the institution's integrity (Malbin and Benjamin 1992; Mayhew 1974). By promoting shortened careers, term limits remove those incentives and the likelihood that anyone will perform those essential tasks.

Finally, many charge that term limits will undercut the ability of legislatures to govern by shifting power and authority to governors and the bureaucracy. Legislatures populated by inexperienced members who see their political and personal futures elsewhere may be less willing and able to perform meaningful oversight of public agencies. And as term limits undercut legislative professionalism, the states' lawmaking institutions may cede control over the policy agenda to the governors as legislatures become even more fragmented and less able to act collectively. Yet, as Malbin and Benjamin (1992: 217) observe, the irony of term limits for governors is that by weakening legislative leadership, term limits may also undercut the governors' ability to realize their legislative goals. "Insofar as term limitations weaken the capacity of legislative leaders to provide disciplined majorities, they are likely to make it harder, not easier, for governors to achieve their objectives."

Although term limits are likely to have a significant and potentially debilitating impact on both members and the institutions in which they serve, two considerations suggest that the impacts of limits may not be as profound and far-reaching as some predict. In the first place, term limits are likely to have their greatest impact where limits are more restrictive (shorter terms and lifetime limits) and in those legislatures that are more professional. Citizen legislatures are not likely to feel many of the effects of limits. Second, and more importantly, there already is evidence that legislatures in a number of term limit states are adapting to limits in ways that mitigate their more negative effects on the institution. Legislative leaders in the Michigan House, for example, faced with lots of new faces and the prospect of higher turnover, have worked hard to bring members "up to snuff" on policy issues and have reduced the number of committee assignments so that members will have the time necessary to specialize and develop expertise in a policy area (Gurwitt 1996). In a number of states, efforts have been made to bring new members into positions of committee and leadership responsibility earlier in their terms, so that when those members actually assume key leadership posts they will have the experience and expertise to lead. In California, for instance, following the 1994 election Speaker Willie Brown appointed a number of freshman members to key committees and increased the number of leadership positions available to second-termers (Hodson et al. 1995). Similarly, in 1994 the speaker of the Arkansas House, Bobby Hogue, appointed a number of freshman chairs of legislative committees (Gurwitt 1996). Moreover, the Florida House, which has historically rotated leadership by limiting the speaker to a single term, demonstrates that even where there is a high turnover of leadership, legislative leaders can nonetheless exert considerable influence and effectively counter the state's governor.

Women and Minorities

As we have seen, state legislatures are populated by a new kind of lawmaker, one who is more professional, better educated, and more assertive. That legislator is also more likely to be a minority and/or a woman. Although state legislatures remain white, male domains, the last two decades have seen a dramatic increase in the number of blacks, Hispanics, and women serving in state legislatures. Between 1969 and 1993, for example, the number of women serving in state legislatures increased fourfold, jumping from just 300 in the late 1960s to over 1500 in 1997. By 1995, women constituted 21 percent of all state legislators. And as we saw in Chapter 2, African Americans and Hispanics have enjoyed similar increases as well. By the mid-1990s, more than 500 blacks served in their state legislatures and Hispanics held more than 10 percent of the seats in the state legislatures of Arizona, Colorado, New Mexico, and Texas (Rosenthal 1996).

Although both minorities and women have enjoyed considerable success in reaching office, that in and of itself is no guarantee that blacks, Hispanics, and women will enjoy a positive or productive legislative experience. Legislatures are not egalitarian institutions. Nor is there any reason to believe that discrimination and fundamental conflicts disappear once these new members assume office. Nonetheless, a review of the evidence on women and blacks (unfortunately too little evidence is available on Hispanic state legislators to discuss them further) suggests that women and minorities have enjoyed some success both on a personal plane and in terms of representing larger interests. Nonetheless, barriers remain.

In the case of women, recent evidence indicates that the role of women in state legislatures is changing in fundamental ways and that the increased representation of women is having a real effect on what occurs in America's statehouses. In reviewing what little is known about the status of women serving in state legislatures in years past, Sue Thomas (1991: 959) concludes: "Evidence indicates that, in the past, women state legislators tended to participate less than their male colleagues in the normal range of legislative behaviors such as speaking in committees and on the floor, bargaining with their colleagues for political goals, and meeting with lobbyists. They were also less aggressive in pursuing issues."

Much of that has changed. First, the differences between men and women lawmakers in terms of activity levels and behavior have diminished. Based on their study of legislators in a dozen states, Sue Thomas and Susan Welch (1991: 450) report that "women and men legislators are reasonably similar in terms of mean levels of floor and committee speaking, meeting with lobbyists, bargaining activity, and having difficulty bargaining." Second, the evidence from those twelve states also indicates somewhat less balkanization in the committee assignments given to male and female legislators. Although women were still more likely to sit on health and welfare committees and less likely to serve on business or economic committees, those assignments apparently reflected personal preferences and not discrimination. Moreover, women proved equally likely to serve on their legislature's budget committees. Third, and equally important, although men still introduced and passed more legislation, women were just as likely as men to pass priority bills.

At the same time, the available evidence suggests that women often bring different priorities to the states' legislatures. In general, women are more likely to introduce and support legislation focusing on women's issues, civil rights, education, health, poverty, and children (Thomas and Welch 1991; Bratton and Haynie 1992). Women also bring new styles of leadership. The number of women serving in leadership posts has increased appreciably, from just 8 percent of all leaders in 1979 to 17.7 percent in 1991 (Jewell and Whicker 1994). Malcolm Jewell and Marcia Whicker's study of legislative leadership illustrates that those women typically exhibit a style of leadership style that is more geared to building consensus and, secondarily, coordination. Male leaders, in contrast, stressed coordination and, to a lesser extent, a command style of leadership and were much less oriented to building consensus. Gender differences also appeared with respect to the leadership goals of men and women. The women in the sample were somewhat more likely to pursue policy goals and less oriented to political power.

Although women have made considerable gains in recent years, problems still remain. Pockets of discrimination still exist, and women are often held to higher standards than men. A study of the conversational dynamics of committee hearings in Colorado in the late 1980s is particularly revealing of the problems women frequently face once they have achieved office. Content analysis of the text of a dozen committee hearings in the Colorado House indicated that women tended to speak less often, spoke later in the hearing process, and were interrupted more often than their male counterparts, a pattern that held even among females who chaired committees. Not only did men tend to dominate committee hearings, but as the proportion of women increased, male members became more verbally aggressive and sought more often to dominate the proceedings (Kathlene 1994).

Although there are only a handful of studies that look at how blacks have fared as legislators, what data exist indicate that, like their female counterparts, blacks are having an impact on their state legislatures and achieving some notable successes. But, like female legislators, blacks face serious constraints as well.

There is evidence, for example, that black legislators carry into office an often unique set of priorities. A comparison of the bill introduction behavior of black and white legislators in Arkansas, Maryland, and North Carolina revealed that black legislators are typically more likely to introduce legislation dealing with women's issues (e.g., family leave or day care), children, poverty, education, and civil rights (Bratton and Haynie 1992). At the same time, a survey of state legislators in the early 1990s suggests that black legislators frequently share many of the policy priorities of their white colleagues—at least at first glance. As part of a national survey of black and white legislators throughout the country, respondents were asked to identify what they felt were the most important issues facing their state. Their responses are outlined in Table 5.4 and suggest that black and white lawmakers are surprisingly similar in their overall policy priorities. In each case, legislators stressed the importance of education, the economy, and health care and the need to attend to the state's budget problems. But there are differences here as well. Whites were generally more concerned with budget issues and the overall economy. In contrast, blacks were more likely to cite unemployment as an area of special concern. Moreover, it is likely that blacks and whites bring different solutions to bear on these issues. Not unexpectedly, blacks were generally more liberal than whites, a difference that remains when only Democrats are included in the analysis. Even within the same party, blacks were more likely to place themselves to

TABLE 5.4 A Comparison of Black and White Legislators' Policy Priorities, Preference for Level of Government, Perceptions of Black Progress, and Ideology, 1991–1992

	Black Legislators		White Legislators	
Most important issue				
	Education	22%	Budget	29%
	Budget	17	Education	21
	Economy	11	Economy	19
	Unemployment	10	Health	9
	Health	8	Taxes	8
Preferred level of government				
	Local	4%		4%
	State	59		77
	Federal	37		19
Black progress in state in last 10 years (% reporting considerable progress)				
	Jobs	8%		35%
	Politics	36		62
	Education	15		38
	Housing	10		29

Ideology								
Black	11%	21%	33%	23%	10%	1%	1%	Avg. 3.1
Liberal	1	2	3	4	5	6	7	Conservative
White	1%	5%	17%	22%	33%	19%	3%	Avg. 4.5

SOURCE: Compiled from James Button and David Hedge, "The Quality of Black Legislative Life: Black-White Comparisons," presented at the annual meeting of the American Political Science Association, September 2–5, 1993, Washington, D.C.; and James Button and David Hedge, "Legislative Life in the 1990s: A Comparison of Black and White State Legislators," *Legislative Studies Quarterly,* 21 (1996): 199–218.

the left of center. And as the table makes clear, blacks were more likely than whites to turn to the federal government for policy solutions. Equally important, a comparison of black and white legislators reveals often dramatic differences in perceptions of black progress. As the data illustrate, white legislators were much more likely to report that blacks had made considerable progress in jobs, politics, education, and housing in recent years, a tendency that was even more pronounced among blacks and whites serving in the South.

Although an increase in black representation has brought new issues and policy approaches into America's statehouses, the important question remains as to whether black constituents and those blacks who represent them are able to successfully promote those policy stances. David

Hedge and James Button's survey of African American lawmakers in the early 1990s (reported in Hedge, Button, and Spear 1992, 1996) provides some insight into that issue and offers reason for both optimism and pessimism. On the one hand, there was a great deal of satisfaction among black lawmakers, and many reported that they had gained power and influence within their legislature. Nearly 90 percent expressed satisfaction with their legislative careers and 40 percent indicated they were very satisfied with those careers. Similar numbers reported satisfaction with their committee assignments. Several black lawmakers also chaired committees (30 percent) or held a formal leadership position (28 percent). In addition, sizable numbers maintained that blacks had a great deal of influence in their legislature (24 percent) and that issues important to African Americans always received a fair hearing (24 percent) and were very likely to become law (21 percent).

Those findings notwithstanding, the responses of black lawmakers to Hedge and Button's survey suggest problems as well. First, many African American lawmakers expressed some dissatisfaction with the party. Nearly twice as many lawmakers reported that they had only a little influence over party affairs as did those reporting a great deal of influence. Second, black lawmakers also reported a substantial amount of discrimination. Over 60 percent indicated that they had either been the victim of or had observed at least one instance of discrimination during the most recent legislative session. Sizable numbers reported at least some discrimination in party affairs (76 percent) and the committee system (61 percent) as well.

Additional analysis pointed to a number of conditions that either detracted from or contributed to the black legislative experience. First, the quality of black legislative life was generally lower in the states of the Deep South—Alabama, Louisiana, Mississippi, South Carolina, and Georgia. Second, more senior members and, to a lesser extent, those blacks who held a party leadership position reported a more positive legislative life. Third, blacks serving black majority districts often reported a lower quality of legislative life. African Americans who represented black majority districts were less satisfied with their committee assignments, reported less black influence over party affairs, and perceived less black influence within their legislatures. Fourth, women were often doubly disadvantaged by reason of their gender and race. Women were much more likely to report discrimination and were less likely to perceive blacks as having influence in the legislature. Finally, the racial climate of the state might well have been the most important determinant of how blacks fared within the nation's state legislatures during the period included in the study. Blacks who reported more strained race relationships within their state consistently reported a lower quality of legislative life (Hedge, Button, and Spear 1996).

Hedge and Button's research also indicates that the black caucuses that exist in many state legislatures also contribute to black influence. As part of their survey, black state legislators were asked to discuss the influence of the black caucus on a range of legislative activities. The responses indicate that members typically viewed their caucus as influential in terms of developing legislation and socializing members. Black lawmakers were particularly likely to point to the role the caucus played in passing legislation important to African Americans. Cheryl Miller's (1990) study of the black caucus in North Carolina further demonstrates the ability of the black caucus to move issues of importance to African Americans on and off the legislative agenda. In 1987, the black caucus was able to obtain passage of four of the five issue areas they targeted for legislative effort. The caucus was also instrumental in obtaining committee chairmanships for its members.

Legislative Assertiveness

Given the kinds of changes that we have outlined so far, it should hardly come as a surprise that state legislatures are becoming increasingly assertive, particularly in terms of their relationship with the executive branch. Today, legislatures contend on a nearly equal basis with the governor and state agencies over budget issues, policy development, and increasingly, the day-to-day management of state government (Rosenthal 1990).

Nowhere is that more evident than in the area of legislative oversight of executive branch behavior. Although legislatures in the past have been loath to perform the oversight function, a number of developments, including divided control of state government, greater state involvement in complex and contentious policy issues, greater legislative professionalism, the public's dissatisfaction with government, and the states' fiscal woes, have led to a renewed interest in performing that task. Over the last decade or so, lawmakers have increasingly engaged in four types of oversight.

First, state legislatures are devoting greater energy and staff to various forms of evaluation and program review. Modeled after the U.S. Congress's General Accounting Office, evaluation units currently exist in more than forty states and perform various forms of analysis, including evaluations of existing programs as well as efforts to identify the likely consequences of alternative legislative proposals (Jones 1987).

Second, state lawmakers have sought to gain additional control over the use of federal funds by state agencies. As the states became more dependent upon federal dollars in the 1970s, state legislatures were increasingly bypassed in the decisions being made about how to use those funds. By 1981, thirty-six states had addressed that problem by requiring that federal funds be appropriated within the state budget. In addition, twenty-three states have adopted special provisions to give state law-makers greater control over federal block grant funding (Bowman and Kearney 1986).

Third, by the mid-1980s more than two-thirds of the states had adopted sunset provisions that required the automatic termination of agencies, usually regulatory agencies, after a specified period of time unless explicitly reauthorized by the legislature. Although considered time consuming and costly (Pound 1982), what little evidence exists suggests that their use has had a positive impact on legislative oversight. William Lyons and Patricia Freeman (1984) surveyed state lawmakers in Tennessee in 1981 in order to assess the impact of the state's adoption of sunset provisions on the oversight process. Their findings indicated that sunset review provisions made agency officials more "conscious of legislative authority," increased the legislature's commitment to engage in oversight, and increased cooperation and understanding between the executive and legislative branches.

Fourth, over the past few decades, state lawmakers have become more involved in an additional form of oversight, committee review of administrative rule making. By the early 1990s, all but a handful of states provided for legislative review of administration regulations in one form or the other. In sixteen states, lawmakers can exercise a legislative veto to invalidate an administrative action (Gormley 1993). Other states grant reviewing committees only advisory powers (Council of State Governments 1992). Despite the potential importance of this form of legislative oversight, little information exists concerning its impact. Marcus Ethridge's (1984a and 1984b) analysis of state rule review is suggestive of both the causes and consequences of legislative oversight. Ethridge proposes that interest in rule review reflects not so much the desire of state legislatures to better understand agency actions, but rather changing interest group politics. In particular, the success of public advocacy groups throughout the states in shaping administrative decisions has led client or regulated groups, those that had traditionally benefited from regulation, to seek relief from their legislatures. At that point rule review simply represents an opportunity for regulated groups to regain the regulatory advantage. Analysis of oversight activity in Wisconsin, Tennessee, and Michigan provides some support for Ethridge's assertion. In each of those states agency proposals that were subsequently disapproved by the respective oversight committees were more likely (relative to approved proposals) to entail restrictions on the actions of regulated interests.

Evidence of greater legislative assertiveness is also found in the rate at which legislatures have overridden gubernatorial vetoes. Although the frequency with which governors have vetoed legislation has held constant over the past few decades at about 5 percent of all legislation, the willingness of legislatures to challenge their governors has increased somewhat in recent years. In 1947, vetoes were overridden by legislatures in less than 2 percent of all cases. Nearly fifty years later, lawmakers were slightly more likely to override their governor's vetoes, doing so in 3.2 percent of all cases (Beyle 1993). Moreover, an examination of veto politics in the 1990s indicates considerable variation across the states. In 1991, for example, nearly two-thirds of the legislatures chose not to override any of their governors' vetoes when given a chance. In contrast, lawmakers overrode at least 10 percent of the vetoes in thirteen states (Council of State Governments 1992).

Table 5.5 provides additional insight into this form of legislative assertiveness and offers support for the notion that legislative reform has contributed to greater conflict between governors and their legislatures. In Chapter 4, measures of gubernatorial veto behavior were used to reference conflict between governors and their legislatures and the ability of governors to persevere in the face of recalcitrant lawmakers. That same data can be used to examine the impact of legislative reform on interbranch conflict and the propensity for lawmakers to emerge victorious from that conflict. Once again, the rate at which governors veto legislation is used as a measure of conflict. In addition, the percentage of vetoes overridden in 1991 is employed as a measure of the legislatures' assertiveness and their ability to compete successfully with the executive branch. Peverill Squire's (1992) index of legislative professionalism is used to measure legislative reform. Squire's index includes measures of state legislative pay, length of session, and staffing, all relative to comparable figures for the U.S. Congress.

The regression analysis reported in Table 5.5 estimates the influence of legislative professionalism on veto dynamics while controlling for those aspects of the governorship that proved important in Chapter 4. As the table indicates, even after controlling for the formal and informal resources of the states' governors, states with more-professional legislatures experience a much higher rate of vetoes and interbranch conflict. At the same time, greater professionalism is not associated with the rate at which legislatures choose to override the governor's vetoes. Instead, as we saw in Chapter 4, legislative overrides reflect various gubernatorial resources, most notably the governor's budget-making powers, his or her prior service in the legislature, and the number of legislators who share the governor's party label. Taken together, the coefficients in Table 5.5 suggest, at least tentatively, that more-professional legislatures may find themselves more frequently in conflict with their governors, but that professionalism, in and of itself, does not ensure that the legislature will prevail.

TABLE 5.5   Legislative Professionalism and Legislative-Executive Conflict,
1991 (entries are standardized regression coefficients, t-ratios in parentheses)

	# of Vetoes 1991 (n = 49)	% Vetoes Overridden (n = 47)
Legislative professionalism	.19+	.09
	(1.31)	(.64)
Gubernatorial Resources		
Veto authority	.23+	
	(1.39)	
Budget-cutting authority	–.41**	
	(–2.83)	
Budget-making authority		–.29*
		(–2.03)
Prior service in legislature	–.22+	–.22+
	(–1.57)	(–1.55)
Age when first elected	.24*	
	(1.66)	
Party margin in legislature		–.22+
		(–1.48)
Adj. R^2	.20	.11
F	3.45**	2.41+

+ significant at .10 level.
* significant at .05 level.
** significant at .01 level.

Implications for Governing

Implicit in most discussions of legislative reform is the assumption that changes in membership, structures, and procedures will impact on how (and how well) legislatures perform various functions including representation, policymaking, and legislative oversight. Early advocates of reform contended that reformed institutions would be more responsive to their publics and more capable of making coherent and effective policies. More recently, a number of analysts worry that recent reforms and other developments, particularly those that "congressionalize" state legislatures, might actually detract from the governing capacity of state governments. Unfortunately, there is little empirical evidence that systematically sorts out the implications of legislative change for the ability of legislatures to govern in a responsible and responsive manner. Nonetheless, a review of those changes, together with the available empirical and anecdotal evidence, suggests that changes in the past several decades have both contributed to and detracted from the character and quality of what legislatures do.

On the positive side of the ledger, even the most skeptical observer would agree that a number of developments have promoted both statehouse democracy and legislative policymaking coherence. Reapportionment and the increase in the number of minorities and women serving as members have ensured that legislatures today are more diverse and more likely to address a wider range of interests and policy issues. And in those legislatures where power has been distributed more widely to committees and to individual members, the ability of various interests to connect with and to be heard by state legislatures is enhanced. Recorded votes, better media coverage, and sunshine laws have also allowed citizens to see more clearly what their legislatures do.

Other changes have probably made legislatures more responsible as well. Institutional reforms of the kinds we documented earlier, including longer sessions, procedural reforms, and an increase in specialized staff, have afforded many legislatures the time and resources they need to tackle difficult policy questions in a more efficient manner. In addition, the rise of legislative careerism has meant that more legislators are more involved in and more informed about legislative deliberations than ever before. Carol Weissert's discovery of policy entrepreneurs is particularly heartening. Greater reliance on the committee systems, together with greater careerism and increases in professional staff, also hold out the promise that legislatures will develop ongoing, technical capabilities that rival the executive branch. The fact that legislatures have become more assertive vis-à-vis the governor contributes as well to policy responsibility by improving the quality of oversight and providing an additional source of policy ideas and innovation.

Support for the notion that legislative reforms have had a positive impact on the ability of legislatures to govern is found in a relatively small, somewhat scattered series of studies that look at the impact of legislative professionalism on policy outputs and outcomes. Taken together, those studies suggest that legislative reforms have improved both the quality of statehouse democracy and legislative responsibility. Research by Harmon Ziegler (1983), for example, indicates that legislatures that are more professional are less susceptible to the blandishments of interest groups, in part because those institutions are less dependent on those groups for information. Although his findings might, at first glance, be interpreted as suggesting that professional legislatures are *less* responsive to citizen demands, for those who fear that state legislatures have become *too* responsive to special interests, Ziegler's findings should be reassuring. Legislatures that are captured by narrow interests are, after all, less able to listen to their constituents or broader public opinion. Indeed, there is some reason to believe that more-professional legislatures are more capable of translating public opinion into public policies. Robert Jackson's (1992) analysis of how political variables condition the fit between opinion and policy suggests the possibility that professional legislatures are better at converting citizen preferences into public policies. Although the relationship between an interactive term for professionalism and public opinion and policy liberalism falls short of statistical significance (t-value = 1.68) his data indicate a slight tendency for the fit between opinion and policy to be stronger in states with more-professional legislatures.

There is also evidence that an increase in professionalism has made for more responsible governance by promoting greater policy autonomy, activity, and effectiveness. As we saw in Table 5.5, for example, more-professional legislatures tend to clash with their governors more often, a finding that suggests that professionalism leads to greater legislative assertiveness. Similarly, Joel Thompson (1986b) finds that more-professional legislatures are more self-reliant and autonomous vis-à-vis their governors. Based on his analysis of budget politics, policy initiation, and legislative oversight in several states, Thompson (p. 40) concludes that "it appears that reformed legislatures are more capable legislatures—more capable of making independent budgetary decisions, more capable of obtaining information about policies and proposing new or alternative policies, and more capable of overseeing the implementation of those policies once they have been made."

There is also data to suggest that professionalism promotes greater policy activism and coherence. Although early studies found little evidence that professionalism influenced state policy outputs once social and economic factors were controlled for (see, most notably, Ritt 1973 and Karnig and Sigelman 1975), more recent analysis indicates that such a linkage does indeed exist. Research reported in the early 1990s demonstrates that legislative professionalism produces greater policy liberalism (see, most recently, Jackson 1992) and contributes to the quality of environmental protection (Ringquist 1993) and economic development (Brace 1993). Indeed, Evan Ringquist's (1993: 119) analysis of environmental programming in the states leads him to conclude that "the single best predictor of air program strength in the states is legislative professionalism."

Table 5.6 presents additional evidence concerning the link between professionalism and public policy. In developing the regression estimates in the table, Squire's (1992) index of legislative professionalism is used together with a series of measures that reflect some of the more important policy developments in the 1980s, including Keon Chi and Dennis Grady's (1989) index of innovation and measures reflecting state efforts during the mid-1980s in the areas of environmental protection, economic development, and educational reform. The innovation index is based on reports from key government informants in each state and reflects the rate at which particular states are cited as a source of innovation across several policy areas. The environmental measure is an overall ranking of

TABLE 5.6   Legislative Professionalism and Public Policy in the 1980s: An Initial Assessment (entries are standardized regression coefficients, t ratios in parentheses, n = 47).

	Policy Innovativeness	Environmental Programming	Economic Development	Educational Reform
Legislative professionalism	.64** (5.21)	.33* (2.88)	.39* (2.59)	−.28 (−1.60)
Public ideology	.08 (.50)	.03 (.24)	.15 (.81)	.12 (.56)
Per capita income	.09 (.58)	.54** (3.95)	.11 (.60)	.18 (.84)
Adjusted R²	.51	.58	.26	.01
F	16.75**	22.42**	6.51**	1.12

   ** significant at .001 level
    * significant at .01 level

state programs generated by the Fund for Renewable Energy and Environment (Ridley 1987) that takes into account state regulatory efforts in the areas of air, water, and hazardous and solid waste. The economic development score is a ranking of state economic development activities, including taxation, regulation, international marketing, and workforce development, provided by the Corporation for Enterprise Development (CED 1990). The education variable is also provided by CED and simply counts whether states had adopted one or more of a half dozen educational innovations by the mid-1980s, including student competency tests and statewide curriculum standards. In each case, the variables have been recoded so that a higher value indicates greater state effort. The most striking finding in Table 5.6 is the consistent relationship between legislative professionalism and policy innovation and activism, even after controlling for state wealth and public opinion.[3] States with more-professional legislatures tend to be viewed by key informants as more innovative. They also tend to be states with more highly regarded economic development and environmental management programs. The one exception is education. States with more-professional legislatures actually adopted somewhat *fewer* educational reforms during the mid-1980s. That finding notwithstanding, the evidence in Table 5.6 together with the other research summarized previously provides strong support for the notion that reformed legislatures are willing and able to act in an autonomous, innovative, and effective manner.

Not everyone agrees, however, that legislative reforms and other developments have produced better governance. In a very compelling and insightful series of chapters, Rosenthal (1989, 1993, and 1996) has argued that many of the changes I have noted in this chapter have actually made legislatures less capable of governing. Writing in the early 1990s, he notes (pp. 97–98): "While the current legislative record in representation, participation, and production is a good one, there is an additional function that the legislature can be expected to perform. The legislature should provide a process that is authoritative, deliberative, and open—a process that is capable of resolving conflict and building consensus. That process and the legislature as an institution are in jeopardy."

In particular, Rosenthal argues that the growing inability of legislatures to function as truly deliberative bodies grows out of the emerging careerism that has come to characterize many legislatures and which has produced a preoccupation with reelection, parochialism, partisanship, and a corresponding fragmentation of legislative power and authority. The result, he contends (1989: 97–98), is that "state legislatures also face the prospect of an unraveling of organizational coherence and approaching paralysis. The result would be a declining ability to fashion a consensus, not with respect to narrowly focused matters, but on statewide policies." More recently, Rosenthal (1996) has argued that state legislatures are becoming "deinstitutionalized," as turnover appears to be on the increase, as informal norms, including institutional loyalty, decline in importance, and as legislatures become permeable and responsive to external pressures.

Rosenthal is not alone in his concern about the institutional well-being of state legislatures. As we have seen, the public still holds many legislatures in low esteem, and there is no shortage of commentary declaring the state legislature as "An Embattled Institution" (Ehrenhalt 1992) and as "Our Beleaguered Institution" (Hansen 1994). Those headlines reflect a number of pathologies, some of which flow from the growing professionalism of state legislatures. During the late 1980s and early 1990s, scandals rocked a number of statehouses, including Kentucky, Arizona, and Michigan, and many worry that the latest round of campaign finance and ethics reforms, while impressive in many instances, only begins to address the fundamental problems of money and influence in state politics. We have also seen that interest groups are ever more present and influential in state governments and that legislatures all too often are unable to resist those pressures. And any number of developments, including careerism and, ironically, term limits have made leadership of an increasingly fragmented legislatures much more difficult. There also seems to be a breakdown of legislative norms, as members grow more parochial and as institutional loyalties diminish. As Weberg (1997: 29) notes: "The legislator of the 21st century, regardless of party affiliation, will likely care much more about things political than those institutional.

Those legislators will have a narrower policy focus and limited legislative experience. They won't know the legislative process and its traditions very well, and they won't have the time or the inclination to learn them—especially in term-limited states."

More broadly, if the conventional wisdom concerning the link between decentralization and responsibility is valid, then many of the changes that have characterized the evolution of state legislatures in recent decades—careerism, candidate-centered elections, a redistribution of responsibility to committees and legislative staff, declining institutional loyalty, and the increasing importance of lobbyists and PACs—have contributed to decentralization and, in doing so, made it more difficult for legislatures to act in a responsible fashion. As I argue in the first chapter, although they can be very responsive to political interests, decentralized institutions are less able to act in a timely fashion, reach necessary compromises, and craft legislation that makes nonincremental change. All of this suggests an irony of reform. On the one hand, recent changes have enhanced the institutional capacity of the states. Legislatures today have more resources and expertise that can be brought to bear on important policy issues. On the other hand, many of those same changes have undercut both the ability and willingness of legislatures to address those issues as those resources are refocused on partisan or individual concerns.

Conclusions

Three things are apparent from a review of state legislatures in recent decades. First, legislatures have changed dramatically in a fairly short period of time. Legislatures currently devote more time and institutional resources to address some of the more complex problems facing America. Their membership is changing as well. The numbers of women and minorities have increased dramatically. There is also a new kind of legislator serving throughout the states. Currently, members are more professional, more likely to view the job of lawmaker as a full-time career, and less willing to defer to others. Given those changes, it is not surprising that legislatures are becoming more assertive as institutions, often to the discomfort of their governors.

Second, those changes have impacted on the legislatures' capacity to govern. But not in a uniform fashion. Some reforms and developments—the increase in staff and greater professionalism, for instance—are likely to promote greater policy responsibility and coherence by increasing institutional capacity. Others, including reapportionment and the increase in the rate at which minorities and women are represented, should increase the responsiveness of legislatures to a wider range of interests. Not every change in how legislatures do their business has had a positive impact on governing, however. As we have seen, there is some concern that a new generation of members may be contributing to a more decentralized and individualized lawmaking institution, where institutional resources are reallocated to securing reelection. In addition, as we saw in this chapter and in Chapter 3, many states still need to attend to issues of ethics, campaign finance, and the behavior of legislative lobbyists. More broadly, long-time students of America's legislatures worry that legislatures are becoming too fragmented, too partisan, and too concerned with reelection to govern wisely. And as legislatures develop as institutions and become more assertive, the likelihood of conflict with the executive and judicial branches increases.

Finally, it is clear that state legislatures will continue to evolve in response to changes from both within and without the institution. Within legislatures and despite many of the changes that we have noted, party leaders may be finding new ways to assert themselves and to promote greater unity and centralization. Certainly as party leaders take a more active role in fund-raising, they will have the leverage to do so. The character of America's legislatures will no doubt change as well in response to recent political trends and developments, most notably term limits, the new Republican majorities that were swept into office in 1994, and recent efforts to shift even greater responsibility for governing to the states. How all of that will unfold is anyone's guess, but one thing is certain: These and other developments will have significant impacts on the ability of legislatures to listen to their citizens and to fashion coherent and effective policies.

NOTES

1. Term limits went into effect in 1996 in both houses of the Maine legislature and the California Assembly. In 1998, limits will go into effect in the California senate and in the lower chamber in eight additional states. Limits will go into effect in the remaining chambers between 2000 and 2007.

2. In February 1996, the Nebraska supreme court struck down the term limits Nebraskans had imposed on their legislators in an earlier statewide initiative.

3. Per capita income in 1987 is used to measure state wealth and Erikson, Wright, and McIver's (1993) estimate of the public's ideology during 1976–1988 is used to gauge public opinion.

6

The Courts

Although governors and legislatures figure prominently in most discussions of the states' resurgence, the states' courts have also undergone fundamental change. Indeed, analysts at the Advisory Commission on Intergovernmental Relations (ACIR) (1982: 105) maintain that "perhaps in no other aspect of state government has improvement been so marked as in the judicial branch." The resurgence of the courts has been evidenced in a variety of ways: structural and personnel reforms, a search for alternative dispute resolution devices, greater judicial activism, and the adoption of new technologies for managing and transmitting information.

Given this volume's concern with the larger question of the states' capacity to govern, this chapter focuses on three areas of change—judicial reforms, the increasing presence of women and minorities on the states' courts, and an increased willingness on the part of many state supreme courts to make public policy. As we shall see, over the past several decades the states have put into place a series of reforms aimed at both streamlining the courts and ensuring that the men and women who serve on the courts are both qualified and held accountable. In addition, efforts have been made to increase the rate at which women and minorities serve on state courts. There is also some evidence that many of the states' courts are seeking to play a more prominent policymaking role, joining the ranks of governors and legislators in fashioning innovative solutions to state policy problems. Although the record in each of those areas is mixed and the courts' actions have engendered controversy and resistance, it is clear that by the 1990s many of the states' courts had emerged as viable partners in the governing of the American states.

Judicial Reform

Modern efforts to reform state courts date back to the 1940s with the adoption of merit selection for judges in Missouri (ACIR 1982). But the pace of reform accelerated in the 1970s as nearly every state put into place changes in the organization and staffing of the courts. Those changes were a response to a court system that had changed little since the eighteenth and nineteenth centuries and that suffered a series of maladies. As researchers at the ACIR (1982: 98) note:

> Critics have pointed to fragmented and confusing systems with no central administrative organization; unqualified judges, often chosen more for party service than judicial merit; continuance in office of senile, arbitrary, or corrupt judges; conflict of interest of judges who devoted only part of their time to the courts; the unequal financing of courts in various parts of a state; and long delays in litigation, among other deficiencies.

Two sets of reforms have been particularly important. One set focuses on the structure of the judiciary. The other speaks to the character of those who serve on the courts.

Structural Reforms

The organization of most state courts developed in a fairly haphazard fashion over the past two hundred years. Prior to the reforms of the past several decades, state court systems had changed little since their creation. The result was state court systems

> characterized by overlapping jurisdictions and confusing, complex judicial organizations that functioned with difficulty. The resulting proliferation and duplication of courts meant both wasted resources and uneven justice. . . . Furthermore, no one was actually responsible for the operation or supervision of a state's judiciary as a whole. The fragmented character of the courts and the lack of data, communication, and skilled administrators resulted in an inefficient use of judicial manpower that no overall court authority had the power to remedy. (ACIR 1982: 98)

Although there is much debate over how to correct these and other problems with the courts, reformers have generally agreed on two related areas of structural reforms which, taken together, provide for a more streamlined and centralized state court system.

Consolidation. For many, the most needed reforms are those that simplify and consolidate otherwise fragmented systems of justice. By reducing the number and types of courts, reformers hope to reduce the amount of jurisdictional overlap and confusion. Although prescriptions vary, reform models typically propose a single supreme court, an intermediate appellate court, and a small number of general and specialized trial courts. At the trial level, advocates of consolidation would, for example, create a general consolidated county court to replace a system where there are separate courts for family matters, small claims, divorce, juvenile, and traffic (Glick 1982). Despite the seeming appeal of consolidation, the record to date has been mixed. Currently thirty-nine states have added intermediate appellate courts in an attempt to alleviate the case loads of their supreme courts (Tarr 1994a). In addition, several states have worked at consolidating the lower courts by eliminating specialized and administratively separate trial courts. By the mid-1970s, forty-one states agreed with reformers that there should only be one trial court of general jurisdiction. In addition, nearly half of the states had one or no trial courts of limited jurisdiction. However, only four states limited themselves to a single trial court, and only twelve states had no separately administered specialized courts (Berkson 1978).

Centralization. A second and related area of structural reform aims at achieving some level of centralization of state court systems on grounds of both efficiency and fairness. Proponents of centralized management have proposed that administrative responsibility over the entire state court system should be placed in the hands of the states' supreme courts and professional court administrators. Under such a system, the states' highest courts and their administrative offices would assume responsibility for, among other things, financial management of the states' court systems, the assignment and transfer of judges, establishing standards for the qualification and selection of judges, and the collection and dissemination of data on the operations of the courts. Relatedly, proponents of centralization advocate some degree of centralized rule making by the states' highest courts or, alternately, a judicial council. Under centralized rule making, a state's supreme court or judicial council would set uniform procedures for court operations throughout the state. Finally, many have proposed centralized budgeting and state assumption of court costs. Reformers, for example, have urged the states to adopt a single, statewide consolidated budget for the entire judicial system. Movement to a centralized budget would enhance both the power and the autonomy of the states' judicial branches and their supreme courts. Under most proposals, a centralized budget would not be part of the executive budget and not subject to revision by the states' legislatures. Reformers have also proposed that state governments shoulder most of the responsibility for financing the state courts. Greater assumption by the states of court costs promises a more efficient allocation of resources and reduces the likelihood of disparities between jurisdictions.

Over the past few decades, a fair amount of centralization has been achieved.

- Currently, every state has a professional court administrator.
- By the mid-1980s thirty-two states had given their supreme courts exclusive authority over procedural rule making and eight provided the courts partial authority (ACIR 1982).

- In recent years there has been a substantial increase in state assumption of court costs. In 1970, only a handful of states assumed all or practically all of the expenses of state court operations. By the mid-1980s, over half of the states did so and nearly every state had increased the state share of judicial expenditures (Lim 1986).
- Three-quarters of the states allow their supreme courts to transfer judges (Glick 1982).

Personnel Reforms

A second set of reforms addresses the individuals who serve within the judicial system. Over the past several decades, a number of states have adopted a series of reforms that aim at ensuring a qualified, nonpartisan judiciary. Perhaps the simplest are requirements that individuals have some legal training before they assume the bench. Surprisingly, as recently as 1955, sixteen states still did not have any legal training requirements for judges of the supreme and appellate courts. By the early 1980s, only a handful of states lacked minimal requirements in terms of legal training or experience.

Second, and perhaps more important, are changes in how judges are selected. Reformers have argued that to ensure qualified and nonpartisan judiciaries, judges should be selected on the basis of merit. Under the Missouri Plan, first proposed by the American Bar Association in 1937, justices are appointed by governors from a short list of three to six candidates submitted by a nominating commission, which ostensibly selects individuals on professional, not partisan grounds. Judges who are selected in this fashion serve for a specified period of time and then must stand for reelection in so-called retention elections—contests in which they are the only candidates on the ballot and in which voters indicate whether the individual should remain in office. Today, over one-third of the states use merit plans to select their supreme court justices. Equally important, the number of states relying on explicitly partisan elections has fallen to just eleven (Tarr 1994a).

A final set of personnel reforms concerns judicial discipline and removal. Historically, the states have relied on three traditional mechanisms for removing justices for misconduct—impeachment, popular recall, and legislative address. In practice those methods have proven to be "unwieldy, expensive, and difficult" (ACIR 1982), and as a result, several states have turned to alternative means of ensuring that incompetent judges do not remain in office. A number of states have, for example, imposed a mandatory retirement age on all members of the bench. Despite legal challenges on the basis of age discrimination, mandatory retirement age has been upheld in several instances (Knoebel 1990). In addition, by the early 1980s nearly every state had established some kind of state disciplinary commission to monitor and, in some cases, sanction judicial misconduct (Glick 1982).

The Consequences of Reform

As we have seen, advocates of structural and personnel reforms maintain that changes in the courts will not only produce better judges but also promote greater efficiency, equity, accountability, and judicial independence. Efficiency is achieved by avoiding duplication and providing some flexibility in assigning justices to various court areas where there is the greatest need for their services. Proponents also maintain that centralization of rule-making authority and budgets provides greater equity and accountability. For its part, merit selection ensures an independent judiciary and reduces the role of politics, while still providing that judges are held accountable for their actions on the bench.

Not everyone shares those views. Some contend, for example, that the centralization of state court systems ignores the limits of hierarchy, including a tendency toward rigidity and a stifling of innovation and cooperation (see, most notably, Gallas 1976 and Saari 1976). Critics also point out the problems inherent in implementing court reforms, including the resistance of lower court justices and local actors and the lack of effective sanctions (Tarr 1981; Glick 1982). In a parallel fashion, some contend that a shift toward greater state financing will lessen local influence and autonomy and encourage bean counting, red tape, and fiscal uncertainties (Hudzik 1985). Other analysts are skeptical that merit selection will reduce the role of politics in nominating judges (Bowman and Kearney 1996), whereas others charge that retention elections insulate judges from popular control (Hall and Aspin 1987).

The evidence to date supports both those who commend reform and those who remain skeptical about its effects. For the most part, research to date has concentrated on two aspects of reform—judicial selection, with a particular emphasis on the "merits" of merit selection, and the creation of intermediate appellate courts. With respect to merit selection, the available evidence indicates that its adoption has had little impact on the character, composition, and decisions of the states' highest courts. A study of sitting judges in the early 1980s, for example, discovered that once the effects of region were controlled, merit selection produced few differences in the background characteristics (e.g., education) of judges (Glick and Emmert 1987). That finding, in turn, casts doubt on the assumption that merit plans will produce more qualified justices. Relatedly, there is little reason to believe that judges will subsequently be held accountable by the voting public for their actions on the court. Few citizens actually vote in retention elections and only rarely are judges turned from office. Of the 1,864 retention elections held between 1964 and 1984, for example, the average affirmative vote was 77 percent and in only 22 instances were judges defeated (Hall and Aspin 1987). More recent analysis yields similar results; between 1980 and 1990, only thirty-four judges (1.3 percent) failed to win their retention races and the average margin of approval was 74 percent (Luskin et al. 1994).

Nor is there much evidence that the adoption of merit selection alters the character of judicial decisions. Analysis of dissent rates between 1961 and 1967, for instance, uncovered few differences between alternative methods of judicial selection. Although dissent rates were lower on those courts in which justices were appointed, a comparison of dissent rates between elected courts and courts that had adopted the Missouri Plan revealed no differences in the rates of dissent (Canon and Jaros 1970). Similarly, a fifty-state study of state supreme court decisions during that same period found no relationship between the method of judicial recruitment and the success rates of various groups, including state agencies, corporations, and criminal defendants (Atkins and Glick 1974). Yet another study found little evidence of a direct link between professionalism (measured in part by judicial salaries and method of selection) and the adoption of tort reform (Canon and Baum 1981).

At the same time, other studies indicate that at least some aspects of how judges are selected and the conditions under which they serve influence the character of the decisions they make. A study of the reputations of state supreme courts, for instance, found a consistent link between judicial professionalism and the rate at which state courts are cited by others. In particular, more professional courts, measured in terms of judicial selection, salaries, tenure, and court organization and administration, tended to be cited more often by other courts in the mid-1970s (Caldeira 1983). In addition, research reported by Melinda Hall and Paul Brace indicates that how state supreme court justices are selected *does* shape the character of decisionmaking on the courts. Drawing upon a neo-institutional perspective, the researchers contend that judges who must periodically face voters tend to be less risk averse and subsequently more likely to cast dissenting votes on all but the most publicly salient issues. Support for their hypotheses is found in a number of contexts. In looking at the rates of dissent in forty-eight states in 1966, 1973, and 1981, they find that dissent rates are lower in those states in which justices are appointed by their governors or legislatures (Hall and Brace 1989; Brace and Hall 1990). Subsequent analysis by Brace and Hall (1995) suggests that how judges are selected can indirectly affect judicial decisionmaking as well. Analysis of the individual votes on death penalty cases of supreme court justices in eight states from 1986 through 1988 indicated that whether justices were elected not only exerted a direct influence on individual decisions but also conditioned the influence of other variables. Where judges had to stand for reelection, greater party competition was associated with a greater likelihood that justices would support the death penalty. Analysis of individual justices' death penalty votes in six states in the 1980s uncovered similar tendencies: The effects of partisan competition on dissent rates varied depending on whether justices were selected on partisan ballots. In states using partisan ballots, competition promoted greater dissent. Where those ballots were absent, however, partisan competition tended to yield lower rates of dissent (Brace and Hall 1993). Although Hall and Brace's research does not speak directly to the impacts of merit selection, their analysis is a useful reminder that the institutional character of the courts, in this case method of selection, matters.

So too does the evidence concerning the impact of intermediate courts of appeal. A study of the Maryland Supreme Court, for instance, indicated substantial change in the workings of the court following the creation of an intermediate court in 1967. Following its creation, the high court's caseload not only dropped precipitously for the next several years, but so too did the number of criminal appeals. In addition, as a more manageable caseload allowed the court to more carefully consider the cases before it, the justices wrote longer opinions, cited more federal and state cases, and reversed a larger percentage of lower court decisions (Tolley 1992). Similarly, Hall and Brace's analysis of dissent rates cited earlier finds a much higher rate of dissent in those states with an intermediate court, a finding that they attribute to the reduced nondiscretionary caseload in states with an intermediate court (Hall and Brace 1989; Brace and Hall 1990). Finally, analysis of dissent rates in the fifty states in the mid-1960s suggests that the adoption of an intermediate court of appeals heightens the influence of the court's social and political environment on supreme court decisionmaking. In particular, supreme courts in those states with intermediate courts were more responsive to external influences, including a diverse population and a more competitive political system (Canon and Jaros 1970).

Women and Minorities on the Bench

Despite the often substantial changes that have occurred in state judicial systems, women, blacks, and other minorities still make up a very small percentage of those who serve on the bench. Although the number of women and minorities serving as judges has increased in recent years (in 1991 Minnesota became the first state supreme court with a female majority), those groups are still substantially underrepresented in nearly every state. Nationally, by the mid-1990s, women represented only 18 percent of all supreme court justices and only one state high court judge in twelve was African American (n=17), Asian (5), or Hispanic (6) (Gray and Eisinger 1997). Clearly a lack of minority representation matters. Women state supreme court justices are often more likely to adopt an outsider role by staking out positions on criminal rights, economic liberties, and gender issues that are either more conservative or more liberal than their male counterparts (Allen and Wall 1987). And, although the available research (see, e.g., Uhlman 1978) fails to uncover a relationship between race and judicial decisions, denying ethnic and racial minorities access to the bench is no more acceptable than denying those groups representation in their states' legislatures.

Why have women, blacks, and other minorities fared so poorly in the judicial branch, particularly in light of significant progress in many state legislatures and the Congress? Those tendencies reflect both contextual and structural considerations (Graham 1990a). Contextually, the lack of representation probably reflects the historically low rate at which women and blacks practiced law in most states. According to one source, the best predictor of the rate at which African Americans serve as justices is the percentage of the state's attorneys that are black (Alozie 1988).

Structurally, critics maintain that the various means by which justices are selected, most notably at-large elections but merit plans as well, systematically exclude blacks (and perhaps women) from their state's highest courts. Civil rights activists have long charged that in a world of racial voting (i.e., where whites vote for whites and blacks for blacks) at-large elections, whether they are used to elect legislators or judges, effectively bar blacks from holding public office by diluting the black vote. Merit plans have been challenged as well on the grounds that minorities lack representation on the states' nominating commissions and therefore are less likely to be appointed by their governors. A review of the relevant literature offers some, but not complete, support for critics of elections and merit plans. Graham's (1990a and 1990b) analysis of black judicial representation in thirty-six states is particularly instructive. Although Graham initially found that the formal method of selection seemingly had little effect on black representation (see Dubois 1983, Alozie 1988, and Luskin et al. 1994 for similar results concerning women and racial and ethnic minorities) a more careful analysis of how justices were *actually* selected revealed that blacks are less likely to serve as justices where elections and merit plans are used. In particular, although most black justices served in states that ostensibly rely on some form of election to fill the bench, most of the black justices serving in those states were in fact initially appointed by their governor to fill seats vacated between elections.

Over the last decade or so, minorities have successfully challenged judicial selection schemes on the grounds that they violate Section 2 of the Voting Rights Act (Haydel 1989; McDuff 1989; and Smith and Garmel 1992).

In 1991, civil rights activists won a major victory when the U.S. Supreme Court ruled in *Chisom v. Roemer* and *Houston Lawyers v. Texas Attorney General* that the Voting Rights Act as amended in 1982 applied to judicial elections. As a result of those and earlier rulings, a number of states, primarily in the South, have developed alternatives to at-large districting schemes. In 1987, for example, lawmakers in North Carolina eliminated a number of large, multijudge districts and replaced them with smaller, single-member districts (Jacob 1996). Similarly, in 1988 a federal judge created single-member judicial districts after the Mississippi legislature failed to adopt an alternative to the existing at-large plan of electing justices. In Illinois, lawmakers in the early 1990s adopted an unusual remedy in response to a challenge to their state's system of at-large elections. Under the Illinois plan, lower court judges in Cook County would be initially selected in fifteen single-member districts, six of which would have a black or Hispanic majority, but would subsequently stand for retention in at-large elections (Smith and Garmel 1992; Luskin et al. 1994). In Georgia, an agreement was reached that would have replaced the state's system of elected judges with a merit selection plan. Under the agreement, by 1994 no fewer than twenty-five African Americans would serve as state superior court judges and by 1995 the judicial nominating committee would become the sole nominator for judges (Smith and Garmel 1992). In 1994, no fewer than ten states faced challenges to their judicial selection schemes (Luskin et al. 1994).

Those victories aside, many challenges have been denied by the federal courts, and there is still considerable ambiguity as to when various selection plans run afoul of the Voting Rights Act. In 1992, for instance, federal district courts in Alabama and Florida denied challenges to those states' at-large selection schemes on the grounds that plaintiffs had failed to demonstrate the existence of the three prerequisites established by the U.S. Supreme Court in 1986 in *Thornburgh v. Gingles* as necessary to prove a violation of the Voting Rights Act. In Alabama, the court ruled that although the plaintiffs had demonstrated that African Americans were politically cohesive, they had failed to prove that blacks constituted a sufficiently large and geographically compact block of voters to warrant a single-member district or that black candidates were typically defeated by the white majority. In Florida, the plaintiff's challenge was denied on the grounds that they had failed to demonstrate racial voting (Smith and Garmel 1992). In 1994, the agreement reached earlier in the state of Georgia was struck down by the federal courts as an unwarranted usurpation of the state's legislative power (Gray and Eisinger 1997). The Supreme Court's recent rulings in *Shaw v. Reno* and *Miller v. Johnson* concerning the use of minority access districts will no doubt add to the current legal ambiguity surrounding judicial selection methods and minority protection under the Voting Rights Act.

State Supreme Courts and Public Policy

In addition to the judicial reforms outlined previously, there has been a noticeable increase in recent decades in the willingness and ability of many state supreme courts to tackle difficult and often controversial policy and political issues, often to the dismay of various interest groups and elected officials. State courts have made it less difficult for individuals to seek tort relief; expanded the rights of women and minorities, gays, the handicapped, juveniles, criminal defendants, and the mentally and terminally ill; and effectively reshaped the operations of state prisons and public schools. In the 1970s and 1980s those rulings had a definite liberal bent, particularly in the areas of civil liberties and economic issues. By the 1990s, however, the states' courts, responding to a new wave of conservatism in the American states, moved to the right.

Legal experts tell us that the states' supreme courts have a number of avenues for making public policy: (1) interpretations of state statutes and administrative orders; (2) consideration of precedents and common law doctrine in those areas that do not involve legislation; (3) judicial review of legislation in terms of its constitutionality under federal and state constitutions; and (4) judicial innovation (Glick 1991; Baum 1996). Many of the states' supreme courts have availed themselves of each of those opportunities. In the late 1950s and early 1960s, for instance, a number of states moved quickly to rewrite legal precedent in the area of tort reform and product liability law (more on this later). More recently, supreme courts in more than a dozen states have created new legal policy in terms of the rights of the terminally or seriously ill to end life-prolonging medical treatment (Glick 1991).

Research from a number of quarters suggests that the states' highest courts have been particularly active in exercising their right of judicial review. One study uncovered more than 3,200 challenges to state law across the fifty states between 1981 and 1985 (Emmert 1988, reported in Glick 1991; Emmert and Traut 1992). As one would expect, the largest number of cases involved criminal law, as defendants made last-ditch efforts to overturn their convictions. In addition, however, plaintiffs challenged state laws involving economic regulation (24 percent), private disputes (15 percent), civil rights/liberties (8 percent), and intergovernmental relations (8 percent). Equally important, state courts have frequently agreed with plaintiffs. During the five-year period included in the study, state courts overturned 22.7 percent of all state laws challenged. Although the courts accepted those challenges in only 9 percent of criminal appeals, the rate at which state law was overturned was much higher in other areas of the law. Nearly a quarter of all challenges involving economic regulation and private property matters were declared unconstitutional, as were

TABLE 6.1   The Willingness of State Supreme Courts to Declare State Laws
Unconstitutional, 1981–1985 (number in parentheses represents the proportion
of constitutional challenges upheld by the state's supreme court)

Most Willing	Least Willing
South Carolina (46%)	North Carolina (3%)
Pennsylvania (39)	Iowa (3)
West Virginia (39)	Wyoming (5)
Maryland (38)	Delaware (10)
Alaska (37)	New Mexico (11)
Washington (36)	Arizona (13)
Texas (36)	Colorado (14)
Alabama (35)	Connecticut (14)
Kentucky (33)	Georgia (15)
Oklahoma (32)	Mississippi (15)
Wisconsin (32)	

SOURCE: Compiled from Henry Glick, "Policy Making and State Supreme
Courts," in Gates and Johnson, eds., *The American Courts: A Critical Assessment*
(Washington, D.C.: CQ Press, 1991), pp. 100–101.

34 and 39 percent, respectively, of civil rights/liberty and intergovernmental cases. Not surprisingly, there is a fair amount of variation across
the states. According to the data, the number of challenges over the five-
year period ranged from a low of 25 or fewer in five states (Vermont,
Virginia, Delaware, Hawaii, and Texas) to over 100 challenges in four of
the states (Georgia, Louisiana, Colorado, and Florida). And as Table 6.1
indicates, some state courts, most notably those in South Carolina,
Pennsylvania, and West Virginia, proved much more willing to declare
state laws unconstitutional, whereas others, including North Carolina,
Iowa, and Wyoming, only rarely agreed with plaintiffs.

In most cases, challenges to state law are based on either federal constitutional grounds (34 percent) or a combination of state and federal
grounds (44 percent; see Emmert and Traut 1992). In an increasing number of instances, however, both litigants and the courts are basing challenges to state laws solely on state constitutional grounds. There is evidence, for example, that the willingness of state courts to use their own
constitutions to afford individuals additional rights beyond those guaranteed by the U.S. Constitution began to increase dramatically in the
1970s and 1980s. One study found that the number of such cases went
from just 3 in the 1950s to 177 in the first half of the 1980s (Collins, Galie,
and Kincaid 1986). A more recent analysis of judicial review cases indicates that the proportion of challenges based exclusively on state grounds
had increased from 22 percent in the first half of the 1980s to 28 percent
during the period 1987–1992 (Kramer 1996). Those and similar trends

have been cited as evidence of a "new judicial federalism" in which state courts "exercise their long dormant authority to base the protection of individual rights on independent interpretations of state constitutional rights rather than U.S. constitutional rights" (Kincaid 1988: 163).

The most visible (and controversial) of the new judicial federalism cases are a series of decisions by state courts in the areas of school finance, criminal law, and privacy rights that relied on the states' constitutions to grant litigants additional rights beyond those provided by the U.S. Supreme Court. For many, those decisions were viewed as an antidote to the growing conservatism of the U.S. Supreme Court under Chief Justices Burger and Rehnquist and signaled a growing trend toward more liberal, activist states courts. A more careful review, however, suggests that most challenges to state law that rely solely on state constitutional grounds do not involve civil liberty cases but deal instead with issues "in which the federal constitution may be least relevant" (Glick 1991: 105). Moreover, sifting through judicial review cases, scholars have learned that where there exists analogous federal and state law (which is typically the case in civil liberty suits) litigants and state courts only rarely base their challenges and decisions solely on state constitutional grounds. Less than 5 percent of due process challenges brought before state supreme courts in the first half of the 1980s, for example, were based exclusively on state constitutional law. Only 18 percent of criminal rights cases and 14 percent of bill of rights cases were based solely on state grounds. More generally, where challenges involve both federal and state law, state courts only rarely base their rulings on state law alone. Of the 194 cases involving challenges on both federal and state grounds in which the court overturned state law between 1981–1985, less than 30 percent of those decisions relied exclusively on state grounds, whereas two-thirds were based on both federal and state grounds (Emmert and Traut 1992). Moreover, state courts in the 1990s are likely to be even less willing to use state grounds in those cases involving state and federal challenges (Kramer 1996).

Taken together, recent studies challenge earlier portraits of the new judicial federalism. As it turns out, the new judicial federalism cases only rarely extend individual rights beyond federal guarantees; many of those cases frequently involve matters of minimal interest to the federal courts (e.g., state laws concerning taxing and spending or technical provisions of the law); and as we shall see shortly, often as not state courts have taken a conservative stance. Nonetheless, a review of individual cases indicates that in a number (albeit a small number) of cases, state courts have reached important and far-reaching decisions under the guise of the new federalism in a variety of areas including criminal law, free speech, school finance, and the rights of women. Accordingly, many would agree with Alan Tarr's conclusion (1994b: 78) that although the impacts of a new judicial federalism to date have been limited, nevertheless, having had the experience of interpreting state guarantees and having seen the creation of a body of precedent on which they can draw, neither will state courts return to (an earlier) era's neglect of state protections or thoughtlessly assume that federal and state guarantees offer equivalent protection. Although they may learn from the rulings of the U.S. Supreme Court, they will not slavishly imitate them. Moreover, at times the justices of the U.S. Supreme Court may learn from the initiatives of their sister courts in the "laboratories" of the states. The new judicial federalism may be new no longer, but there is reason to believe that it will not soon disappear.

The willingness of the states' supreme courts to engage in policymaking, including the new judicial federalism of the 1970s and 1980s, is due to a number of factors. Ironically, part of that willingness reflects the state courts' relationship with the U.S. Supreme Court (what Tarr and Porter [1988] refer to as the vertical dimension of judicial federalism). Much of the states' activism in recent years is a legacy of the Warren Court's activism of nearly three decades ago. As Lawrence Baum (1993: 154) notes, "The Warren Court did much to reshape the thinking of lawyers by showing that protection of civil liberties could be an appropriate role for the courts. As judges who received their legal training in the 1960s join the state supreme courts, many bring with them an expectation that the courts should play such a role." That activism also reflects the more conservative bent of the Burger/Rehnquist courts. In a much cited *Harvard Law Review* article, Justice William Brennan in 1977 explicitly encouraged the states to find independent state grounds on which to base additional protection of individual rights in the face of the Court's growing conservatism on matters concerning criminal procedure. In that sense, recent state decisions that take a liberal tack, most notably in the area of criminal procedures, are seen as a means of mitigating the U.S. Supreme Court's recent retreat on doctrines established during the liberal Warren Court. Relatedly, the states' activism in the 1980s also reflected the lack of consensus found in the Supreme Court as Warren Court holdovers, most notably Brennan and Marshall, consistently dissented from rulings inconsistent with those made earlier. Some have argued that a lack of consensus has produced vague and less than persuasive Supreme Court decisions and the need for clarification at the state level (see, e.g., Kincaid 1988).

The willingness of the states' supreme courts to venture into policymaking also reflects the courts' relationship with one another (horizontal judicial federalism). Although there is no legal obligation for state courts to rely on the decisions of their counterparts in other states, for a variety of reasons—a reliance on precedent and similar policy concerns and substantive laws—they do. Indeed, Baum (1993) and others suggest that a momentum often develops; once a doctrine is adopted by a number of states, many others follow almost as a matter of course. Tort reform provides an excellent example. Following landmark decisions in New Jersey,

Michigan, and California in the late 1950s and early 1960s, rulings that
substantially increased the liability of manufacturers for defective products, states moved with "unprecedented speed" to adopt similar doctrines; five did so in 1965, seven in the following two years, five more in
1968–1969 and six in 1970–1971 (Baum and Cannon 1982). Analysis of
right-to-die cases in the fifteen or so states that had ruled on that issue by
the early 1990s indicates that the diffusion of legal innovations is not necessarily uniform, however. As Henry Glick (1991: 107) discovered "instead of a single, uniform innovation, state supreme courts soon produced several different streams of policy and substantially reinvented the
policy during the diffusion process, with very different impacts on later
adopting courts."

Much of the impetus for judicial policymaking comes from within the
states themselves. Many of the elements of the courts' policymaking activities are found in the unique constitutional and legal environment in
which state courts operate. Unlike the federal constitution, state constitutions are much more explicit about limits on their legislatures. In many
instances it is the courts that are responsible for enforcing those restrictions, a role that necessarily increases their policy role (Galie 1987).
Similarly, state constitutions are often more explicit in outlining individual rights. State supreme court activism in the area of educational finance
is an example. States whose constitutions are more explicit about the educational "rights" of the public and that include equal protection and due
process guarantees that go beyond federal standards tend more often to
strike down their state system of funding education (Swinford 1991). In
addition, because state constitutions often give the state supreme courts
broad supervisory powers over the judiciary system, including authority
concerning rules of evidence and discovery, those courts are freer from
legislative intrusions and in a better position to ensure individual rights.

More broadly, there is good reason to believe that the policymaking activities of the states' supreme courts have been and will continue to be
conditioned by the larger political environment in which the courts operate. In particular, there is evidence to suggest that judicial decisions
often reflect the ideological character of the state. Gregory Caldeira's
(1983) analysis of the reputation of state supreme courts in the mid-1970s,
for example, finds a strong bivariate relationship between his measure of
state policy liberalism and the rate at which state courts are cited by others. Similarly, using the political ideology of the state's congressional delegation as an indicator of state ideology, Hall and Brace (1996: 250) discover that "justices in liberal states are less likely than justices in
conservative states to support the imposition of the death penalty." There
is also evidence to suggest that activism responds to the public's ideology. Herbert Jacob (1996), for instance, reports a moderately strong rela-

tionship between the public's ideology and the willingness of state courts to expand privacy rights. As one would expect, supreme courts located within states with more liberal publics were more likely to expand privacy rights.

Judicial activity in three areas—tort reform, education, and criminal law procedure—are discussed next in order to more fully illustrate the impact and limits of recent judicial activism.[1] Taken together they illustrate the complexities and conflicts associated with this aspect of the states' resurgence.

Tort Reform

Tort reform—in particular, product liability law—has long been the subject of state court rulings. Until the last two to three decades, state courts typically relied on two legal doctrines to limit relief to consumers who suffered death, injury, or damage from a faulty product. Under the negligence rule, plaintiffs had to prove not only that they had suffered as a result of a defective product, but that the injury was foreseeable *and* that the manufacturer had neglected to take corrective action. Consumer relief was also limited by the privity rule, which limited liability to those who sold the product directly to the consumer. State courts set limits on each of these doctrines early in the twentieth century, but it was not until the late 1950s and early 1960s that activist courts in Michigan (1958), New Jersey (1960), and California (1963) completely rejected each of those rules (Baum 1993). In its 1963 ruling in *Greenman v. Yuba Power Products*, the California court provided that manufacturers were strictly liable for any damages resulting from a defective product. Over the next dozen years, the majority of the states moved quickly to adopt this stricter view of liability (Baum and Canon 1982). What accounted for the dramatic changes in tort doctrine? A number of factors were apparently at play. First, developments associated with the industrial revolution, most notably an increase in work-related injuries and the number of consumer products available on the market, created both a need for relief as well as a heightened awareness of the problem. Second, the courts' decisions also grew out of changes in legal philosophy, including a growing acceptance of the notion that individuals should be liable for their actions. Third, tort reform reflects a larger willingness on the part of state supreme court justices to set aside the doctrine of *stare decisis* in favor of greater assertiveness and activism (Tarr 1994a).

Not surprisingly, the courts' decisions have produced a great deal of controversy and backlash, and the issue of tort reform has spilled over, often in a dramatic fashion, into the states' politics. In recent years, business interests, insurance companies, and some in the medical community have joined forces to challenge what they see as a dangerous pro-plaintiff trend in the state courts. One approach defendant groups have taken is to mount advertising and information campaigns aimed at convincing judges, policymakers, and the public that new liability doctrines promote excessive and often unwarranted litigation and undercut America's economic competitiveness (Baum 1996). A more direct approach has been attempts by defendant groups to replace pro-plaintiff justices with judges likely to take a pro-business approach. Those efforts have often transformed judicial elections in states such as Alabama, Michigan, North Carolina, and Texas into expensive, heated contests pitting defendant groups against the states' trial lawyers. The politics of tort reform have been particularly intense in Alabama, a state whose court has a reputation for being unusually generous to plaintiffs in liability cases. Over the past several years, elections for Alabama's highest courts have dominated state electoral politics, as both sides of the tort debate have sought to elect justices favorable to their positions. In 1994, business groups succeeded in narrowly defeating the chief justice. Two years later, trial lawyers and defendant groups spent an estimated $5 million in a race for a seat on the state's supreme court that ultimately led to the defeat of the incumbent Democratic justice. Tort warfare is likely to continue in Alabama in 1998 when the terms of three justices will expire (Rossakoff 1996).

By all counts, the opposition of defendant groups has proven effective. Several states have enacted changes in product liability law aimed at making it more difficult or less lucrative for litigants to sue. For their part, the supreme courts in a number of states are moving more cautiously in liability suits and, in some instances, have issued rulings making it more difficult to win liability claims (Baum 1996). And in 1995, each house of the U.S. Congress passed legislation limiting liability suits in both federal and state cases.

Criminal Law

Criminal law procedure provides a second example of state court activism and illustrates the importance of the vertical dimension of judicial federalism. Over the past three decades, a number of state courts have moved to broaden the protections afforded criminal defendants on independent state constitutional grounds. They have done so ostensibly in reaction to the narrowing of those protections by the Burger/Rehnquist Courts. Barry Latzer's (1991) analysis of state supreme court decisions, for example, uncovered over 700 instances between the late 1960s and 1989 in which the courts based their rulings in criminal procedures cases on state constitutional grounds. In many instances, those decisions expanded or protected the rights of criminal defendants. Four states—California, Colorado, Massachusetts, and Oregon—overturned their state's death penalty. In addition, a number of states moved to reinstate defendant protection from unreasonable search and seizure following the U.S. Supreme Court's adoption of "good faith" exceptions to the exclusionary rule (Baum 1993).

Although state court rulings in this area have indeed been innovative and demonstrate the courts' resurgence and assertiveness, those rulings need to be placed in perspective. In the first instance, many of the more liberal rulings have met with stiff opposition from legislators and citizens. Voters in a number of states have used initiatives and retention elections to challenge more liberal criminal law rulings. In Massachusetts (1982) and California (1972), for example, voters reestablished the death penalty in the wake of their state supreme court's decision to overturn it (Baum 1993). In 1982, Florida and California adopted constitutional amendments to narrow the exclusionary rule in their states, again in reaction to what was perceived as liberal rulings by the states' highest courts. In addition, a number of judges have faced challenges in subsequent elections for their decisions on criminal law, most notably the death penalty. The defeat of California's Chief Justice Rose Bird and two of her colleagues in their retention elections during the 1980s is largely attributable to their opposition to the death penalty and a well-organized campaign to punish them for that opposition.

Lazter's analysis of state supreme courts and criminal law procedure is particularly instructive. Although Lazter counted more than 200 instances in which courts in forty-four states relied on independent state grounds to reject U.S. Supreme Court doctrine, state courts were twice as likely to *adopt* the Court's doctrine. Table 6.2 highlights that tendency. As part of his analysis, Lazter identifies "high rejectors and adopters." High rejectors are state supreme courts that disagreed with the Supreme Court at least three-quarters of the time, whereas high adopters agreed with the high court at the 75 percent rate. As the table illustrates, the number of high adopters far surpasses the number who regularly reject U.S. Supreme Court doctrine. Only four states fall into the high rejection grouping, and of these, two (Florida and California) do so only until the early 1980s. In contrast, twenty-two states are listed in the table as high adopters. Lazter concludes that "the conservative Burger/Rehnquist majority is 'winning.' That is, the New Federalism has not been a repudiation of its approach and an endorsement of the more defendant-oriented Brennan-Marshall perspective" (p. 194).

Lazter's analysis suggests that if state courts have become more active, they often do so in a conservative fashion. To account for that complex-

TABLE 6.2   The States and the U.S. Supreme Court: Rejection and Adoption of
Supreme Court Doctrine by State Courts

Rejecting States	*Adopting States*
California (before 1983)	Illinois
Alaska	Nebraska
Florida (before 1983)	Iowa
Massachusetts	Wisconsin
	North Carolina
	Connecticut
	Maryland
	Delaware
	Wyoming
	Missouri
	Kansas
	Ohio
	Florida (after 1983)
	Texas
	Kentucky
	New Hampshire
	North Dakota
	Michigan
	South Dakota
	Utah
	Idaho
	Maine

NOTE: Includes states that had rendered five or more state constitutional rulings in criminal cases between the late 1960s and 1989 and had disagreed (rejecting states) or agreed (adopting states) with U.S. Supreme Court doctrine at
least 75% of the time. States listed by rate of rejection or adoption.

SOURCE: Compiled from Barry Latzer, "The Hidden Conservatism of the State
Court Revolution," *Judicature* 74 (1991): 190–197.

ity, Lazter draws upon a framework initially developed by Tarr and
Porter (1988). In particular, Lazter maintains that more active, yet conservative, state court doctrine reflects the vertical and horizontal dimensions
of judicial federalism as well as intrastate pressures on state supreme
courts. In terms of the states' relations with the U.S. Supreme Court, "the
general thrust of vertical federalism has been to pressure state courts to
adopt U.S. Supreme Court decisions" (p. 195), but to do so from independent constitutional grounds. The pressure to rely on state constitutional precepts reflects the horizontal dimension of judicial federalism.
According to Lazter, the increasing tendency to rule on state constitutional grounds stems, to a large degree, from a tendency on the part of
state courts to attend to and emulate developments in other states. As

New York, California, and others increasingly turned to their own state constitutions in reaching decisions, many of the remaining states adopted the practice in an effort to avoid appearing backward or out of touch with the latest developments in state law. That those decisions would take on a conservative tinge, however, is further explained by the states' internal politics and the backlash in many states to more liberal state and federal rulings in the area of criminal law and the rights of the accused.

Education Finance

A third area in which state courts have exhibited greater activism in recent years is educational finance. Traditionally, public schools have relied on the local property tax to finance education. The result is often glaringly disparate funding levels between more and less affluent districts. In the late 1960s and early 1970s, those inequalities were challenged in federal court on grounds that they violated the equal protection clause of the Fourteenth Amendment. However, after winning their case at the federal district court level, litigants were denied relief by the U.S. Supreme Court. In *San Antonio Independent School District v. Rodriguez* (1973), the Supreme Court overruled the lower court's decision and, on a 5–4 vote, ruled that the U.S. Constitution did not require equal educational funding. Challenges to inequity in school finance and quality did not end there, however. Even before the Rodriguez ruling, parents from low-income districts had begun to seek relief from their state courts and on state constitutional grounds.

In 1973, just days after the Rodriguez ruling, the New Jersey Supreme Court ruled in *Robinson v. Cahill* (1973) that the state's system of educational finance violated the state's constitutional guarantee of a "thorough and efficient education." The Robinson case was very important and has become a landmark decision. Not only did the decision revive the campaign to reform school finance, but it demonstrated that the state courts could, and in many cases would, independently rule on the issue with little review from the federal courts (Tarr 1994a). Over the next two decades, supreme courts in over half the states agreed to hear cases challenging school finance plans and in fourteen instances declared those plans invalid (Baum 1996). Those challenges occurred in two waves. In the 1970s and early 1980s, critics challenged finance schemes on equity grounds, pointing to the often substantial disparities that existed between a state's richest and poorest school districts. During those years, the states' courts issued seventeen decisions and, in seven cases, overturned school financing arrangements. Prompted by the first wave of challenges, altogether twenty-eight states passed education finance reforms between 1971 and 1981 (Goertz 1996). Despite those efforts, funding inequities among school districts remained largely unchanged (Odden 1992), and in the late 1980s and early 1990s, a second wave of finance challenges occurred. The second wave of challenges not only addressed questions of equity, but educational adequacy as well. In Kentucky, for example, the court ruled the state's educational system invalid for failing to meet the state constitution's mandate for a "thorough and efficient" education (Lewis and Maruna 1996). Between 1989 and 1994, the states' courts issued fourteen decisions on education finance and in nine instances (Alabama, Arizona, Kentucky, Massachusetts, Missouri, Montana, New Jersey, Tennessee, and Texas) ruled that state funding systems were unconstitutional (Goertz 1996).

But mandating educational change and actually achieving it are two different things. In the final analysis, state supreme courts cannot effect educational reform on their own. The effectiveness of their decisions rests in large part on the willingness of the other branches to comply with court rulings. Asking states to redesign their systems of finance not only proves to be costly but generates considerable political conflict. And requiring that schools provide an adequate or quality education requires not only resources but ideas and workable solutions to the problems of American education. Often, the most the courts can do is to set an agenda for other state policymakers to address as they can and will (Tarr 1994a). Given these difficulties, it is not surprising that many states have moved slowly to correct the problems of educational finance. With the exception of a few states, such as Kentucky, state legislatures and governors have not only delayed in responding to the court's mandates but have often sought ways of circumventing court-ordered changes. In West Virginia, for example, it took the state ten years to comply with the 1979 decision that declared the state's system of school finance unconstitutional, as policymakers wrestled with the issue of property tax reassessment and the state's lack of resources. Similarly, in New Jersey several years passed before finance reforms were passed and implemented (Tarr 1994a).

Summary

A review of state court actions in three areas illustrates both the potential and constraints of the states' supreme courts as policymakers. On the one hand, more assertive courts have effected a great deal of change in their states. Educational and tort reforms are just two of several areas in which the courts have precipitated larger and far-reaching changes in state policy. And by choosing to act, state courts in some instances have offered an alternative to an increasingly conservative U.S. Supreme Court.

On the other hand, a review of the three policy areas reveals a number of factors that mitigate the impact of more active supreme courts as agents of policy change. First, the evidence makes clear that not all state courts have been active or, for that matter, liberal. The reader will note that supreme courts in slightly less than half of the states have chosen not to rule on the constitutionality of their schools' funding. And as the cases of education funding and criminal procedure illustrate, even when state courts do choose to address those issues, they are as likely as not to side with the status quo. State court decisions in those areas are particularly instructive because they demonstrate that activism and policy liberalism are not one and the same. Frequently state courts have become more active in the sense of choosing to rule on broader matters of law and policy but in doing so have adopted conservative doctrine. What that suggests is that as the states and their legislatures and governors become more conservative in the years ahead, so too will those who are selected to serve on the states' supreme courts. If that occurs and state courts continue to be active, the result may well be a new round of conservative rulings. There is some evidence that this is already occurring. In recent years, for example, state courts in both North Dakota and New Hampshire have issued conservative rulings that expand individual property rights.

Second, the case of education funding demonstrates how dependent the courts are on other branches to realize mandated changes. Although the courts have some sanctioning authority (at one point the New Jersey court simply closed down the state's school system), more typically they must negotiate with legislatures and governors to find workable solutions to the problems they have identified. Moreover, in many cases, challenges and opposition to court rulings have produced delays in compliance and, in the area of criminal law and tort reform, ultimate reversals in state policy.

Third, state court activism is necessarily constrained by the federal system in which it operates. The trend toward the development of independent state constitutional doctrine is limited in a couple of ways. Most of the significant constitutional issues that state courts might consider have already been decided by the U.S. Supreme Court. Under the supremacy clause of the U.S. Constitution those decisions are binding on the states. Relatedly, state courts must consider Supreme Court doctrine in order to ensure that federal minimal standards have been met (Lazter 1991).

Implications for Governing

As we have seen, the states' courts have undergone considerable change in recent years. Among other things, several states have attempted to restructure their court systems through consolidation and centralization, put into place reforms intended to ensure that more qualified individuals serve as judges, seen an increase in the number of women and minorities serving on the courts, and seen their courts become more willing to review a wider range of policy issues. Although the evidence is mixed, there is some reason to believe those changes have mattered; in many instances, judicial reforms have influenced the character of judicial decisions, and judicial activism has frequently altered the nature of state policy.

The larger question is whether those changes have contributed to the quality of governing in the states. As was the case with governors, legislatures, and demand-side changes, the record to date suggests that judicial reforms and developments over the past several decades have promoted statehouse democracy and the ability of state governments to govern wisely in many but not all instances.

In terms of statehouse democracy and responsiveness, the courts have attempted to walk a fine line between accountability and responsibility. A number of reforms have sought to reduce the role of politics and partisanship in judicial decisions, while promoting accountability. Clearly, for many that was the rationale for merit plans. As we have seen, however, those efforts have not been very successful. Evidence from a number of quarters suggests that merit plans have had little impact on the kinds of individuals who serve on the courts. The evidence on accountability is particularly troublesome. In addition, despite recent gains, women and minorities still serve on the states' highest courts in unacceptably small numbers. More broadly, judicial elections in California, Texas, Alabama, and elsewhere illustrate how politically charged state judicial elections can become and how interest groups often are able to shape the decisions of the states' highest courts. Nonetheless, evidence of a link between public opinion and the ideological thrust of the courts is particularly heartening and demonstrates that, limits on recent reforms aside, the courts do listen to their publics. And that, ultimately, bodes well for the quality of statehouse democracy.

Similar conclusions can be reached concerning the ability of the states' supreme courts to fashion coherent workable policies. Although merit plans have probably had little impact on the caliber of sitting justices, other structural reforms, most notably the creation of intermediate appellate courts, have provided the states' supreme courts with a critical resource—time and smaller caseloads—essential for becoming deliberative norm-enforcement and policymaking institutions. In addition, the courts' rulings in the area of tort reform, school finance, civil liberties, criminal law, and other areas are clear evidence of the courts' willingness and ability to assert their policymaking role. And although those rulings have often generated considerable controversy and resistance, the fact of the matter is that many of those decisions filled a vacuum created by the inaction of the states' governors and legislators. School finance decisions in a number of states, for instance, have provided the impetus for much needed and larger educational reforms. Similarly, recent right-to-die decisions have been reached because interest groups and state lawmakers were unable to find acceptable political solutions to an important policy issue.

At the same time, our review of the courts as policymakers demonstrates that the courts, not unlike the governors and legislatures, face a number of limits. As the case of education financing reveals, the courts are frequently dependent upon others to implement their decrees, others who often lack the capacity and the will to carry out the courts' decisions. In addition, a more careful review of the new judicial federalism indicates that the states' courts are exercising more restraint than scholars initially perceived. Moreover, the courts' experiences in the areas of tort reform and criminal law illustrate how other political actors, including state legislators, interest groups, the federal courts, and the U.S. Congress, can alter, indeed nullify the actions of the states' highest courts.

NOTES

1. This section builds upon a similar discussion provided by Baum (1993 and 1996).

7

Summary and Conclusions

$\mathbf{A}$s the 1990s come to a close, it is increasingly clear that the political landscape of American politics has undergone fundamental change. Nowhere is that more evident than in the reordering of American federalism. As the nation moves into the twenty-first century, more and more of the governing of America will move to the states. A devolution of authority began during the Reagan years, but political developments in the 1990s, most notably Republican victories in 1994 and presidential politics in 1996, promised to accelerate the rate at which state governments assume greater responsibility for governing the nation.

Coupled with that development is the sense among observers that state governments, long perceived as the weakest link in American politics, are now perhaps the strongest. That conclusion reflects fundamental changes in the character of state politics and government, changes many argue increase substantially the governing capacity of the states. On the demand side of government, more citizens have more opportunities to participate in politics and policy than ever before. On the supply side, legislatures have become more professional and representative, a new kind of governor armed with more formal powers and resources has emerged, and state courts have restructured themselves and, in many cases, become more active participants in state politics and policy. In addition, the states are increasingly serving as policy laboratories producing innovative solutions to pressing problems of public policy.

Others take a less benign view of recent political changes, however, and offer a second and more problematic perspective on the states' ability to govern, one in which state politics and government suffer the same kinds of problems—partisanship, political deadlock, and inordinate interest group influence—that characterize national politics. Many worry, for example, that demand-side changes have worked disproportionately to the advantage of organized interests and accentuate the role and influence of money in state electoral politics. Others submit that as each of the three branches of state government become stronger, greater institutional conflict and stalemate will occur, particularly as divided government becomes the norm. Still others are concerned that legislatures have become fragmented, captured by their members and lobbyists, too partisan, and less able to serve as responsible deliberative bodies.

In short, as America enters the new century, two views of the states' ability to govern and govern wisely have emerged—an optimistic perspective that is becoming the new conventional wisdom of American political thought and a second, more pessimistic view that questions whether state governments are as ready to govern as many imagine. As it turns out, the evidence to date provides support for *both* perspectives. Indeed, if there is one overarching conclusion that can be drawn from the dozens of studies reviewed in the preceding chapters, it is that political changes in the American states have both contributed to *and* detracted from the quality of statehouse democracy and the ability of the states to govern in a responsible manner.

In the pages that follow I take one last look at the resurgence of the states and the implications of that development for American government in an effort to pull together what has been said so far. I begin by summarizing the implications for statehouse democracy and policy responsibility of the various supply- and demand-side changes outlined throughout the text. The chapter ends with some concluding remarks concerning the ability of the states to govern in the twenty-first century.

Political Change and Statehouse Democracy

Many of the momentous changes that have occurred throughout the American states touch on the ability of the states to govern in a democratic fashion. Changes on both the supply and demand sides of state governments both promote and inhibit statehouse democracy. Table 7.1 summarizes what we have learned to date about those impacts. As the table indicates, a number of changes have had a net positive impact on statehouse democracy. On the demand side, several reforms and developments have increased the ability of citizens and groups to access, influence, and participate in government. In the early 1960s and beginning with its decision in *Baker v. Carr*, the U.S. Supreme Court instigated a reapportionment revolution that ultimately gave urban America greater representation in the states' legislatures and, in many instances, altered the character of state policy. Equally important, federal civil rights policies produced a second revolution in state politics by guaranteeing racial and ethnic minorities the right to vote and hold office. The results have often been dramatic. By the 1990s, racial and ethnic minorities served in state government and the Congress in record numbers. More recently,

TABLE 7.1   Demand- and Supply-Side Changes and Statehouse Democracy

	Impact on Statehouse Democracy
Demand-side changes	
Reapportionment	Positive
Civil rights policy	Positive
Electoral reforms	Positive
Increased use of initiative and referendum	Mixed
Citizen participation requirements	Positive
Transformed electoral politics	Mixed
Political party resurgence	Mixed
Changing interest group politics	Mixed
Supply-side changes	
Governors	
Centralizing reforms	Positive
Candidate-centered campaigns	Positive
Legislatures	
Increases in women/minorities	Positive
Decentralization	Positive
Professionalism	Positive
Judicial reforms	Mixed

state and federal authorities have sought to simplify the act of voting for millions of Americans by making it easier to register and, in many states, allowing individuals to vote by mail or prior to election day. Not only have state and federal laws promoted higher rates of voter turnout, but in doing so, they have produced taxing and spending policies that are more progressive and generous to the poor. Other reforms and developments have allowed citizens to more directly influence government. Open meeting laws, public hearing requirements, and proxy advocates are being used more frequently throughout the states to afford citizens more opportunities to offer input into government between and in addition to elections.

Changes on the supply side of state government have also had a positive impact on statehouse democracy. Although the changing character of the states' governors speaks more directly to policy responsibility, reforms that reduce executive branch fragmentation and give America's governors more control over the executive branch provide citizens with more of an opportunity to hold governors accountable for their and the executive branch's action. And, as gubernatorial races become more candidate-centered, voters will have even more opportunity to do so. A number of changes within legislatures have contributed to the quality of representation as well. Most important perhaps is the increase in the number of women and minorities that serve as lawmakers. In addition, as power within legislatures becomes more widely distributed, the ability of various interests to have a place at the legislature's "table" is increased. Moreover, greater legislative professionalism often makes it easier for legislators to resist the blandishments of lobbyists and the organized interests they represent. More professional legislators are also better able (and often more willing) to attend to the concerns and interests of their constituents.

The impact of other developments on statehouse democracy has been more variable. The increasing use of the initiative and referendum has, for instance, allowed citizens in a number of states to directly influence public policy by placing issues on the ballot (most notably term limits and taxing and spending limitations) that otherwise would not have made it onto the states' policy agenda. At the same time, direct democracy has, more often than not, fallen short of its goals. The available evidence suggests that turnout is generally no higher in issue elections than it is in candidate elections and there is little reason to believe, except in the most unusual cases, that initiatives and referenda have promoted a more open and informed discussion of public issues. More seriously, there is a concern that direct democracy has become just one more opportunity for well-funded interest groups to exert inordinate influence over state governments. Relatedly, although the changing nature of interest group politics has often ensured that a wider range of interests will influence the decisions of state government, on balance the increasing influence of lobbyists and PACs has probably detracted from more than it has contributed to the quality of statehouse democracy, as lawmakers become too dependent on PAC contributions and too responsive to interest group pressures. State party reforms have been a mixed blessing as well. As I argued in Chapter 3, the resurgent state parties have the potential to serve as a centripetal force in an increasingly fragmented system of state politics. As state party organizations grow stronger, as leadership and party PACs become more involved in raising and distributing campaign funds, and as some measure of national-state party integration takes place, the opportunity for parties to play an organizing role in both elections and governing increases. Unfortunately, the record to date suggests that this opportunity is largely foregone. The emergence of leadership PACs, for example, often undermines state party organizations, preempts the local parties, and further fragments the parties. And although an infusion of national party moneys into state party coffers appears, at first glance, to represent an opportunity for integrating the nation's political parties, a closer look reveals that state parties are often no better off once elections are over and national party money and personnel pull out.

The changing contours of the states' electoral politics have had a mixed effect on the quality of representation as well. On the one hand, as fewer voters rely on party cues, as campaigns become candidate-centered, and as lawmakers and governors become more visible, ordinary citizens have more opportunities to identify and assess the performance of those they elect. On the other hand, other elements of the transformation of the states' electoral dynamics make it more difficult for citizens to participate in those activities. In particular, as campaigns become more expensive and as organized groups and the money they offer become an increasing part of both governing and electioneering, ordinary citizens are more likely to be crowded out of the electoral system, as both candidates and significant influences on elected officials.

The impact of recent changes within the state courts on statehouse democracy is difficult to gauge. On balance, those changes have contributed little to the quality of representation. The adoption of merit plans, for example, has not increased voter interest, information, or turnout in judicial elections. Moreover, recent elections in Alabama, Texas, and elsewhere raise the possibility that the inordinate interest group influence that we have witnessed in those states may become more prevalent in judicial races, particularly as the courts issue more rulings of interest to organized groups. In addition, and despite recent gains, women and minorities are still underrepresented on most courts. At the same time, evidence that examines the fit between public opinion and state supreme court decisions provides some reason to believe that many, perhaps most, state courts are mindful of what their publics want.

Political Change and Policy Responsibility

The quality of state government is measured not only in how representative and democratic it is, but also whether and to what extent governing is carried out in a coherent and effective manner. There is considerable disagreement as to what constitutes responsible government and, in particular, what institutional arrangements and processes are necessary for achieving it. However, there is some consensus that, at a minimum, effective governing requires that governments act in a timely fashion to resolve conflicts and avoid stalemate and, ultimately, produce innovative and effective policy solutions. Against those very general benchmarks, it is fair to conclude that political and institutional developments at the state level in recent decades have, at one and the same time, made state governments more *and* less responsible. Those who serve in state governments are more professional and capable and have more of the resources they need to develop and implement coherent public policies. Over the past several decades, the American states have frequently served as policy laboratories where new ideas and innovations have been developed and diffused to other states. At the same time, other aspects of

TABLE 7.2   Demand- and Supply-Side Changes and Policy Responsibility

	Impact on Policy Responsibility
Demand-side changes	
Proliferation of interest groups	Negative
Transformed electoral politics	Negative
Increased use of initiative and referendum	Mixed
Supply-side changes	
Governors	
Increases in formal powers/resources	Positive
New kind of governor	Positive
Legislatures	
Greater professionalism	Positive
Procedural reforms	Positive
Increase in staff	Positive
Legislative assertiveness	Mixed
Careerism	Mixed
Greater partisanship	Negative
Term limits	Negative
The Courts	
Structural reforms	Positive
Judicial activism	Positive
Interinstitutional conflict	Negative
Divided government	Negative

the states' political development on both the supply and demand side of government have promoted greater political fragmentation and decentralization and, in doing so, have made it more difficult for state policy actors to govern and to govern wisely. The implications for policy responsibility of demand- and supply-side changes are summarized in Table 7.2.

An enduring legacy of many of the changes that have occurred on the demand side of state governments is that more people and groups have more opportunities to influence government than ever before. And that makes for better statehouse democracy. Yet, as the states' political systems become open to a wider range of interests, those interests need to be accommodated in the actions and decisions of state government, and the potential for conflict, stalemate, and policy incoherence necessarily increases. The problem is made worse by the proliferation of interest groups and changing state electoral politics. As we saw in Chapter 3, the number of lobbyists and PACs has increased dramatically in recent years. One estimate indicates that as many as 42,000 lobbyists currently ply their trades in the states' capitals. In addition, a much wider range of interests are now represented in the states' interest group systems. Those groups are well funded, and are highly effective at pressing their claims. Moreover, divided control of state government, greater institutional assertiveness and rivalry, and a decentralization of power within many legislatures provide organized interests more venues than ever to do so. Transformed state electoral politics represent an additional centrifugal force on state politics and governing. As state elections become candidate-centered and as more individuals make lawmaking a career, the incentive to avoid difficult and controversial decisions and to concentrate on "bringing home the bacon" to constituents becomes more prevalent and compelling.

More particularly, the tendencies toward decentralization that emerge from the demand side of state government and politics undercut policy responsibility in at least two ways. First, the combination of reelection-oriented lawmakers and active and well-organized interest groups places pressures on state governments to traffic in particularized benefits. In doing that, state governments are not only likely to spend more than they can afford but they are also likely to substitute a patchwork of programs that address parochial and specialized interests for coherent policies that systematically and comprehensively address major policy problems. Second, as the number and diversity of organized interests continues to climb, state lawmakers will find it increasingly difficult to fashion consensus on the difficult policy issues facing their states. As the conflict between competing groups grows more intense and more difficult to resolve, one of two equally distasteful policymaking results—stalemate or incrementalism—is likely to occur. Ideally, transformed and resurgent state parties might serve as an antidote to decentralizing tendencies in state politics and government. Unfortunately, the emergence of LCCs and national-state party integration may actually undercut the ability of state parties to serve as a centralizing force in state politics.

For their part, initiatives have been a mixed blessing for responsibility. While direct democracy has usefully expanded the states' policy agenda, some worry that it produces bad policy as a result of inordinate interest group influence, a lack of information among ordinary citizens, and how decisions are structured.

In terms of responsibility, the more important changes have occurred on the supply side of government. A number of developments within each branch of state government have increased substantially the states' ability to govern by bringing more qualified and energetic individuals to state government and giving them the resources they need to carry out their many responsibilities. Governors now have more of the formal powers and resources they need to develop, sell, and implement major policy initiatives. Today's governors are also younger, better prepared in terms of prior government service, and as the recent case of welfare reform illustrates, emerging as an important source of policy innovation. The governing capacity of state legislatures has increased as well. State legislatures are increasingly populated by full-time professionals, many of whom serve as policy entrepreneurs. In the 1990s, legislatures have more time, use that time more efficiently, and can draw upon the expertise of specialized staff. Today's legislatures are typically more active as policy innovators and in performing their oversight responsibilities. For their part, the states' highest courts have benefited from structural changes, most notably the creation of intermediate appellate courts, that allow high court justices to attend more carefully to difficult policy issues that come before the court. In addition, many state courts have proven more than willing to set legal precedent and public policy in a number of policy areas, including tort reform, education, and civil liberties. Research from a number of quarters illustrates that those developments contribute to policy responsibility. States with more professional legislatures are more assertive and independent from their governors and more likely to develop innovative policies that are ultimately effective. Similar findings obtain for the governors. Increases in the formal powers and resources of the states' governors have often yielded innovative and effective policies. Finally, although the evidence is mixed, there is some reason to believe that various attempts at reforming the judiciary have contributed to the quality of judicial decisionmaking.

Although many of the changes that have occurred on the supply side of government have made state governments more responsible, many of those developments, as well as others, have also made governing more problematic. There is, for example, some concern that as legislatures mature they may become less able to function as deliberative bodies capable of fashioning solutions to difficult policy problems. Ironically, a key element of that incapacity is the careerism that comes with the greater professionalism of many state legislatures. Although careerism produces a more capable legislator in many instances, it also promotes a fixation on reelection, greater partisanship, and heightened parochialism as individual members seek to exploit institutional resources to pursue their electoral needs. More broadly, a number of developments within legislatures, including careerism, candidate-centered elections, a redistribution of responsibility to committees and legislative staff, declining institutional loyalty, and the increasing importance of lobbyists and PACs, make legislatures more fragmented and decentralized. Decentralized legislatures, in turn, find it much more difficult to reach consensus and are less willing to legislate in the broader interests of the state. A further irony is found in the adoption of term limits in a number of states. Although term limits may reduce legislative careerism, there is little reason to believe their adoption will promote greater policy responsibility and good reason for suspecting that limits will detract from responsibility as legislatures become populated by more inexperienced members who are less committed to their institutions and more dependent on their staff, the executive branch, and lobbyists for information and expertise.

There is also the concern that as legislators, the courts, and the governors come into their own, greater conflict will occur as the respective branches assert their institutional wills. The problem is made worse by the increasing presence of divided government. Although the evidence here is also mixed, there is reason to suspect that divided government will undercut policy responsibility either by contributing to conflict and stalemate or, alternatively, fiscal irresponsibility.

The States and Governing in the Twenty-First Century: Some Concluding Thoughts

A review of the record to date indicates that state governments are neither as capable and representative as the new conventional wisdom of American federalism might suggest nor as dysfunctional and inept as cynics might maintain. As we have seen, there is no shortage of evidence to support (and refute) each perspective. So what can be concluded about the ability of the states to govern in the next century? Clearly, the states are better prepared to govern than they have been for a long time. Indeed, the principal conclusion that can be drawn from the states' evolution is that the performance gap between state and federal authorities that was so glaring just three decades ago has, for the most part, closed. A history of politics and policy in America in the 1970s, 1980s, and 1990s illustrates not only the limits of the federal government but the capabilities of the American states as well. As the federal government wrestles with its deficit, divided government, and the attendant conflict and stalemate those things produce, state governments must increasingly turn inward to their revitalized institutions to find novel solutions to policy problems that have eluded federal authorities. For good or bad, those trends will continue.

At the same time, it would be premature to assume, as many do, that state governments are necessarily *better* able to govern than their federal counterparts. As we saw throughout the chapters, state governments share many of the same political pathologies—political gridlock, partisanship, ethical problems, and PAC-dominated politics—that plague national politics. And many analysts agree that the states' budgets are more fragile than the robust economy of the mid-1990s would indicate. None of this should come as a surprise to the reader. After all, state governments share the same constitutional framework as the national government, and state politics and political figures are as susceptible to the decentralizing pressures of organized interests and political ambition that Americans have come to associate with politics as usual in the nation's capital. Relatedly, both federal and state authorities face the same skeptical electorate. The nearly universal adoption of term limits in those states with initiatives illustrates how much Americans distrust public officials at *all* levels of government.

Those problems aside, as the relative capacities of state and federal governments converge, there is the potential for both governments to become true partners in governance, something the nation has rarely achieved. However, this partnership will require not only capable governments, but something that may prove even more elusive in today's political climate—consensus on how responsibility for governing should be apportioned within our federal system of government. As it turns out, there is some agreement among many in academe and in government on a "sorting out" theory that would place redistributive responsibilities at the federal level while delegating development programs (e.g., education, infrastructure, economic development) to the state and local level (see, most notably, Peterson 1995; Rivlin 1992). According to this view, market forces and the necessity to compete for both citizens and firms make state and local governments ideal candidates to take the lead in development issues, while those same forces compel a federal presence in redistributing wealth in society. Unfortunately, there is little evidence that those who actually make the decisions, Congress and the president, will heed that advice or, for that matter, draw upon an alternative set of principles for dividing up the responsibility for governing. Instead, the division of authority between the national and subnational governments will continue to reflect the tugging and pulling of partisan politics. As we saw in the case of welfare, fundamental decisions about who will do what have more to do with presidential politics, the federal deficit, and public opinion than any attempt to fashion agreement on a larger paradigm for parceling out responsibility in our much changed federal system. Finding that agreement may be the crucial challenge of American federalism and governance in the next century.

References

CHAPTER 1 — INTRODUCTION

Bingham, Richard D., and David Hedge. 1991. *State and Local Government in a Changing Society*, 2nd ed. New York: McGraw-Hill.

Brace, Paul. 1993. *State Government and Economic Performance*. Baltimore: Johns Hopkins University Press.

Cutler, Lloyd N. 1985. "To Form a Government." In Donald L. Robinson, ed., *Reforming American Government: The Bicentennial Papers of the Committee on the Constitutional System*. Boulder: Westview Press.

Dye, Thomas R. 1988. "A Theory of Competitive Federalism." Presented at the annual meeting of the Southern Political Science Association, Atlanta, November 3–5.

Erikson, Robert S., Gerald C. Wright, and John P. McIver. 1993. *Statehouse Democracy: Public Opinion and Policy in the American States*. New York: Cambridge University Press.

Fiorina, Morris. 1996. *Divided Government*, 2nd ed. Needham Heights, MA: Simon & Schuster.

"Governors Add Conservative Themes to Their Agendas for Next Few Years: States Look for Ways to Cut Taxes, Reform Welfare, Shrink Government." *Washington Post*, January 29, 95: A18.

Hill, Kim Quaile. 1994. *Democracy in the Fifty States*. Lincoln: University of Nebraska Press.

Meyer, Michael. 1992. "Another Lost Generation." *Newsweek*, May 4: 70–72.

Nathan, Richard P. 1996. "The Role of the States in American Federalism." In Carl Van Horn, ed., *The State of the States*, 3rd ed. Washington, DC: CQ Press.

Osborne, David. 1988. *Laboratories of Democracy: A New Breed of Governor Creates Models for National Growth*. Boston: Harvard Business School Press.

Peirce, Neal. 1991. "State Leadership for the Nation." *The Journal of State Government* (Jan./March): 27–29.

Ridley, Scott. 1987. *The State of the States*. Washington, DC: Fund for Renewable Energy and the Environment.

Rieselbach, Leroy N. 1994. *Congressional Reform: The Changing Modern Congress*. Washington, DC: CQ Press.

Rivlin, Alice M. 1992. *Reviving the American Dream: The Economy, the States, and the Federal Government*. Washington, DC: Brookings Institution.

Robinson, Donald L., ed. 1985. *Reforming American Government: The Bicentennial Papers of the Committee on the Constitutional System*. Boulder: Westview Press.

Strawn, Julie, Sheila Dacey, and Linda McCart. 1994. *Final Report: The National Governors' Association Survey of State Welfare Reforms*. Washington, DC: National Governors' Association.

Van Horn, Carl E. 1989. "The Quiet Revolution." In Carl E. Van Horn, ed., *The State of the States*. Washington, DC: CQ Press.

_____. 1996a. "The Quiet Revolution." In Carl E. Van Horn, ed., *The State of the States*, 3rd ed. Washington, DC: CQ Press.

_____. 1996b. "Power to the States." In Carl E. Van Horn, ed., *The State of the States*, 3rd ed. Washington, DC: CQ Press.

Victor, Kirk. 1990."State-Style Safety." *National Journal*, February 24: 440–443.

Weaver, R. Kent, and Bert A. Rockman, eds. 1993. *Do Institutions Matter? Government Capabilities in the United States and Abroad*. Washington, DC: Brookings Institution.

Wilson, Woodrow. 1981. *Congressional Government: A Study in American Politics*. Baltimore: Johns Hopkins University Press.

CHAPTER 2—DEMAND-SIDE CHANGES:
ELECTIONS AND CITIZEN PARTICIPATION

Advisory Commission on Intergovernmental Relations (ACIR). 1980. *Citizen Participation in the American Federal System*. Washington, DC: U.S. Government Printing Office.

AllPolitics. 1996a. "Ballot Measures by State." On-line posting. Available: http://allpolitics.com/1996/news/9610/31/ballots. (October 31, 1996).

_____. 1996b. "Ballot Measures by Topic." On-line posting. http://all-politics.com/1996/news/9611/02/ballots. (November 2, 1996).

Barnes, James A. 1990. "Losing the Initiative." *National Journal*, September 1: 2046–2047.

Bennett, Stephen Earl, and David Resnick. 1990. "The Implications of Nonvoting for Democracy in the United States." *American Journal of Political Science* 34: 771–802.

Beyle, Thad. 1996. "Governors: The Middlemen and Women in Our Political System." In Virginia Gray and Herbert Jacob, eds., *Politics in the American States*, 6th ed. Washington, DC: CQ Press.

Bibby, John F., and Thomas M. Holbrook. 1996. "Parties and Elections." In Virginia Gray and Herbert Jacob, eds., *Politics in the American States*, 6th ed. Washington, DC: CQ Press.

Bingham, Richard D., and David Hedge. 1991. *State and Local Government in a Changing Society*. New York: McGraw-Hill.

Bowman, Ann O'M., and Richard C. Kearney. 1996. *State and Local Government*. Boston: Houghton Mifflin.

Bullock, Charles S., III. 1992. "Minorities in State Legislatures." In Gary F. Moncrief and Joel A. Thompson, eds., *Changing Patterns in State Legislative Careers*. Ann Arbor: University of Michigan Press.

Busch, Andrew E. 1996. "Early Voting: Convenient, but . . . ?" On-line posting. Available: http://www.ncsl.org.ote96/earlyart.html. (November 6).

Cavanaugh, Thomas. 1991. "When Turnout Matters: Mobilization and Conversion as Determinants of Election Outcomes." In William Crotty, ed., *Political Participation and American Democracy*. New York: Greenwood Press.

Cronin, Thomas E. 1988. "Public Opinion and Direct Democracy." *PS: Political Science and Politics* 22: 612–619.

_____. 1989. *Direct Democracy*. Cambridge: Harvard University Press.

Davidson, Chandler. 1992. "The Voting Rights Act: A Brief History." In Bernard Grofman and Chandler Davidson, eds., *Controversies in Minority Voting*. Washington, DC: Brookings Institution.

Dye, Thomas R. 1965. "Malapportionment and Public Policy in the States." *Journal of Politics* 27: 586–601.

_____. 1994. *Politics in States and Communities*. Englewood Cliffs, NJ: Prentice Hall.

Erikson, Robert. 1971. "The Partisan Impact of State Legislative Reapportionment." *Midwest Journal of Political Science* 15: 57–71.

Everson, David H. 1981. "The Effects of Initiatives on Voter Turnout: A Comparative State Analysis." *Western Political Quarterly* 34: 415–425.

Feig, Douglas G. 1978. "Expenditures in the American States: The Impact of Court-Ordered Legislative Reapportionment." *American Politics Quarterly* 6: 309–315.

Fenster, Mark J. 1994. "The Impact of Allowing Day of Registration Voting on Turnout in U.S. Elections from 1960 to 1992: A Research Note." *American Politics Quarterly* 22: 74–87.

Foster, David. 1994. "States Get Creative to Raise Voter Turnout." *Nation's Cities Weekly*. October 31: 10.

Frederickson, G., and Y. H. Cho. 1974. "Legislative Apportionment and Fiscal Policy in the American States." *Western Political Quarterly* 27: 18.

Glass, David, Peverill Squire, and Raymond Wolfinger. 1984. "Voter Turnout: An International Comparison." *Public Opinion* (December/January): 49–55.

Godschalk, D., and B. Stiftel. 1981. "Making Waves: Public Participation in State Planning." *Journal of Applied Behavioral Science* 17: 597–614.

Gormley, William T., Jr. 1983. *The Politics of Public Utility Regulation*. Pittsburgh: University of Pittsburgh Press.

_____. 1986. "The Representation Revolution: Reforming State Regulation Through Public Representation." *Administration & Society* 18: 179–196.

_____. 1989. *Taming the Bureaucracy*. Princeton: Princeton University Press.

_____. 1993. "Accountability Battles in State Administration." In Carl E. Van Horn, ed., *The State of the States*, 2nd ed. Washington, DC: CQ Press.

Gray, Virginia, and Peter Eisinger. 1997. *American States and Cities*. New York: Addison-Wesley.

Grofman, Bernard, and Lisa Handley. 1991. "The Impact of the Voting Rights Act on Black Representation in Southern State Legislatures." *Legislative Studies Quarterly* 16: 111–128.

Herrmann, Frederick M., and Ronald D. Michaelson. 1994. "Financing State and Local Elections: Recent Developments." In Council of State Governments, *The Book of the States*. Lexington, KY: Council of State Governments.

Hill, Kim Quaile. 1994. *Democracy in the Fifty States*. Lincoln: University of Nebraska Press.

Hill, Kim Quaile, and Jan E. Leighley. 1992. "The Policy Consequences of Class Bias in State Electorates." *American Journal of Political Science* 36: 351–365.

Hill, Kim Quaile, Jan E. Leighley, and Angela Hinton-Anderson. 1995. "Lower-Class Mobilization and Policy Linkage in the U.S. States." *American Journal of Political Science* 39: 75–86.

Hofferbert, Richard I. 1966. "The Relation Between Public Policy and Some Structural and Environmental Variables in the American States." *American Political Science Review* 60: 73–82.

Idelson, Holly. 1996. "Minority-District Decisions Lay No Clear Guidelines." *Congressional Quarterly Weekly Report* June 15: 1679.

Jacob, Herbert. 1964. "The Consequences of Malapportionment: A Note of Caution." *Social Forces* 43: 256–261.

Joint Center for Political and Economic Studies. 1993. *Black Elected Officials: A National Roster 1993*. Washington, DC: Joint Center for Political and Economic Studies.

Kehler, David, and Robert M. Stern. 1994. "Initiatives in the 1980s and 1990s." In Council of State Governments, *The Book of the States*. Lexington, KY: Council of State Governments.

Knack, Stephen. 1995. "Does 'Motor Voter' Work? Evidence from State-Level Data." *Journal of Politics* 57: 796–811.

Maggiotto, Michael A., Manning J. Dauer, Steven G. Koven, Joan S. Carver, Joel Gottlieb. 1985. "The Impact of Reapportionment on Public Policy: The Case of Florida, 1960–1980." *American Politics Quarterly* 13: 101–121.

Magleby, David B. 1984. *Direct Legislation*. Baltimore: Johns Hopkins University Press.

_____ . 1988. "Taking the Initiative: Direct Legislation and Direct Democracy in the 1980s." *PS: Political Science and Politics* 21: 601–607.

Martinez, Michael D. 1997. "Don't Tax You, Don't Tax Me, Tax the Fella Behind the Tree: Partisan and Turnout Effects on Tax Policy." *Social Science Quarterly* 78: 895–906.

Mazmanian, Daniel, and Paul Sabatier. 1980. "A Multivariate Model of Public Policy Making." *American Journal of Political Science* 24: 439–468.

Moore, W. John. 1988. "Election Day Lawmaking." *National Journal*, September 17: 2296–2301.

National Association of Latino Elected and Appointed Officials (NALEO). 1994. *National Roster of Hispanic Elected Officials*. Washington, DC: NALEO.

Neal, Tommy. 1992. "The Sky-High Cost of Campaigns." *State Legislatures* (May): 16–22.

Oliver, J. Eric. 1996. "The Effects of Eligibility Restrictions and Party Activity on Absentee Voting and Overall Turnout." *American Journal of Political Science* 40: 498–513.

O'Rourke, Timothy G. 1980. *The Impact of Reapportionment*. New Brunswick: Transaction Books.

Parker, Paul E., and James T. Przybylski. 1993. "It's in the Mail—Present Use and Future Prospects of Mail Elections." *State and Local Government Review* 25: 97–106.

Patterson, Samuel. 1976. "American State Legislatures and Public Policy." In Herbert Jacob and Kenneth Vines, eds., *Politics in the American States*, 3rd ed. Boston: Little, Brown.

PBS. 1996. "The People and the Power Game—The Unelected: Lobbies and the Media." Hedrick Smith Productions.

Peterson, Paul E., and Mark Rom. 1989. "American Federalism, Welfare Policy, and Residential Choices." *American Political Science Review* 83: 711–728.

Piven, Frances Fox, and Richard A. Cloward. 1996. "Northern Bourbons: A Preliminary Report on the National Voter Registration Act." *PS: Political Science & Politics* 29: 39–42.

Rhine, Staci L. 1995. "Registration Reform and Turnout Change in the American States." *American Politics Quarterly* 23: 409–426.

Ringquist, Evan J., Kim Quaile Hill, Jan E. Leighley, and Angela Hinton-Anderson. 1997. "Lower-Class Mobilization and Policy Linkage in the States: A Correction." *American Journal of Political Science* 41: 339–344.

Rosenbaum, Walter A. 1983. "The Politics of Public Participation in Hazardous Waste Management." In James P. Lester and Ann O'M. Bowman, eds., *The Politics of Hazardous Waste Management*. Durham, NC: Duke University Press.

Rosener, Judy. 1982. "Making Bureaucrats Responsive: A Study of the Impact of Citizen Participation and Staff Recommendations on Regulatory Decision Making." *Public Administration Review* 42: 339–345.

Rosenstone, Steven J., and Raymond E. Wolfinger. 1978. "The Effect of Registration Laws on Voter Turnout." *American Political Science Review* 72: 22–45.

Saffell, David C. 1982. "Reapportionment and Public Policy: State Legislators' Perspectives." In Bernard Grofman, Arend Lijphart, Robert B. McKay, and Howard A. Scarrow, eds., *Representation and Redistricting Issues*. San Diego: DC Heath.

Schutz, Howard. 1983. "Effects of Increased Citizen Membership on Occupational Licensing Boards in California." *Policy Studies Journal* 2: 504–516.

Salmore, Stephen A., and Barbara G. Salmore. 1993. "The Transformation of State Electoral Politics." In Carl E. Van Horn, ed., *The State of the States*, 2nd ed. Washington, DC: CQ Press.

Teixeira, Ruy A. 1992. *The Disappearing American Voter*. Washington, DC: Brookings Institution.

Zisk, Betty H. 1987. *Money, Media, and the Grass Roots*. Newbury Park, CA: Sage Publications.

CHAPTER 3—DEMAND-SIDE CHANGES: POLITICAL PARTIES AND INTEREST GROUPS

Advisory Commission on Intergovernmental Relations (ACIR). 1986. *The Transformation in American Politics: Implications for Federalism*. Washington, DC: U.S. Government Printing Office.

Alexander, Herbert E. 1991. *Reform and Reality, The Financing of State and Local Campaigns*. New York: Twentieth Century Fund Press.

Bernstein, Marver. 1955. *Regulating Business by Independent Commission*. Princeton: Princeton University Press.

Berry, William D. 1984. "An Alternative to the Capture Theory of Regulation." *American Journal of Political Science* 28: 524 558.

Bibby, John F. 1994. "State Party Organizations: Coping and Adapting." In L. Sandy Maisel, ed., *The Parties Respond: Changes in American Parties and Campaigns*, 2nd ed. Boulder: Westview Press.

Bibby, John F., and Thomas M. Holbrook. 1996. "Parties and Elections." In Virginia Gray and Herbert Jacob, eds., *Politics in the American States: A Comparative Analysis*, 6th ed. Washington, DC: CQ Press.

Biersack, Robert. 1994. "Hard Facts and Soft Money: State Party Finance in the 1992 Federal Elections." In Daniel M. Shea and John C. Green, eds., *The State of the Parties: The Changing Role of Contemporary American Parties*. Lanham, MD: Rowman & Littlefield Publishers.

Boulard, Gary. 1996. "Lobbyists as Outlaws." *State Legislatures* (January): 20–25.

Bullock, Joyce. 1994. "State Lobby Laws in the 1990s." In Council of State Governments, *The Book of the States 1994–95*. Lexington, KY.: Council of State Governments.

Chi, Keon S. 1992. "Financing State and Local Elections: Trends and Issues." In Council of State Governments, *The Book of the States 1992–93*. Lexington, KY: Council of State Governments.

Cingranelli, David L. 1993. "New York: Powerful Groups and Powerful Parties." In Ronald J. Hrebenar and Clive S. Thomas, eds., *Interest Group Politics in the Northeastern States*. University Park, PA: The Pennsylvania State University Press.

Conlan, Timothy, Ann Martino, and Robert Dilger. 1984. "State Parties in the 1980s: Adaptation, Resurgence, and Continuing Constraints." *Intergovernmental Perspective*. 10: 6–13.

Cotter, Cornelius P., James L. Gibson, John F. Bibby, and Robert J. Huckshorn. 1984. *Party Organizations in American Politics*. New York: Praeger Publishers.

Council of State Governments. 1996. *The Book of the States 1996–97*. Lexington, KY: Council of State Governments.

Downs, Anthony. 1957. *An Economic Theory of Democracy*. New York: Harper.

Erickson, Robert S., Gerald C. Wright, and John P. McIver. 1993. *Statehouse Democracy: Public Opinion and Policy in the American States*. Cambridge: Cambridge University Press.

Gibson, James L., Cornelius P. Cotter, John F. Bibby, and Robert J. Huckshorn. 1983. "Assessing Party Organizational Strength." *American Journal of Political Science* 27: 193–222.

Gierzynski, Anthony. 1992. *Legislative Party Campaign Committees in the American States*. Lexington: The University of Kentucky Press.

Gormley, William. 1982. "Alternative Models of the Regulatory Process." *Western Political Quarterly* 35: 297–317.

_____ . 1983. *The Politics of Public Utility Regulation*. Pittsburgh: University of Pittsburgh Press.

Gray, Virginia, and David Lowery. 1993. "The Diversity of State Interest Groups Systems." *Political Research Quarterly* 46: 81–97.

_____ . 1995. "Interest Representation and Democratic Gridlock." *Legislative Studies Quarterly* 20: 531–552.

Gurwitt, Rob. 1992. "The Mirage of Campaign Reform." *Governing* (August): 48–55.

Hall, Richard L., and Frank W. Wayman. 1990. "Buying Time: Moneyed Interests and the Mobilization of Bias in Congressional Committees." *American Political Science Review* 84: 797–820.

Herrmann, Frederick M., and Ronald D. Michaelson. 1994. "Financing State and Local Elections: Recent Developments." In Council of State Governments, *The Book of the States 1994–95*. Lexington, KY: Council of State Governments.

Hill, Kim Quaile. 1994. *Democracy in the Fifty States*. Lincoln: University of Nebraska Press.

Hodgkin, Douglas I. 1993. "Maine: From the Big Three to Diversity." In Ronald J. Hrebenar and Clive S. Thomas, eds., *Interest Group Politics in the Northeastern States*. University Park: Pennsylvania State University Press.

Hrebenar, Ronald J., and Clive S. Thomas, eds. 1987. *Interest Group Politics in the American West*. Salt Lake City: University of Utah Press.

_____ . 1992. *Interest Group Politics in the Southern States*. Tuscaloosa: University of Alabama Press.

_____ . 1993a. *Interest Group Politics in the Midwestern States*. Ames: Iowa State University Press.

_____ . 1993b. *Interest Group Politics in the Northeastern States*. University Park: Pennsylvania State University Press.

Huntington, Samuel. 1952. "The Marasmus of the ICC: The Commission, the Railroads, and the Public Interest." *Yale Law Journal* 61: 467–509.

Jackson, Robert. 1992. "Effects of Public Opinion and Political System Characteristics on State Policy Outputs." *Publius: The Journal of Federalism* 22: 31–46.

Judd, Alan. 1996. "Buying Influence." *Gainesville Sun*, February 18: G–1+.

Lester, James P., James L. Franke, Ann O'M. Bowman, and Kenneth W. Kramer. 1983. "Hazardous Wastes, Politics, and Public Policy: A Comparative State Analysis." *Western Political Quarterly* 36: 257–281.

Lippincott, Ronald C., and Larry W. Thomas. 1993. "Maryland: The Struggle for Power in the Midst of Change, Complexity, and Institutional Constraints." In Ronald J. Hrebenar and Clive S. Thomas, eds., *Interest Group Politics in the Northeastern States*. University Park: Pennsylvania State University Press.

Meier, Kenneth J. 1987. "The Political Economy of Consumer Protection: An Examination of State Legislation." *Western Political Quarterly* 40: 343–359.

Moore, W. John. 1987. "Have Smarts, Will Travel." *National Journal* 19: 3020–3025.

Morehouse, Sarah McCally. 1981. *State Politics, Parties, and Policy*. New York: Holt, Rinehart and Winston.

Neal, Tommy. 1992. "The Sky-High Cost of Campaigns." *State Legislatures* (May): 16–22.

_____ . 1995. *Campaign Finance, Lobbying, and Ethics Legislation 1994*. Denver: National Conference of State Legislatures.

_____ . 1996. *Campaign Finance, Lobbying, and Ethics Legislation 1995*. Denver: National Conference of State Legislatures.

Opheim, Cynthia. 1991. "Explaining the Differences in State Lobby Regulation." *The Western Political Quarterly* 44: 405–421.

Patterson, Samuel C. 1993. "The Persistence of State Parties." In Carl E. Van Horn, ed., *The State of the States*, 2nd ed. Washington, DC: CQ Press.

Peterson, Walfred H. 1987. "Washington: The Impact of Public Disclosure Laws." In Ronald J. Hrebenar and Clive S. Thomas, eds., *Interest Group Politics in the American West*. Salt Lake City: University of Utah Press.

Prochnow, Tyler. 1994. *Campaign Finance Legislation 1993*. Denver: National Conference of State Legislatures.

Ringquist, Evan J. 1993. *Environmental Protection at the State Level: Politics and Progress in Controlling Pollution*. Armonk, NY: M.E. Sharpe.

Rohde, David. 1991. *Parties and Leaders in the Postreform Congress*. Chicago: University of Chicago Press.

Rosenthal, Alan. 1993. *The Third House: Lobbyists and Lobbying in the States*. Washington, DC: CQ Press.

Rosenthal, Cindy Simon. 1994. "Where's the Party?" *State Legislatures* (June): 31–37.

Shea, Daniel M. 1995. *Transforming Democracy: Legislative Campaign Committees and Political Parties*. Albany: State University of New York Press.

Stigler, George. 1971. "The Theory of Economic Regulation." *Bell Journal of Economics and Management Science* 2: 3–21.

Thomas, Clive S., and Ronald J. Hrebenar. 1990. "Interest Groups in the States." In Virginia Gray, Herbert Jacob, and Robert B. Albritton, eds., *Politics in the American States*, 5th ed. Scott Foresman, Little Brown.

_____ . 1991. "Nationalization of Interest Groups and Lobbying in the States." In Allan J. Cigler and Burdett A. Loomis, eds., *Interest Group Politics*, 3rd ed. Washington, DC: CQ Press.

_____ . 1996. "Interest Groups in the States." In Virginia Gray and Herbert Jacob, eds., *Politics in the American States: A Comparative Analysis*, 6th ed. Washington, DC: CQ Press.

Wiggins, Charles W., Keith E. Hamm, and Charles G. Bell. 1992. "Interest-Group and Party Influence Agents in the Legislative Process: A Comparative State Analysis." *The Journal of Politics* 54: 82–100.

Williams, Bruce, and Albert Matheny. 1984. "Testing Theories of Social Regulation: Hazardous Waste Regulations in the American States." *Journal of Politics* 46: 428–459.

Wright, John R. 1996. *Interest Groups and Congress: Lobbying, Contributions, and Influence*. Boston: Allyn and Bacon.

Zeigler, L. Harmon. 1983. "Interest Groups in the States." In Virginia Gray, Herbert Jacob, and Kenneth N. Vines, eds., *Politics in the American States: A Comparative Analysis*, 4th ed. Boston: Little, Brown.

CHAPTER 4 — THE GOVERNORS

Abney, Glenn, and Thomas P. Lauth. 1987. "Perceptions of the Impact of Governors and Legislatures in the State Appropriations Process." *Western Political Quarterly* 40: 335–342.

Alt, James, and Robert Lowry. 1994. "Divided Government, Fiscal Institutions, and Budget Deficits: Evidence from the States." *American Political Science Review* 88: 811–828.

Baranowski, Michael. 1995. "The Formal Powers of the Governor: A Brief Investigation." Presented at the meeting of the Southern Political Science Association, Tampa, November 1–4.

Barrilleaux, Charles, and Robert Crew. 1991. "Political Institutions and Public Policy in the American States." Presented at the annual meeting of the American Political Science Association, Washington, DC, August 29–September 1.

Bernick, E. Lee. 1979. "Gubernatorial Tools: Formal vs. Informal." *Journal of Politics*" 41: 656–664.

Beyle, Thad. 1988. "The Governor as Innovator in the Federal System." *Publius* 18: 131–152.

_____ . 1989. "From Governor to Governors." In Carl E. Van Horn, ed., *The State of the States*. Washington, DC: CQ Press.

_____ . 1990. "Governors." In Virginia Gray, Herbert Jacob, and Robert Albritton, eds., *Politics in the American States*, 5th ed. Foresman, Little, and Brown.

_____ . 1992a. "New Governors in Hard Economic and Political Times." In Thad Beyle, ed., *Governors and Hard Times*. Washington, DC: CQ Press.

_____ . 1992b. "The Executive Branch: Organization and Issues: 1990–91." In Council of State Governments, *The Book of the States 1992–93*. Lexington, KY.: Council of State Governments.

_____ . 1992c. "The Governors, 1990–91." In Council of State Governments, *The Book of the States 1992–93*. Lexington, KY.: Council of State Governments.

_____ . 1993. "Being Governor." In Carl E. Van Horn, ed., *The State of the States*, 2nd ed. Washington, DC: CQ Press.

_____ . 1995a. "Enhancing Executive Leadership in the States." *State and Local Government Review* 27: 18–35.

_____ . 1995b. "Gubernatorial Report Cards: Summer 1994." *Spectrum* (Spring): 14–20.

_____ . 1996a. "Governors: The Middlemen and Women in Our Political System." In Virginia Gray and Herbert Jacob, eds., *Politics in the American States*, 6th ed. Washington, DC: CQ Press.

_____ . 1996b. "Being Governor." In Carl E. Van Horn, ed., *The State of the States*, 3rd ed. Washington, DC: CQ Press.

Bowman, Ann O'M., and Richard C. Kearney. 1986. *The Resurgence of the States*. Englewood Cliffs, NJ: Prentice-Hall.

_____ . 1996. *State and Local Government*, 3rd ed. Boston: Houghton Mifflin.

Brace, Paul. 1993. *State Government and Economic Performance*. Baltimore: Johns Hopkins University Press.

Chi, Keon S., and Dennis O. Grady. 1989. *Innovators in State Governments: Their Organizational and Professional Environment*. Lexington, KY.: Council of State Governments.

Chubb, John E. 1988. "Institutions, the Economy, and the Dynamics of State Elections." *American Political Science Review* 82: 133–154.

Conant, James K. 1992. "Executive Branch Reorganization in the States 1965–91." In Council of State Governments, *The Book of the States 1992–93*. Lexington, KY.: Council of State Governments.

Council of State Governments. 1996. *The Book of the States 1996–97*. Lexington, KY.: Council of State Governments.

Crew, Robert, and Majorie Renee Hill. 1995. "Gubernatorial Influence in State Government Policymaking." Presented at the annual meeting of the Southern Political Science Association.

Dilger, Robert. 1993. "The Governor's Office: A Comparative Analysis." *West Virginia Public Affairs Reporter* 10: 2–12.

_____ . 1994. "Gubernatorial Enabling Resources in West Virginia: A Comparative Analysis." *West Virginia Public Affairs Reporter* 11: 17–22.

Dilger, Robert, George A. Krause, and Randolph R. Moffett. 1995. "State Legislative Professionalism and Gubernatorial Effectiveness." *Legislative Studies Quarterly* 20: 553–565.

Dodd, Lawrence. 1981. "Congress, the Constitution, and the Crisis of Legitimation." In Lawrence Dodd and Bruce Oppenheimer, eds., *Congress Reconsidered*. Washington, DC: CQ Press.

Dometrius, Nelson C. 1979. "Some Consequences of State Reform." *State Government* 54: 93–98.

Dunkelberger, Lloyd. 1994. "MacKay Has Been Much More than a Mere Figurehead," *Gainesville Sun*, October 23: 8A.

Eggers, William D., and John O'Leary. 1994. "Ax Wielders Improve State Governments," *St. Louis Post-Dispatch*, November 23: 7B.

_____ . 1994. "Less Is More: Voters Want a Diet, and Governors Can Cut the Fat." *Roanoke Times & World News*, December 14: A11.

Gable, Richard W. 1992. "California: Pete Wilson, A Centrist in Trouble." In Thad Beyle, ed., *Governors and Hard Times*. Washington, DC: CQ Press.

Ginsberg, Benjamin, and Martin Shefter. 1991. "Electoral Decay and the Power of the American State." In Benjamin Ginsberg and Alan Stone, eds., *Do Elections Matter?* 2nd ed. Armonk, NY: M.E. Sharpe.

"Governors Add Conservative Themes to Their Agendas for Next Few Years: States Look for Ways to Cut Taxes, Reform Welfare, Shrink Government." *Washington Post*, January 29, 1995: A18.

Gray, Virginia, and David Lowery. 1995. "Interest Representation and Democratic Gridlock." *Legislative Studies Quarterly* 20: 531–552.

Hale, Dennis. 1992. "Massachusetts: William F. Weld and the End of Business as Usual." In Thad Beyle, ed., *Governors and Hard Times*. Washington, DC: CQ Press.

Hebert, F. Ted, Jeffrey L. Brudney, and Deil S. Wright. 1983. "Gubernatorial Influence and State Bureaucracy." *American Politics Quarterly* 11: 243–264.

Hedge, David M. 1997. "The Political and Policy Consequences of Institutional Development: The View From the States." Presented at the annual meeting of the Midwest Political Science Association, Chicago, April 10–12.

Holbrook-Provow, Thomas M. 1987. "National Factors in Gubernatorial Elections." *American Politics Quarterly* 15: 471–484.

Meier, Kenneth J. 1980. "Executive Reorganization of Government: Impact on Employment and Expenditures." *American Journal of Political Science* 24: 396–412.

Moe, Terry. 1989. "The Politics of Bureaucratic Structure." In John Chubb and Paul Peterson, eds., *Can the Government Govern?* Washington, DC: Brookings Institution.

Osborne, David. 1988. *Laboratories of Democracy: A New Breed of Governor Creates Models for National Growth*. Cambridge: Harvard Business School Press.

Partin, Randall W. 1995. "Economic Conditions and Gubernatorial Elections: Is the State Executive Held Accountable?" *American Politics Quarterly*. 23: 81–95.

Poterba, James. 1994. "State Responses to Fiscal Crisis: The Effects of Budgetary Institutions and Politics." *Journal of Political Economy* 102: 799–821.

Raimondo, Henry J. 1996. "State Budgeting: Problems, Choices, and Money." In Carl E. Van Horn, ed., *The State of the States*, 3rd ed. Washington, DC: CQ Press.

Ramsey, James R., and Merlin M. Hackbart. 1979. "Budgeting: Inducements and Impediments to Innovations." *State Government* 52: 65–69.

Sabato, Larry. 1978. *Goodbye to Good-time Charlie: The American Governorship Transformed, 1950–75.* Lexington, MA: Lexington Books.

_____ . 1983. *Goodbye to Good-Time Charlie: The American Governor Transformed*, 2nd ed. Washington, DC: CQ Press.

Salmore, Stephen A., and Barbara G. Salmore. 1996. "The Transformation of State Electoral Politics." In Carl E. Van Horn, ed., *The State of the States*, 3rd ed. Washington, DC: CQ Press.

Schick, Allen. 1993. "Governments Versus Budget Deficits." In R. Kent Weaver and Bert A. Rockman, eds., *Do Institutions Matter? Government Capabilities in the United States and Abroad*. Washington, DC: Brookings Institution.

Sigelman, Lee, and Nelson C. Dometrius. 1988. "Governors as Chief Administrators." *American Politics Quarterly* 16: 157–169.

Sigelman, Lee, and Roland Smith. 1981. "Personal, Office, and State Characteristics as Predictors of Gubernatorial Performance." *The Journal of Politics* 43: 169–180.

Simon, Lucinda S. 1986. "Legislatures and Governors: The Wrestling Match." *The Journal of State Government* 59: 1–6.

Sundquist, James. 1992. *Constitutional Reform and Effective Government*. Washington, DC: Brookings Institution.

Svoboda, Craig J. 1995. "Retrospective Voting in Gubernatorial Elections: 1982–1986." *Political Research Quarterly* 48: 135–150.

Sylvester, Kathleen. 1992. "The Weld Experiment." *Governing* (June): 36–40.

Wiggins, Charles W. 1980. "Executive Vetoes and Legislative Overrides in the American States." *The Journal of Politics* 42: 1110–1117.

CHAPTER 5—THE LEGISLATURES

Advisory Commission on Intergovernmental Relations (ACIR). 1982. *State and Local Roles in the Federal System*. Washington, DC: U.S. Government Printing Office.

Beyle, Thad. 1993. "Being Governor." In Carl E. Van Horn, ed., *The State of the States*, 2nd ed. Washington, DC: CQ Press.

Bowman, Ann O'M., and Richard C. Kearney. 1986. *The Resurgence of the States*. Englewood Cliffs, NJ: Prentice-Hall.

Brace, Paul. 1993. *State Government and Economic Performance*. Baltimore: Johns Hopkins University Press.

Bratton, Kathleen, and Kerry Haynie. 1992. "Do Differences Matter? A Study of Race and Gender in State Legislatures." Presented at the annual meeting of the American Political Science Association Chicago, September 3–6.

Breaux, David, and Malcolm Jewell. 1992. "Winning Big: The Incumbency Advantages in State Legislative Races." In Gary Moncrief and Joel A. Thompson, eds., *Changing Patterns in State Legislative Careers*. Ann Arbor: University of Michigan Press.

Button, James, and David Hedge. 1993. "The Quality of Black Legislative Life. Black-White Comparisons." Presented at the annual meeting of the American Political Science Association, September 2–5, Washington, DC.

_____ . 1996. "Legislative Life in the 1990s: A Comparison of Black and White State Legislators." *Legislative Studies Quarterly* 21: 199–218.

Chi, Keon S., and Dennis O. Grady. 1989. *Innovators in State Governments: Their Organizational and Professional Environment*. Lexington, KY.: Council of State Governments.

Citizens Conference on State Legislatures. 1971. *State Legislatures: An Evaluation of Their Effectiveness*. New York: Praeger Publishers.

Corporation for Enterprise Development. 1990. *The 1990 Development Report Card for the States*. Washington, DC: Corporation for Enterprise Development.

Council of State Governments. 1992. *The Book of the States 1992–93*. Lexington, KY.: Council of State Governments.

_____ . 1996. *The Book of the States 1996–97*. Lexington, KY: Council of State Governments.

Ehrenhalt, Alan. 1992. "An Embattled Institution." *Governing* (January): 28–33.

Erickson, Robert S., Gerald Wright, and John P. McIver. 1993. *Statehouse Democracy: Public Opinion and Policy in the American States*. Cambridge: Cambridge University Press.

Ethridge, Marcus. 1984a. "Consequences of Legislative Review of Agency Regulations in Three U.S. States." *Legislative Studies Quarterly* 9: 161–178.

_____ . 1984b. "A Political-Institutional Interpretation of Legislative Oversight Mechanisms and Behavior." *Polity* 17: 340–359.

Francis, Wayne L. 1989. *The Legislative Committee Game*. Columbus: Ohio State University Press.

Freeman, Patricia, and William Lyons. 1992. "Female Legislators: Is There a New Type of Woman in Office?" In Gary Moncrief and Joel A. Thompson, eds., *Changing Patterns in State Legislative Careers*. Ann Arbor: University of Michigan Press.

Goodman, Marshall, Timothy J. Holp, and Eric Rademacher. 1994a. "Legislative Ethics: Reform and Reaction in the States." Presented at the annual meeting of the American Political Science Association, New York, September 1–4.

_____ . 1994b. "State Legislative Ethics: Proactive Reform or Reactive Defense?" Presented at the annual meeting of the Midwest Political Science Association, Chicago, April 14–16.

Goodman, Marshall, Timothy J. Holp, and Karen Ludwig. 1996. "Understanding State Legislative Ethics Reform: The Importance of Political and Institutional Culture." In James S. Bowman, ed., *Public Integrity Annual*, 51–57. Lexington, KY: Council of State Governments.

Gormley, Jr., William T. 1993. "Accountability Battles in State Administration." In Carl E. Van Horn, ed., *The State of the States*, 2nd ed. Washington, DC: CQ Press.

Gurwitt, Rob. 1996. "Greenhorn Government." *Governing* (February): 15–19.

Hamm, Keith. 1986. "Committee Stacking and State Legislative Policy Making: Overrepresentation of Which 'Interesteds'?" Presented at the annual meeting of the American Political Science Association, Washington, DC, August 28–31.

Hamm, Keith, Robert Harmel, and Robert Thompson. 1983. "Ethnic and Partisan Minorities in Two Southern State Legislatures." *Legislative Studies Quarterly* 8: 177–189.

Hansen, Karen. 1994. "Our Beleaguered Institution." *State Legislatures* (January): 12–17.

Hedge, David M., James Button, and Mary Spear. 1992. "Black Leadership in the 1990s." Presented at the annual meeting of the American Political Science Association, Chicago, September 3–6.

_____ . 1996. "Accounting for the Quality of Black Legislative Life: The View from the States." *American Journal of Political Science* 40: 82–98.

Hodson, Timothy, Rich Jones, Karl Kurtz, and Gary Moncrief. 1995. "Leaders and Limits: Changing Patterns of State Legislative Leadership Under Term Limits." *Spectrum* (Summer): 6–15.

Jackson, Robert. 1992. "Effects of Public Opinion and Political System Characteristics on State Policy Outputs." *Publius: The Journal of Federalism* 22: 31–46.

Jewell, Malcolm, and Marcia Whicker. 1994. *Legislative Leadership in the American States.* Ann Arbor: University of Michigan Press.

Jones, Rich. 1987. "Keeping an Eye on State Agencies." *State Legislatures* (July): 20–23.

_____ . 1990. "The State Legislatures." In Council of State Governments, *The Book of the States 1990–91.* Lexington, KY: Council of State Governments.

_____ . 1992. "The State Legislatures." In Council of State Governments, *The Book of the States 1992–93.* Lexington, KY: Council of State Governments.

_____ . 1994. "State Legislatures." In Council of State Governments, *The Book of the States 1994–95.* Lexington, KY: Council of State Governments.

Karnig, Albert, and Lee Sigelman. 1975. "State Legislative Reform and Public Policy." *Western Political Quarterly* 28: 548–553.

Kathlene, Lyn. 1994. "Power and Influence in State Legislative Policymaking: The Interaction of Gender and Position in Committee Hearing Debates." *American Political Science Review* 88: 560–576.

Kurtz, Karl. 1990. "The Changing Legislatures (Lobbyists Beware)." In Public Affairs Council, *Leveraging State Government Relations.* Washington, DC: Public Affairs Council.

Kurtz, Karl T., ed. 1993. "The Old Statehouse, She Ain't What She Used to Be." Edited transcript of concurrent session conducted at the annual meeting of the National Conference of State Legislatures, San Diego, July 26.

Luttbeg, Norman R. 1992. *Comparing the States and Communities.* New York: HarperCollins.

Lyons, William, and Patricia Freeman. 1984. "Sunset Legislation and the Legislative Process in Tennessee." *Legislative Studies Quarterly* 9: 151–159.

Malbin, Michael J., and Gerald Benjamin. 1992. "Legislatures After Term Limits." In Gerald Benjamin and Michael J. Malbin, eds., *Limiting Legislative Terms.* Washington, DC: CQ Press.

Mayhew, David R. 1974. *Congress: The Electoral Connection.* New Haven: Yale University Press.

McCubbins, Matthew, and Thomas Schwartz. 1984. "Congressional Oversight Overlooked: Police Patrols Versus Fire Alarms." *American Journal of Political Science* 28: 165–179.

Miller, Cheryl M. 1990. "Agenda-Setting by State Legislative Black Caucuses: Policy Priorities and Factors of Success." *Policy Studies Review* 9: 339 354.

Moncrief, Gary, Joel Thompson, and Karl Kurtz. 1993. "The Old Statehouse Ain't What It Used to Be: Veteran State Legislators' Perceptions of Institutional Change." Presented at the annual meeting of the American Political Science Association, Washington, DC, September 2–5.

Moncrief, Gary, Joel Thompson, Michael Haddon, and Robert Hoyer. 1992. "For Whom the Bell Tolls: Term Limits and State Legislatures." *Legislative Studies Quarterly* 17: 37–47.

Neal, Tommy. 1992. "The Sky-High Cost of Campaigns." *State Legislatures* (May): 16–20.

_____ . 1995. *Campaign Finance, Lobbying, and Ethics Legislation 1994*. Denver, Colorado: National Conference of State Legislatures.

_____ . 1996. *Campaign Finance, Lobbying, and Ethics Legislation 1995*. Denver, Colorado: National Conference of State Legislatures.

Nelson, Albert J. 1991. *Emerging Influentials in State Legislatures: Women, Blacks, and Hispanics*. New York: Praeger.

Niemi, Richard, and Laura Winsky. 1987. "Membership Turnover in U.S. State Legislatures: Trends and Effects of Districting." *Legislative Studies Quarterly* 12: 115–124.

Opheim, Cynthia. 1994. "The Effect of U.S. State Legislative Term Limits Revisited." *Legislative Studies Quarterly* 19: 49–59.

Patterson, Samuel C. 1990. "State Legislators and the Legislatures." In Virginia Gray, Herbert Jacob, and Robert B. Albritton, eds., *Politics in the American States*, 5th ed. Glenview, IL: Scott Foresman, Little Brown.

_____ . 1996. "Legislative Politics in the States." In Virginia Gray and Herbert Jacob. eds., *Politics in the American States*, 6th ed. Washington, DC: CQ Press.

Pound, William. 1982. "The State Legislatures." In Council of State Governments, *The Book of the States 1982–83*. Lexington, KY: Council of State Governments.

_____ . 1986. "The State Legislatures." In Council of State Governments, *The Book of the States 1986–87*. Lexington, KY: Council of State Governments.

_____ . 1992. "State Legislative Careers: Twenty-Five Years of Reform." In Gary F. Moncrief and Joel A. Thompson, eds., *Changing Patterns in State Legislative Careers*. Ann Arbor: University of Michigan Press.

Prochnow, Tyler. 1994. *Campaign Finance Legislation 1993*. Denver, Colorado: National Conference of State Legislatures.

Ridley, Scott. 1987. *The State of the States*. Washington, DC: Fund for Renewable Energy and the Environment.

Rieselbach, Leroy N. 1977. *Congressional Reform in the Seventies*. Morristown, NJ: General Learning Press.

Ringquist, Evan J. 1993. *Environmental Protection at the State Level: Politics and Progress in Controlling Pollution*. Armonk, NY: M.E. Sharpe.

Ritt, Leonard. 1973. "State Legislative Reform: Does It Matter?" *American Politics Quarterly* 1: 499–509.

Rosenthal, Alan. 1981. *Legislative Life*. New York: Harper & Row.

_____ . 1986. "The Consequences of Constituency Service." *State Government* 59: 25–29.

_____ . 1989. "The Legislative Institution: Transformed and at Risk." In Carl E. Van Horn. ed., *The State of the States*. Washington, DC: CQ Press.

_____ . 1990. *Governors & Legislatures: Contending Powers*. Washington, DC: CQ Press.

_____ . 1992. "The Effects of Term Limits on Legislatures: A Comment." In Gerald Benjamin and Michael J. Malbin, eds., *Limiting Legislative Terms*. Washington, DC: CQ Press.

_____ . 1993. "The Legislative Institution: In Transition and at Risk." In Carl E. Van Horn, ed., *The State of the States*, 2nd ed. Washington, DC: CQ Press.

_____ . 1996. "The Legislature: Unraveling of Institutional Fabric." In Carl E. Van Horn, ed., *The State of the States*, 3rd ed. Washington, DC: CQ Press.

Squire, Peverill. 1988. "Career Opportunities and Membership Stability in Legislatures." *Legislative Studies Quarterly* 13: 65–82.

_____ . 1992. "Legislative Professionalism and Membership Diversity in State Legislatures." *Legislative Studies Quarterly* 17: 69–79.

Thomas, Sue. 1991. "The Impact of Women on State Legislative Policies." *Journal of Politics* 53: 958–975.

Thomas, Sue, and Susan Welch. 1991. "The Impact of Gender on Activities and Priorities of State Legislators." *Western Political Quarterly* 44: 445–456.

Thompson, Joel A. 1986a. "Bringing Home the Bacon: The Politics of Pork Barrel in the North Carolina Legislature." *Legislative Studies Quarterly* 11: 91–107.

_____ . 1986b. "State Legislative Reform: Another Look, One More Time, Again." *Legislative Studies Quarterly* 19: 27–41.

Thompson, Joel A., and Gary Moncrief. 1993. "The Implications of Term Limits for Women and Minorities: Some Evidence from the States." *Social Science Quarterly* 74: 355–364.

Weberg, Brian. 1988. "The Coming of Age of Legislative Staffs." *State Legislatures* (August): 24–27.

_____ . 1997. "New Age Dawns for Legislative Staff." *State Legislatures* (January): 26–31.

Weissert, Carol. 1991. "Policy Entrepreneurs, Policy Opportunists, and Legislative Effectiveness." *American Politics Quarterly* 19: 262–274.

Zeigler, Harmon L. 1983. "Interest Groups in the States." In Virginia Gray, Herbert Jacob, and Kenneth N. Vines, eds., *Politics in the American States*, 4th ed. Boston: Little, Brown.

CHAPTER 6—THE COURTS

Advisory Commission on Intergovernmental Relations (ACIR). 1982. *State and Local Roles in the Federal System*. Washington, DC: U.S. Government Printing Office.

Allen, David W., and Diane E. Wall. 1987. "The Behavior of Women State Supreme Court Justices: Are They Tokens or Outsiders?" *Justice System Journal* 12: 232–244.

Alozie, Nicholas O. 1988. "Black Representation on State Judiciaries." *Social Science Quarterly* 69: 979–986.

Aspin, Larry T., and William K. Hall. 1994. "Retention Elections and Judicial Behavior." *Judicature* 77: 306–315.

Atkins, Burt M., and Henry R. Glick. 1974. "Formal Judicial Recruitment and State Supreme Court Decisions." *American Politics Quarterly* 2: 427–449.

_____ . 1976. "Environmental and Structural Variables as Determinants of Issues in State Courts of Last Resort." *American Journal of Political Science* 20: 97–111.

Baum, Lawrence. 1989. "State Supreme Courts: Activism and Accountability." In Carl E. Van Horn, ed., *The State of the States*. Washington, DC: CQ Press.

_____ . 1993. "Making Judicial Policies in the Political Arena." In Carl E. Van Horn, ed., *The State of the States*, 2nd ed. Washington, DC: CQ Press.

_____ . 1996. "Supreme Courts in the Policy Process." In Carl E. Van Horn, ed., *The State of the States*, 3rd ed. Washington, DC: CQ Press.

Baum, Lawrence, and Bradley C. Canon. 1982. "State Supreme Courts as Activists: New Doctrines in the Law of Torts." In Mary Cornelia Porter and G. Alan Tarr, eds., *State Supreme Courts: Policymakers in the Federal System*. Westport, CT: Greenwood Press.

Berkson, Larry. 1977–78. "Unified Court Systems: A Ranking of the States." *Justice System Journal* 3: 264–280.

Bowman, Ann O'M., and Richard C. Kearney. 1986. *The Resurgence of the States*. Englewood Cliffs, NJ: Prentice-Hall.

_____ . 1996. *State and Local Government*, 3rd ed. Boston: Houghton Mifflin.

Brace, Paul, and Melinda Gann Hall. 1990. "Neo-Institutionalism and Dissent in State Supreme Courts." *Journal of Politics* 52: 54–69.

_____ . 1993. "Integrated Models of Judicial Dissent." *Journal of Politics* 55: 914–935.

_____ . 1995. "Studying Courts Comparatively: The View from the American States." *Political Research Quarterly* 48: 5–28.

Caldeira, Gregory A. 1983. "On the Reputation of State Supreme Courts." *Political Behavior* 5: 83–108.

Canon, Bradley C., and Lawrence Baum. 1981. "Patterns of Adoption of Tort Law Innovations: An Application of Diffusion Theory to Judicial Doctrines." *American Political Science Review* 75: 975–987.

Canon, Bradley C., and Dean Jaros. 1970. "External Variables, Institutional Structure, and Dissent on State Supreme Courts." *Polity* 4: 175–200.

Collins, Ronald K. L., Peter Galie, and John Kincaid. 1986. "State High Courts, State Constitutions, and Individual Rights Litigation Since 1980: A Judicial Survey." *Publius* 16: 141–161.

Dubois, Philip L. 1980. *From Ballot to Bench: Judicial Elections and the Quest for Accountability*. Austin: University of Texas Press.

_____ . 1983. "The Influence of Selection System on the Characteristics of a Trial Court Bench: The Case of California." *Justice System Journal* 8: 59–87.

Emmert, Craig F., and Carol Ann Traut. 1992. "State Supreme Courts, State Constitutions, and Judicial Policymaking." *Justice System Journal* 16: 37–48.

Fino, Susan P. 1987. *The Role of State Supreme Courts in the New Judicial Federalism*. Westport, CT: Greenwood Press.

Flango, Victor E., and Craig R. Ducat. 1979. "What Difference Does Method of Judicial Selection Make? Selection Procedures in State Courts of Last Resort." *Justice System Journal* 5: 25–44.

Galie, Peter J. 1987. "State Supreme Courts, Judicial Federalism, and the Other Constitutions." *Judicature* 71: 100–110.

Gallas, Geoff. 1976. "The Conventional Wisdom of State Court Administration: A Critical Assessment and Alternative Approach." *Justice System Journal* 2: 35–55.

Glick, Henry R. 1981. "Innovation in State Judicial Administration: Effects on Court Management and Organization." *American Politics Quarterly* 9: 49–69.

_____ . 1982. "Supreme Courts in State Judicial Administration." In Mary Cornelia Porter and B. Alan Tarr, eds., *State Supreme Courts: Policymakers in the Federal System*. Westport, CT: Greenwood Press.

_____ . 1991. "Policy Making and State Supreme Courts." In John B. Gates and Charles A. Johnson, eds., *The American Courts: A Critical Assessment*. Washington, DC: CQ Press.

Glick, Henry R., and Craig F. Emmert. 1987. "Selection Systems and Judicial Characteristics: The Recruitment of State Supreme Court Justices." *Judicature* 70: 228–235.

Goertz, Margaret E. 1996. "State Education Policies in the 1990s." In Carl E. Van Horn, ed., *The State of the States*, 3rd ed. Washington, DC: CQ Press.

Graham, Barbara L. 1990a. "Do Judicial Selection Systems Matter? A Study of Black Representation on State Courts." *American Politics Quarterly* 18: 316–336.

_____ . 1990b. "Judicial Recruitment and Racial Diversity on State Courts: An Overview." *Judicature* 74: 28–34.

Gray, Virginia, and Peter Eisinger. 1997. *American States and Cities*. New York: Longman.

Hall, Melinda Gann. 1995. "Justices as Representatives: Elections and Judicial Politics in the American States." *American Politics Quarterly* 23: 485–503.

Hall, Melinda Gann, and Paul Brace. 1989. "Order in the Courts: A Neo-Institutional Approach to Judicial Consensus." *Western Political Quarterly* 42: 391–407.

_____ . 1992. "Toward an Integrated Model of Judicial Voting Behavior." *American Politics Quarterly* 20: 147–168.

_____ . 1996. "Justices' Responses to Case Facts." *American Politics Quarterly* 24: 237–261.

Hall, William K., and Larry T. Aspin. 1987. "What Twenty Years of Judicial Retention Elections Have Told Us." *Judicature* 70: 340–347.

Haydel, Judith. 1989. "Section 2 of the Voting Rights Act of 1965: A Challenge to State Judicial Election Systems." *Judicature* 73: 68–73.

Hudzik, John K. 1985. "Rethinking the Consequences of State Financing." *Justice System Journal* 10: 135–158.

Jacob, Herbert. 1996. "Courts: The Least Visible Branch." In Virginia Gray and Herbert Jacob, eds., *Politics in the American States: A Comparative Analysis*, 6th ed. Washington, DC: CQ Press.

Kincaid, John. 1988. "The New Judicial Federalism." *The Journal of State Government* 60: 163–169.

Knoebel, Dixie. 1990. "State of the Judiciary." In Council of State Governments, *The Book of the States 1990–91*. Lexington, KY: Council of State Governments.

Kramer, Paul A. 1996. "Waiting for Godot? The New Judicial Federalism 1987–1992: Reality or Hoax?" Paper presented at the 1996 annual meeting of the American Political Science Association, San Francisco, August 29–September 1.

Latzer, Barry. 1991. "The Hidden Conservatism of the State Court 'Revolution.'" *Judicature* 74: 190–197.

Lewis, Dan A., and Shadd Maruna. 1996. "The Politics of Education." In Virginia Gray and Herbert Jacob, eds., *Politics in the American States*, 6th ed. Washington, DC: CQ Press.

Lim, Marcia J. 1986. "State of the Judiciary." In Council of State Governments, *The Book of the States 1986–87*. Lexington, KY: Council of State Governments.

Luskin, Robert C., Christopher N. Bratcher, Christopher B. Jordan, Tracy K. Renner, and Kris S. Seago. 1994. "How Minority Judges Fare in Retention Elections." *Judicature* 77: 316–321.

McDuff, Robert. 1989. "The Voting Rights Act and Judicial Elections Litigation: The Plaintiffs' Perspective." *Judicature* 73: 82–86.

Odden, Allan R. 1992. "School Finance and Educational Reform: An Overview. In Allan R. Odden, ed., *Rethinking School Finance*. San Francisco: Jossey-Bass.

Russakoff, Dale. 1996. "When Courts Become Political Battlegrounds," *Washington Post National Weekly Edition*, December 9–15: 29.

Saari, David J. 1976. "Modern Court Management: Trends in Court Organization Concepts, 1976." *Justice System Journal* 2: 19–33.

Smith, Nancy J., and Julie Garmel. 1992. "Judicial Election and Selection Procedures Challenged Under the Voting Rights Act." *Judicature* 76: 154–156.

Swinford, Bill. 1991. "A Predictive Model of Decision Making in State Supreme Courts: The School Financing Cases." *American Politics Quarterly* 19: 336–352.

Tarr, G. Alan. 1981. "Court Unification and Court Performance: A Preliminary Assessment." *Judicature* 64: 356–368.

_____. 1994a. *Judicial Process and Judicial Policymaking*. St. Paul: West Publishing.

_____. 1994b. "The Past and Future of the New Judicial Federalism." *Publius* 24: 63–79.

Tarr, G. Alan, and Mary Cornelia Porter. 1988. *State Supreme Courts in State and Nation*. New Haven: Yale University Press.

Tolley, Michael C. 1992. "The Impact of Form on Substance: Court Reform and the Work of the Maryland Court of Appeals." *Justice System Journal* 15: 765–781.

Uhlman, Thomas M. 1978. "Black Elite Decision Making: The Case of Trial Judges." *American Journal of Political Science* 22: 884–895.

CHAPTER 7—SUMMARY AND CONCLUSIONS

Peterson, Paul E. 1995. *The Price of Federalism*. Washington, DC: Brookings Institution.

Rivlin, Alice M. 1992. *Reviving the American Dream: The Economy, the States, and the Federal Government*. Washington, DC: Brookings Institution.

Index